Conscious Ascendance

Full consciousness for spiritual ascendance and empowerment

Kenneth E. Bartle

aotf
publishing

ISBN: 978-0-6455837-0-0 (sc)
ISBN: 978-0-6455837-1-7(e)

For rights and permissions, please contact:
Kenneth E. Bartle

bartle@iinet.net.au — http://aotf.site

Disclaimer

The author of this book does not directly or indirectly dispense medical or psychological advice or prescribe the use of any technique as a form of treatment for physical, emotional, or medical problems without the advice of a physician or psychologist. In the event you use any of the information in this book for yourself, which is your constitutional right, neither the author nor publisher assume responsibility for your actions.

Because this book disavows the subjects of legal positivism, statute laws, and government itself, it does not infer, offer or give any legal advice whatsoever. This book has no need for the legalese of lawyers, attorneys or (legal) practitioners. Its focus is the study of Man and the orderliness of his activities, his rights, respects, and responsibilities. Refer to 'Definitions' in the Appendix.

Examples used herein portend potential outcomes, not actual results. They are not intended to represent or guarantee that anyone will achieve the same or similar results, since each individual's success depends on his or her intent, application, valued-desire, and motivation.

All diagrams are for illustration of idea only; not to be construed as advisory recommendations. All ideas and material presented are entirely those of the author, generally written and formatted in Australian English, but using indented paragraphs in lieu of separation for economy and more universally accepted presentation.

Because of the dynamic nature of the Internet, any web addresses or links contained in this book may have changed since publication and may no longer be valid. The views expressed in this work are solely those of the author.

Conscious Ascendance

Table of Chapters

Table of Diagrams

Introduction

Academics freely admit not knowing what consciousness is. Neuroscience fails also, thus people are trapped in an intellectual vacancy. Countless 'new agers' and spiritual healers offer lectures, sessions, podcasts and webinars that purportedly raise our consciousness, frequencies or vibrations, yet none first define consciousness! Meanwhile, science tells us that everything is energy, and that reality is an illusion, which further testifies to conscious ignorance. 'Panpsychism' adds fuel to that fire. In all, people are trapped without their knowing. Thus stifled, they suffer. Anxiety, stress and trauma run rampant but are considered a mere accident of normality. No escape offers. Ignorance of full consciousness forbids it. This book solves all those problems and more.

"No problem can be solved from the same level of consciousness that created it."— *Albert Einstein*

You are a miracle, and your unique nature is no accident. You have a divine purpose in life and this book shows that path in a way that has never been seen. It describes the conscious process from perception to spiritual revelation, and from infancy through adolescence to adult maturity. Separating the conscious mind from its subconscious counterpart shows how they communicate, what they share, and why. You'll learn how infants can program their subconscious minds with no words, math, or science. How the conscious and subconscious minds swap functions during adolescence, and how our nine higher faculties work collaboratively to support and uphold our lives. This book shows the exact nature and role of free will and how it conducts the whole symphonic orchestra of your mental, emotional and spiritual wellbeing. You can be a winner on the world stage!

This book builds a picture in your mind, much as an artist paints a picture. Each new brush stroke builds on the one before. As the picture develops, the process becomes clear. Full meaning and purpose become transparent as you see how each part corresponds with others. Diagrams further help to cement this picture in your mind. Better yet, the key components of your conscious process can be fully automated to ensure success.

Around 2012 I began researching how the Australian government could be lawfully repurposed, but neither law, common law, nor natural law offered any answers. Undeterred, I turned to human consciousness but found that no one explains what consciousness is, or how it works. With forty-five years of study and practice of Objectivist philosophy under my belt, I engaged in observational science and deductive reasoning. The results blew my mind. The whole picture of the conscious process emerged with unmistakable clarity. Tears of compassion for the human race streamed for several weeks while writing 'Law from Within,' published in 2017.

That book describes human consciousness as never before and revealed twenty natural laws that govern its processes. My understanding has increased since, suggesting a new book explaining the conscious process. This book is it. A third book will deal with the twenty natural laws and how they may establish free, organic societies worldwide. First things first, however, because if freedom is the end goal, knowing exactly how consciousness enables 'self-guidance' before 'self-governance,' is vital.

This knowledge unleashes stupendous personal power, intellectually, emotionally, and spiritually. It will change your life and allow your benefits to run off the charts. When you learn how free will oversees your desires like the conductor of an orchestral masterpiece, you'll marvel at sheer simplicity, beauty beyond words, and esteemed power. Learn how to program your subconscious mind as infants do and your desires are automated while your mental workload subsides to near nil. Myths regarding feelings and emotions, conscience, imagination, and intuition will vanish without your asking. The miracle of your unique nature will blossom like a flower never witnessed before.

"Why didn't I learn this as a kid?" — you might ask. You did. Indeed we all began learning the moment we were born, but we had no intellectual capacity to understand the method. We do now! We have

Introduction

learned to write and speak, and many people have developed acute intellectual abilities. But few understand the pivotal secrets we all perfected during infancy. This book changes that absolutely, so LOOK OUT! All your abilities unite in the power of the complete conscious process!

When you see what is possible and engage with this blessing of nature, remarkable things will happen. Simple examples allow you to play and prove the veracity of simple principles. As you advance with little effort, mental, emotional, and spiritual powers will become natural to you. Knowing no bounds, inventive brilliance will raise inner confidence, yours to enjoy forever.

Resolute calmness will oversee your mental performance, your power, and your satisfaction. You will see straight through bogus ideologies, political correctness and all else intended to throttle your mind and reduce you to a vegetable state. Fears will vanish so much you will wonder why you ever suffered them. Pure clarity of mind will send your success rate soaring while reducing stress, fear and anxiety to near nil. Nothing excels when the exact nature of your being comes into full play!

Observational science and deductive reasoning helped me discover how my described methods produce success. The more I understood this method, the more I realised its power for good and evil. The secret was learning how to direct personal outcomes and benefits so that evil had no entry. Value-based mind programming methods proved their worth repeatedly, leaving no doubt they worked to perfection. As mentioned, joy skyrocketed, and tears of compassion for humanity streamed for weeks. This book testifies continuing success over five years since, without which it would not publish. This advanced knowledge is so distinctive and more pertinent today that it cannot be withheld any longer.

As you practice the simple exercises here shown, and your desires begin to manifest, you'll discover an undreamt ability to choose feelings of joy, happiness, and prosperity in advance. That is a massive statement, yet it gets better. Progressing from simple steps to personal triumph, self-confidence, calmness, peace, and tranquillity will create an inner excitement as your sovereignty emerges.

Stop wishing for such astonishing benefits! Make them yours to keep. This book is not your typical 'listen up, feel-good, gather dust on the shelf type of book. You have in your hands a serious, non-fiction, self-help book for regular revision, its explanatory diagrams each a study in themselves.

Conscious Ascendance

Just as our bodily systems convey nutrients to cells so that you prosper and thrive, so your two minds work similarly. Their secrets are now in your hands, all reducible to just two words! But until you've read this book cover to cover you'll not realise how precious those two words are. They grant access to whatever you most want in life, materially, mentally, emotionally, and spiritually.

Mental orderliness enabled me to write this book and that same orderliness can propel your life to heights unknown. Choose to advance now and you will. Stop now and you will.

There are no hurdles to leap, nothing to undo, no blame or sins to accept. Once you learn the 'value of addition,' subtraction issues will take care of themselves. Creator has gifted you the means to prosper without reservation. Your children's great benefit is a bonus beyond measure! Become a leader in the greatest conscious revolution the world has ever witnessed, all according to your will and no other.

That is freedom! Having already started, make it happen now.

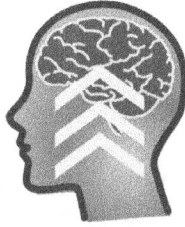

Chapter 1

1. Ignorance and the fundamentals of consciousness

Conscious ignorance traces from Man's beginnings. Very few people know that such ignorance exists, less what might repair it, even less what might eliminate it or prevent its recurrence. Worse yet, we've no idea how that unspeakable tragedy conceals our key to personal benefits.

Tragically, an intellectual void developed because neither academia nor neuroscience defines consciousness. Plausible explanations have arisen to fill this vacuum. But none suffice because none describe what consciousness is to begin. Consequently, mysticisms, theories, ideologies and beliefs abound worldwide, all reliant on believing for support, lacking any factual grounding. When this accepted vocabulary of broad misconceptions thrives unchallenged, ignorance assumes the legitimacy of conscious knowledge. The problem exacerbates as a result, and despite millions joyously raising their frequency or vibrations purportedly, no one explains what consciousness is or how it works.

That circular path needs breaking. This chapter first explores what any proposed remedy must answer in full. It then sets forth the fundamentals to explain and define conscious knowledge.

In common usage, the word 'consciousness' means 'awareness.' Dictionaries define it thus, yet awareness is less than one-tenth of the conscious process! As late as 1989, Stuart Sutherland (1989), a British psychologist, wrote in the International Dictionary of Psychology—

> *"Consciousness is a fascinating but elusive phenomenon. It is impossible to specify what it is, what it does, or why it evolved. Nothing worth reading has been written on it."* —*Stuart Sutherland*[1]

Conscious Ascendance

That tragedy arises from the belief that free will renders consciousness subjective in nature, whereby consciousness cannot be science. Consequently, our human sciences, psychologists and philosophers admit to knowing little about consciousness. Our mental abilities stagnate at the level where animals function, but no one sees it or explains it! Should we awaken to our primitive condition, we've no mental means to overcome that deprivation and thrive as we should.

Science considers that consciousness and physicality are inseparable, whereby consciousness only deals with our physical bodies in a physical environment. 'Materialism' and 'dualism' dominate traditional scientific perspectives, each purportedly providing a framework solution to 'the problem.' Both lead to non-solvable complications, and so the problem remains.

The 'materialist' viewpoint holds that consciousness derives from physical matter but cannot explain how this could work. For example, how do you get consciousness out of non-consciousness?

The 'dualist' view holds that consciousness is separate and distinct from physical matter. So how can consciousness interact and influence the physical world?

David Chalmers, an Australian philosopher and cognitive scientist, puts forward what he calls 'the hard problem of consciousness.' For example—

> *"Science can explain what the machinery of the eye does, but not the spark of brilliant perception or dazzling awareness of something new or profound."—David Chalmers* [2]

Increasing numbers of neuroscientists now accept 'panpsychism.' It holds that consciousness is a fundamental feature of physical matter, in which every single particle in existence has a simple form of consciousness. Further, these particles may come together to form complex phrases that describe consciousness, such as 'human subjective experiences.' Panpsychism does not say that particles think but rather that some inherent subjective experience of consciousness exists even in the tiniest particle.

Observe what results. First, if consciousness is physical, how can imagination exist? The 'materialist' viewpoint is nonsensical. Second, panpsychism attempts to explain how consciousness interacts with the physical world, whence the 'dualist' problem disappears. Both views sound plausible, but neither is.

> *"Panpsychism offers no distinctive predictions or explanations. It finds a place for consciousness in the physical world, but that place is a sort of limbo. Consciousness is indeed a hard nut to crack, but I*

think we should exhaust the other options before we take a metaphysical sledgehammer to it." —*Keith Frankish* [3]

Indeed, because conscious ignorance has profound implications. That science considers consciousness inseparable from physicality, via panpsychism, has taken hold in intellectual circles. How could we be misled so easily? Because it is believed the entire material world is nothing but vibration.

"Everything in Life is Vibration" – Albert Einstein

This belief results in many people speaking of ascending to a 'higher level of consciousness,' also described as 'raising our vibrations.' That should not end the discussion, however. In physics, vibration refers to an oscillation of the parts of a fluid or an elastic solid whose equilibrium becomes disturbed or of an electromagnetic wave. Many say that we experience an ocean of infinite waves surging through our inner sensations and the eternal dance of the countless vibrations within every atom of our body. We correctly conclude, therefore, that the reality of matter, or bodies, do indeed vibrate. If we also conclude that consciousness is physical, as panpsychism postulates, then our thoughts and emotions are vibrations.

Do you see the error? To conclude that the reality of our mind, that consciousness, perception, sensations and feelings are vibrations while not knowing what consciousness is, presents (or delivers) a flawed recipe for mind-control.

"The opinion on 10,000men is of no value if none of them know anything about the subject." —*Marcus Aurelius.*

Consider the opposite viewpoint. If our thoughts, especially their 'values' are spiritual abstracts, not physical manifestations, then vibrations and energy do not apply to consciousness. Make no mistake, however. Such spiritual abstractions may indeed trigger what we call emotions, which may manifest as physical vibrations. But the (abstracted) spiritual source remains independent from the resultant vibratory manifestation.

Cause and effect are not interchangeable. So we may paraphrase Einstein in saying that *"every material thing in life is vibration, but spirituality is not."* Spirituality is the coherent flow of abstracts more accurately.

The unspoken secret is 'value,' as it pertains to life. As later discussed, consciousness switches from material vibrations and energy to spiritual values or their lack, and vice versa. It switches to root 'cause' and leaves resultant 'effects' to themselves, including emotions. All of this will become clear later.

Conscious Ascendance

The mind is not a mechanical phenomenon. Instead, thought is a spiritual medium of value communication. It is a mental process of discovery and learning, from which we choose our actions and behaviour.

Notwithstanding, many people speak of vibration, or energy, as an individual's emotional state. That concept expands to include a place's atmosphere, or the associations of an object experienced as a felt condition. That error brings our entire conscious vocabulary into question and much pseudo science.

Indeed, intensity relates to energy and vibration, but in the spiritual sense, it refers to the word value. Let's explore that thought. Observably, our subconscious mind acts to fulfil our chosen goals. Its role is to uphold your life and thus it must know what you want to do and why. It wants to know what value you place on your proposed actions. Will they uphold your life or depreciate it?

All talk about energy and vibrations is spurious. It diverts our attention from choosing to align our thoughts with our subconscious supplications and turns our focus to manifestations or material outcomes. Spiritual values are vital, but their role is never taught.

Energy is not a constituent element in this spiritual realm, even if it is the actuator. Energy is the ability to perform work, a measure. Spiritualists who talk about the bodies energy fields, or unblocking, harmonising, tuning, aligning, unifying, balancing, channelling, or manipulating subtle energy, are not saying anything meaningful. The new-age culture has transformed the word energy into an element unto itself, like a glowing, hovering, shimmering cloud from which adepts can draw power and feel rejuvenated, else darkness will crush their life. All of that nonsense arises from new-age quackery emerging from forsaken consciousness.

No one questions the woeful tragedy of conscious ignorance that feeds on itself, but they should. The first culprit for our address is 'belief.' Over the past fifty years, that word has knocked the word 'knowledge' clean out of our everyday vocabulary. Beliefs are mental propositions or proposals. They're neither true nor false. No evidence presents, or they would be called knowledge, not beliefs. Such postulates should therefore pass through a process of investigation and enquiry, from possibilities through probabilities to knowledge. At that point, belief cancels. It has served its purpose, much like a shopping trolly where the checkout confirms one's chosen values. Truth is what you take home because of the value it offers.

Very few people use the word knowledge today because 'belief' allows them to say what they consider truthful while avoiding any charge of certainty. Certainty is not intolerance of another's beliefs. Yet it is expected we apologise for 'certainty' to avoid offending someone's feelings.

Chapter 1

'Collective consciousness' or 'unity consciousness,' is often spoken of as though a fog-like flux that wafts between us all, belonging to no one. That commonly held belief stems from 'awareness' as 'consciousness.' But just as there is no collective stomach or liver, so there is no collective mind and no collective consciousness. Like-mindedness among several or many people is not consciousness. Conscious ignorance of this calibre has deprived us of our unalienable right to life.

Jean-Jacques Rousseau, (1712-78), a French philosopher and writer, believed that *while Mans freedom is a fact of nature, people should be taught to consider that it is dangerous; whereby they ought to sacrifice their individual nature to the artificial condition of citizenship.* Furthermore, *natural persons should become artificial persons, that is, citizens—wittingly or unwittingly—willingly, or by legal compulsion.*

That ideology has not changed in three centuries and is still taught today. Additionally, censorship, political correctness, mind control and totalitarian rule all have one aim. That is to censor our thinking ability, maintain ignorance, and block us from sharing information and ideas with others. Authoritarians fear our knowledge like a plague. They cannot succeed without suppressing our ability to work as a powerful group of aware, enlightened people. The result is that we each are victims of deliberate mind control that forces our submission to totalitarian dictatorship.

So-called 'spiritual healers' who speak of energetics or raising our consciousness are no real threat to sociopaths because, as mentioned, none define their subject. Absent any challenge, authoritarian rule presides while conscious ineptitude lives with no end. Ignorance has no challenge and no opposition!

The good news is that the instant truth concerning consciousness reaches a tipping point, centuries of authoritarian rule will end. Consider some hurdles to be overcome.

Consciousness cannot be science so long as 'awareness' and free will are considered 'subjective.' Consciousness does not appear in laboratories whereby science has little choice but to regard consciousness as a matter of ongoing debate amongst non-scientists.

With ninety per cent of the conscious process spurned or at best relegated to cognitive awareness only, we exist in a conscious vacuum. Quantum physics sees this gaping chasm and seeks to fill it.

Thus it holds that everything is energy, whereby reality is nothing but an illusion. Conceptually, identity, and causality collapse, whereby identification vanishes and beliefs replace knowledge.

Consciousness then becomes a mishmash of subjectivity, beliefs, illusion, energetics, vibrations and frequencies. This mentally destructive feat defies comparison. It fosters increased belief in 'unity consciousness,' or mass consciousness, which completely denies the individual faculty of consciousness.

Conscious Ascendance

'Life' exits from all discussion, accordingly. No mind communication is observable. Value transfer remains unseen. Our higher faculties are not united. Three out of nine are not recognised, thereby denied. Unsurprisingly, this distressing condition fuels greed for more material possessions as the only relief possible. In turn, conscious ignorance of this calibre promotes 'collectivism.' The practice or principle of group priority over each individual founds socialism and communism. That is today's condition, despite the remedy being addressed more than two centuries ago.

"If a nation expects to be ignorant and free, in a state of civilisation, it expects what never was and never will be." — Thomas Jefferson

Biological orderliness

We each are an aggregate collection of singular living beings comprising cells, tissues, and organs. Our body is both elementary and complex, organised across six levels in a structural hierarchy.

The chemical level comprises atoms that combine to form molecules and then organelles that make the internal organs of a cell. Some fifty trillion cells vary in size and shape. Some have similar functions, and each type of cell has a set of different tasks.

Tissues are groups of similar cells that function in common. Four basic tissue types each comprise two different cell types. Each tissue has an essential role within the body.

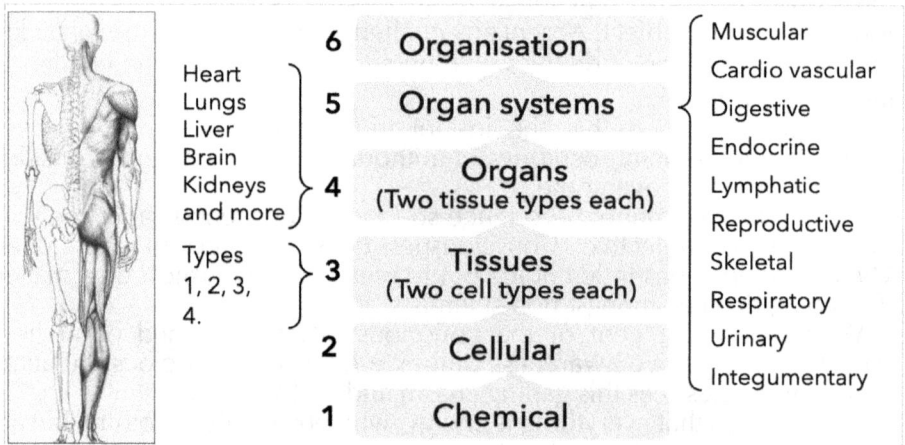

		Muscular
Heart	6 Organisation	Cardio vascular
Lungs	5 Organ systems	Digestive
Liver		Endocrine
Brain	4 Organs	
Kidneys	(Two tissue types each)	Lymphatic
and more		Reproductive
Types	3 Tissues	Skeletal
1, 2, 3, 4.	(Two cell types each)	Respiratory
	2 Cellular	Urinary
		Integumentary
	1 Chemical	

1. Patterns of order in biology

Organs comprise at least two different tissue types, each performing a particular task within the body. One or more organs work together to accomplish a common system purpose, such as the cardiovascular system. The heart and blood vessels work together to circulate blood throughout the body to provide oxygen and nutrients to cells. The organisational level is the highest, uniting all the levels or the being (or organism) as a whole.

That description speaks of enormous complexity, yet, everything functions with orderliness for optimal efficiency. Organs are governed much as processes in a factory are methodically organised and managed. Our heart (hydraulic) and lungs (pneumatic) function as separate entities, yet they work cooperatively to uphold our lives from start to finish, and neither can interfere with the other. Trillions of body cells plus our vital organs and systems all do the same. Accordingly, our whole body functions optimally and efficiently for our benefit.

Our neurological processes and nervous system communicate data across our body functions in an orderly fashion, so we can think, converse, plan, and exercise our choices.

Notice how everything functions in an orderly way. Orderly optimisation refers to 'law,' thus 'natural orderliness' refers to natural law.

Nothing in human biology questions our motives, goals or ambitions. All nature asks is that we choose nutrients to maintain bodily health or suffer and die. Conversation between our two minds testifies to the same orderliness. Free will is in charge because our organs prosper or suffer depending on our choice of what we eat, drink or inhale. All nature asks is that we choose nutrients to maintain bodily health. If we poison or abuse our bodies, we suffer or die.

It seems logical that life-sustaining 'values' must serve as nutrients for our mental, emotional and spiritual life. I speak of values such as truth, honesty, diligence, respect, commitment and the like. We might refer to these as 'virtues,' however, that word may have moral overtones. Consequently I refer to 'life-sustaining values' as 'life values,' and will use that term hereafter.

Isn't it logical we should study how values communicate between the conscious and subconscious minds, just as science considers how vital nutritional elements transport to our bodily organs and systems? Shouldn't we also study how spiritual values can renew our emotional lives, much as our immune system rids toxins and repairs damage?

A somewhat comical observation emerges in passing. If consciousness cannot be a science because free will is 'subjective,' neither can biology because what we ingest (toxins, nutrients or poisons) is also (free choice) 'subjective.'

This discussion points to a huge problem. Our body cells are like those in animals, yet our (conscious) operating systems are vastly different. Animals have no free will. They automatically respond to their immediate conditions and environment. Perception also prompts us to discover, to enquire and then act on our choices. Thus, our operating system is choice-based. We are volitionally conscious beings, not animals or automatons.

Ignorance of this fundamental difference, or its deliberate refusal, allows governments to create an artificial legal environment that coerces or forces us to adapt to its edicts as though that were organic nature itself. To enforce a mental state of animality is criminal, yet we vote for its continuance. Why do we? Because when governments control 'consent,' they manipulate the consent of the governed. You have heard that phrase, I am sure. Most people love it because it comforts them to know that government cares about their safety and security. The opposite is true more often. Our ignorance of consciousness permits devious control of our minds, thereby our consent. Conscious ignorance is our downfall, authoritarian rulers greatest mental weapon.

Ayn Rand wrote that if the benchmark of morality is our devotion to truth, then one who assumes the responsibility of thinking exhibits the most noble, most heroic form of respect for truth. That sounds like work, a task with no paycheck. It is not, as you will discover.

Meanwhile, however, passivity is a disease. It spreads and takes over, weakening strong people and making weak people demented. Passivity is life without power. Some people say that power is a neutral object allowing utilisation for good or evil. Ignore them. Remember that evil has no power but that which it extorts or we admit. Importantly, evil practice is not creative. It is the product of second-handers, utterly reliant on your creativity and power. Outright theft of your efforts is the only power authoritarians have. Coercion is not our consent. We should never sacrifice our intellect or mental power on the altar of what others insist is good, true and rightful. Neither should we give up the truth for an abstract ideology someone has invented. Bogus notions separate us from our power or deny it in full.

"Much of the evil in the world is due to the fact that man is hopelessly unconscious." — Carl Jung

The cure is to define, develop and exercise your power as your Creator intended you should. Real power is dynamically alive. It expresses your understanding of what is true, beneficial, and morally correct. Creative power is our key to a glorious future. Suspending our conscious process cancels it. Take your power back. It is yours, not theirs.

Accept that the brain is physical, but the mind is non-physical. Our minds communicate with each other. Neither science nor technology can address this. They presently have nothing to offer. Observational science and deductive reasoning can, however, provide they employ a rational vocabulary based on reason. Our mind and our spirit can receive information from sources and other derivations. How that information is processed and accepted as 'value' largely depends on you knowing how your conscious operating system works.

Widespread ignorance results from searching for consciousness in the wrong place. Academia and neuroscience should concede that consciousness relates to 'life.' Relieved of that study, psychologists and philosophers could show what this book shows, namely that the object of consciousness is life, equally as scientific as nutrition and anatomy.

The problem of consciousness, however, is essentially unlike any other scientific problem. One reason is that consciousness is unobservable. You can't look inside someone's head and see their feelings and experiences. If consciousness derived from observing a third-person perspective, we would have no grounds for postulating consciousness at all.

So how can science ever explain it (consciousness)? We can establish, for example, that the invisible feeling of hunger is correlated with visible activity in the brain's hypothalamus. But the accumulation of such correlations does not amount to a theory of consciousness. What we ultimately want is to explain why conscious experiences are correlated with brain activity. Why is it that such activity in the hypothalamus comes along with a feeling of hunger?—Phillip Goff Durham University [4]

The answer is clear since conscious experiences correlate with brain activity, and life is of paramount importance. That understanding renders the study of consciousness entirely objective and purposeful, just as nutrition is purposeful. That obliges we deny all who would suppress our body and mind. We should also divorce the new-age gobbledygook that fosters ignorance and strive to become conscious beings in the true sense. That will improve empathy, upgrade your divinity, and allow you to daily access 'Source.'

Take that idea one step further. If the object purpose of consciousness is 'life's sustenance,' physical matter is only a tool to that end. That being so, the 'materialist' viewpoint holding that consciousness derives from physical matter is shattered. Consciousness is the nature of life, while the physical matter is our material means to fulfil it.

'Dualism' is questioned once more. Conscious use of physical matter is vastly different from physical constituents exhibiting consciousness. Life's fulfillment shows that physicality and consciousness are related but are not the same. With 'materialism' and 'dualism' explained as never before, consciousness is spiritual, not material.

Accordingly, conscious study evaluates in life terms, with all challenges not so founded dismissed as irrelevant, fear and all its entrapments sent packing. Knowledge is the only way to redeem ourselves from blind ignorance.

Radical change is imperative to remove oligarchic oppressors from power, thus establishing healthy and harmonious societies in their place. Some hitherto undisclosed knowledge must be present, sufficient to blast widespread ignorance into oblivion and rid overt control forever. Albert Einstein tumbled to it—

> *"No problem can be solved from the same level of consciousness that created it"—Albert Einstein.*

Newfound knowledge that in this book concerns consciousness is dynamic, powerfully so. Once these revelations are known and enacted, our mental, moral, spiritual, financial and political world will bear little resemblance to todays world. With that in mind, let us begin discovery.

The book of Genesis describes that God created plant and animal life and "God created man in His own image; in the image of Creator God — male and female He created them." Each life form is different, and those differences are vital to our understanding of full consciousness.

Plant life is conditional. Plants remain in one place, and are dependent on local nutrients.

Animal life is perceptual. They can move and adapt themselves to nature. (Change colour, grow defensive attributes, hibernate, etc.)

Human life is volitional, and it is spiritual. We adapt nature to ourselves. (We build dams, railroads, houses, and computers.)

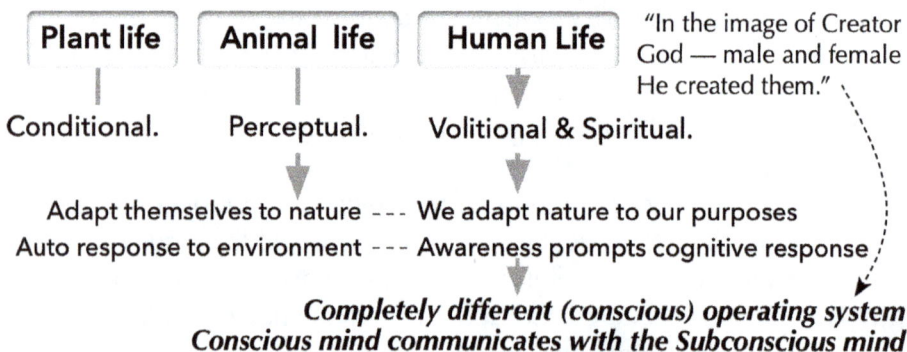

Plant life	Animal life	Human Life	"In the image of Creator God — male and female He created them."
Conditional.	Perceptual.	Volitional & Spiritual.	

Adapt themselves to nature --- We adapt nature to our purposes
Auto response to environment --- Awareness prompts cognitive response

Completely different (conscious) operating system
Conscious mind communicates with the Subconscious mind

2. The untold story of creation

Animals perceptual faculties automatically drive them to an action of some kind. Their primary motivations are fear and food (survival). Mating plays a part, of course. Our perceptual faculty works similarly, but the outcome is different.

Once made aware, we must choose what actions we take. That implies our Creator must have said these (unwritten) words also.

"Let men and women have free will to uphold their life in the manner of their choosing. Let them have a conscious mind that communicates with a subconscious mind, so they may choose their values, and receive reports through feelings and emotions — so they can alter their behaviour or change their values, to advance intellectually, emotionally, morally and spiritually."

That statement is likely the most succinct description of the consciousness process ever written. Between the lines, it tells us that our subconscious perception stops working once we are cognitively aware of something or a condition. Since we cannot automatically respond as animals do, it prompts us to think. Our free will faculty is priceless. It enables us to think and consider, evaluate, and abstract thoughts, thus forming concepts, as later explained.

The fundamental difference between animals and humans is made crystal clear.

- Animals adapt to their environment, *as their nature has determined.*
- Different, we must alter the natural environment to serve our purpose, *as our free will determines.*

Animals automatically respond to their environment. We do so by conscious choice. Thus for ourselves and all animals, consciousness is the operating system of our lives, and life is the goal in both cases.

Awareness is always truthful and accurate. Nonetheless, what we do with that information is up to us. For example, a straight stick or rod half immersed in water appears bent. Is our perception mistaken? No. Because light travels at a different frequency through the air versus water, our perception of the facts is faultless. The reason is that we must deal with the facts of reality, not superficial appearances. In sum, life is our reference base, and nothing disputes it.

Neither consciousness nor free will is separable from 'life,' because both exist to sustain it. To illustrate, we all choose what to eat, what to drink, and what air quality we should breathe. None of those choices affects how our cardio-vascular system functions or how our immune, respiratory, circulatory, or skeletal systems work. Yet every atom in our body depends on the value of what we eat, drink, and inhale.

The same applies to the (valued) quality of thought, including the validity of all information, knowledge, beliefs, superstitions, and ideologies.

Diagram 3 shows the prime difference between ourselves and animals. It shows how cognitive awareness is a sequential part of our human conscious process in that it triggers our free will. 'Perception' is where the similarity stops because 'awareness' prompts us to think. We automatically respond to emergencies like pulling our hands from a flame, otherwise awareness invokes that we learn, and we must. Because our subconscious mind stops work at the point of becoming aware, we've no alternative but to exercise our faculties as our Creator intended we should.

The diagram also shows that for both animals and humans, 'actions' engage the voluntary and involuntary subconscious functions.

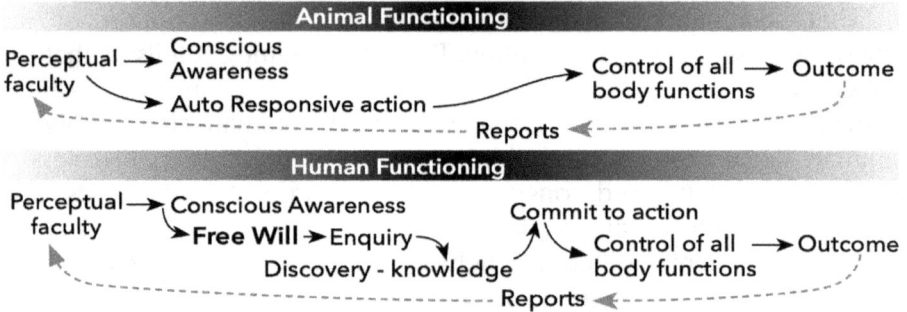

Animal Functioning

Perceptual faculty → Conscious Awareness
↘ Auto Responsive action → Control of all body functions → Outcome
Reports ◄

Human Functioning

Perceptual faculty → Conscious Awareness
↘ Free Will → Enquiry ↘
Discovery - knowledge → Commit to action ↗ ↘ Control of all body functions → Outcome
Reports ◄

3. Auto animal response versus human prompting of free will

Another difference between animals and ourselves poses an important question. Why can many animals see, hear, smell, and feel, having far greater sensibilities than we possess? Animals must have more highly developed faculties because their lives depend on the realities they perceive, not on conscious enquiry and learning as we do. Whatever knowledge they need to survive and thrive comes from their heightened sensory ability and nothing else.

Although our senses are less acute than those of animals, we suffer no deprivation. Fish can swim better than we can, but they cannot build swim pools. Birds can see much further and sharper, but none can build radar systems. Our mental faculties far exceed those of animals, and that blessed ability is ours alone. From that, we learn, lest we should.

Another vital fact emerges concerning our ability to condense information into small, manageable packages. 'Integration' is vitally important. All the essentials combine into one package, whereby we realise packaged information instead of a haphazard jumble of unrelated sensory data. Integration is crucial, later shown comprehensively.

In his book 'Real Answers to Everything,' Australian biologist Jeremy Griffith discusses these matters, explaining—

> *"that once our nerve-based learning system became sufficiently developed for us to become conscious and able to effectively manage events, our conscious intellect was then in a position to wrest control from our gene-based learning system's instincts, that, up until then, had been controlling our lives. Basically, once our self-adjusting conscious mind emerged it was capable of taking over the*

management of our lives from the instinctive orientations we had acquired through the natural selection of genetic traits that adapted us to our environment." — Jeremy Griffith [5]

Griffith also confirms the difference between animal and Man described above.

"The rehabilitation of our environments and our social and political systems requires a rehabilitation of our psychology, not merely as individuals, but as a species—that a spiritual change must be the basis for social reform and the restoration of the earth's ecosystems."—Jeremy Griffith [6]

Griffith effectively outlined this book in one sentence. Accepting his thoughts, let's explore psychological restoration further.

Consider consciousness a mental processing capability as our lungs, heart, liver, and kidneys are processing faculties. Consider also that, at its most basic level, 'consciousness' uses reason and logic to identify that which it seeks and finds. That process is ours alone. It is not communal. Consider also our subconscious mind as the silent partner of our conscious mind. I'll explore their different functions and reunite them later since, in reality, only one mind exists.

First, I ask that you clear your mind of preconceived ideas and beliefs concerning consciousness. That may not be easy at first glance, but readers who free their minds from interference will grasp these explanations more quickly and thoroughly. Your success presents a huge opportunity to begin exercising your will power. Picture your two minds paying rapt attention to all that follows. You will soar in return.

First, consider 'awareness' less than one-tenth of the conscious process. As you read on, a comprehensive picture will build. It will show how many different functions contribute to the interactive process of full consciousness. That totality, and its interoperability, is the operating system of your life. You will soon recognise a vital dynamic that 'awareness' can never explain.

Try visualising consciousness as Creator's wonderful invitation to live a joyous life filled with happiness, excitement, peace and joy. Visualise new revelations presenting details as you progressively continue reading. In all, I promise to paint a picture of yourself as you're never taught or have ever imagined!

For the moment, picture consciousness as the operating system of your life, running on autopilot authored by your free will. Visualise joy and happiness as the natural outcome, with no stress, anxiety or fear. Picture pure bliss beyond anything you've dreamt possible! Dr Zach Bush explains the opportunity you have like this—

Conscious Ascendance

"You are not stuck with the brain you have. Not only can you make it better, you can make it better in a very short time."

The following few pages introduce the conscious process, and the rest of this book expands on it. Necessary for this study, the (free will) cognitive mind must be separate from the (automated) subconscious mind. Our conscious mind, being our brain, is the home of awareness and free will, used for thinking, evaluating, and decision making. The subconscious mind is below awareness, whence 'sub' is the prefix. It accounts for about ninety-two percent of the total, notwithstanding both minds communicate with each other as though one.

Each of us has a conscious mind, and though we cannot see it, still we know we possess it. We are always consciously aware of ourselves save when sleeping. It is this self-knowingness that makes us each an individual. Consciousness is the operational process in which values interchange between your free will cognitive mind and automated subconscious mind. Your thought processor has a three-fold purpose.

1. **First,** it accepts the end product of perception. It holds our awareness in focus. We can choose its information, expand it, learn more from it, polish it, or reject it.

2. **Second,** it engages in investigation, enquiry and discernment. From our study of that process, our free will formulates ideas concerning what we can do further.

3. **Third,** it enables us to reach one of more decisions concerning possible action. It allows us to examine possibilities, explore opportunities, and assess values before we act. The conscious mind (cognitively) interfaces our biology with the world of physicality. Our free will enables us to choose different actions, after which our subconscious mind acknowledges our choices and enacts them. It oversees our activities and regulates our muscles and movements according to our desires. In so doing, it recognises the life-sustaining values we have chosen, whence it interfaces with Source in spiritual or soul terms.

Accordingly, our two minds have three principal functions.

1. **Sensory ability** includes light, sound, and tactile stimuli, plus information from our body parts, joints, muscles, skin and internal organs, including emotions, thoughts, and memories from within ourselves.

2. **Motor functionality.** Our minds integrate, store, and retrieve signals for different mental processes, including thinking, remembering, and experiencing emotions. The subconscious mind monitors all our

processes involuntarily. That maintains muscle tone and balance, breath control, adrenaline realise, sweat secretion, and much more.

3. **Two-way communication.** Communication unites all of our nine higher faculties. (That is fifty percent more than science recognises.) Effectors such as muscles and glands communicate with other parts to control bodily functions in response to changing factors.

Our mind and body thus appear as a convivial society of fifty trillion unique individuals acting in collaboration. Divorcing the (free will) cognitive processes from the automated subconscious functions permits our study of their (cross) communication inside a closed (value-transfer) loop that mimics the body's endocrine system.

Our senses and our intellect exist to grasp the truth. That is their fundamental purpose. Just as our eyes seek light, our subconscious mind seeks the truth, thus possessing it. It desires agreement of itself with a thing or event because truthfulness is fidelity to life, essential to uphold it.

Aristotle (384 BC—322 BC) is the recognised author of classifying the five senses: sight, smell, taste, touch, and hearing. They interface our body and mental processes with the physical environment in which we live. Even though humans are said to possess some fifteen senses, I will deal here only with the five most familiar senses.

Because the subconscious mind receives little attention, we are not conscious of it to the same degree we are of our conscious mind. Both are real nonetheless. It is imperative we understand the relationship that each bears to the other because that shows our every need supplied. In short, we have two different systems working in parallel to achieve the same goals. Conscious awareness manifests in two ways.

1. **Cognitive** awareness pertains to our recognition of material things, events, or circumstances. We recognise awareness as truthful, but that gives no understanding of the founding information. For example, we can walk into a factory or science laboratory and be consciously aware of many objects and things. Yet what they are, what material they are from, or what purpose they serve remains unexplained. We see whole integrated objects, not a haphazard assortment of sensory stimuli. However, problems may arise due to subsequent mistaken explorations, investigations and analyses. That shows us that conscious awareness is not equal to conscious understanding! (Witness those who may sharply retort— *"I'm well aware of that!"*— as if to say, *"I understand perfectly."*)

2. **Sentient** awareness, or sentience, is different. Sentience is our sensory ability to feel or perceive feelings and emotions. 'Sentient consciousness' means being aware of an (abstract) feeling being no less significant than being awre of material things we perceive.

Conscious Ascendance

Neither conscious awareness nor sentient consciousness offers an understanding of a particular thing, event, or feeling. Our perceptual faculty presents enough information to alert our conscious mind that such exists, but not enough to understand its properties.

In sum, while perception alerts us to material matters, our sentient feelings advise success or distress concerning the (spiritual) value we place on our actions. Said differently, perception reports our material progress, while our feelings and emotions report our (value-based) spiritual progress, or lack thereof.

Our choices activate our nervous motor control systems, for example so as to walk or climb, dance or run. Our subconscious mind then monitors our progress each millisecond and makes minor adjustments. All cells and body systems are monitored and adjusted to ensure successful outcomes. Accordingly, values like diligence, respect, fortitude, and patience are high on subconscious minds priority list. Life values are its benchmark.

Every element, system and faculty of our physical, intellectual and spiritual being exists and functions according to its nature, yet none is superior, more dominating, or authoritative. Gender, race, size, colour, thoughts, ideas, and goals all give vital spark to humanity, but none of these differences contradicts or denies the faculties that make us all equal. Indeed, these different appearances and traits testify that our uniqueness shares equality in nature. We are alike in kind but independently unique. And we are independent one from another in body, mind, and soul.

Each of us is different in physical, mental, and spiritual expression from everyone on earth and in all galaxies. Your beauty is yours. Fixed natural laws ensure your difference from others while possessing identical faculties in good health. Consequently, the natural laws that govern our physiological and psychological processes are the same in us all, despite whether we use them or refuse them.

Equality and individual free expression should be the core foundation of our societal structures, taught across the board from infancy. Tragically it is not whereby people must respond to the artificiality of our political environment as though animals.

If we are to become free from this mental crime, we must first understand how consciousness relates to physical reality. Centuries ago, a theory concerning this relationship developed from the work of Plato, Immanuel Kant and René Descartes, all three regarded as among the world's most influential philosophers. Novelist/philosopher Ayn Rand described their theory, saying that—

"The Platonist school begins by reversing the relationship of consciousness to existence, by assuming that reality must conform

to the content of consciousness, not the other way around—on the premise that the presence of any notion in man's mind proves the existence of a corresponding referent in reality."

Plato, often credited as the 'father of modern philosophy,' was not alone in his endeavors. René Descartes (1596 - 1650) added his voice to 'Platonist school.' Rand described his contribution as follows—

"Descartes began with "the prior certainty of consciousness," the belief that the existence of an external world is not self-evident, but must be proved by deduction from the contents of one's consciousness—which means: the concept of consciousness as some faculty other than the faculty of perception—which means: the indiscriminate contents of one's consciousness as the irreducible primary and absolute, to which reality has to conform." —Ayn Rand.

Descartes concluded everything was open to doubt except his conscious experience, thus his existence as a necessary condition. Hence his premise and most famous statement, *Cogito, ergo sum translated as I think, therefore I am.* Ayn Rand named his work the Primacy of Consciousness theory. She added that this theory is the source of collectivism. As a result, subjectivism has become the psychological and political means to herd humanity into conglomerate states enabling governments to rule our minds and body as though we are animals. The primacy of Consciousness philosophies tragically remains taught today in most world universities.

We need to look no further for the source of philosophical disparity and non-sensible confusion that runs rampant today. Why? Consider the first two words of Descartes famous statement — *I think.* Do you see the obvious error? Unless a conscious mind first exists, nothing exists with which to think! The faculty of consciousness precedes all thought.

The relationship between consciousness and existence is clear. 'Existence' is present in every object, all circumstances and events, available for us to understand. Nothing that exists can deny or refute itself. Conscious awareness follows our perception of what exists, including all relationships between all identifiable properties. In simplest terms, cognitive awareness recognises a constituent identity, which prompts our identification of it, and its constituent properties. All conversation and all communication between our two minds rely on existence and its identification, in that order. Thought follows.

That 'existence' precedes 'consciousness' should now be self-evident. Without your consciousness, you cannot be conscious of existence. With this in mind, Rand inverted Descartes statement to read, *'I am, therefore I think.'* She names this principle The 'Primacy of Existence.' In summary, thinking is self-mastery because all thought derives from the prime nature of existence, including the existent nature of our own mind.

Consciousness is quite simple in concept, therefore. Our conscious mind and subconscious mind have different functionalities. Importantly, information is exchanged back and forth between each. Our cognitive and subconscious minds communicate values comprising material goals and desires, being additional to life-sustaining values and virtues. This value data jointly exchanges with the autonomic nervous system when applicable. This value transfer process mimics our endocrine system, thus coordinating with it.

Because consciousness is a communication tool interfacing and connecting the nature of physicality with our spiritual life force, freedom is a prime necessity. It must be free from force and coercion. We may choose differently, but our actions follow the same sequentially repeating the (mental) process. We observe, become aware, investigate, think, evaluate, and then choose what we will do and do it. On completion, we receive a material report via our perceptions, plus a (sentient) feeling which reports concerning success or distress. The conscious process is that simple. It is our operating system of life that transfers life values between our two minds. Our (chosen) thoughts and values are then used in monitoring and regulating the whole process. The same values fuel our conscience, intuition, instincts, feelings and emotions. Thus consciousness is a mental processing faculty, much as our lungs, heart, liver, and kidneys are biological processing faculties. Our conscious process depends on nutritious thoughts and values, just as our digestive system depends on nutritional foods.

Ayn Rand stated that 'consciousness is identification,' which is true in material terms of perception. But the fulness of consciousness goes beyond mere identification. As a communication tool, it connects the nature of physicality with our spiritual life force, according to what we accept as valued truth. However, our values must first be 'identified' before they can be processed. Thus Rand's statement can be expanded to include 'value identification.'

Consciousness belongs to each of us as separate individuals. Others may notice our desires, goals, and our outcomes and share the same qualities, but none but ourselves can process our spiritual values. Consequently, no 'unity consciousness' or 'group consciousness' is possible. 'Awareness' may be shared by many people in common, of course. Witness any game at the ballpark for evidence. Said differently, our human minds are finite while our Creator God of nature is infinite. We cannot comprehend the infinite, but we can grasp particular facts that concern it.

The mind of God is all the mind there is. It is eternal and coexists with the eternal life of God himself. God is spirit, eternally ever-present. Mind is spirit. The essential mind of God is the part of the spirit which knows itself. Similarly, that part of our spiritual knowing, known as our subconscious mind, is a huge blessing. It is that part of the spirit of God placed within each of us so that we may function. The difference is our conscious mind orchestrates the subconscious mind in terms of our choices. We inform the subconscious mind concerning what we choose to value. It then connects with self-knowingness to the spirit or essential mind of God. Thus our subconscious mind is an intermediary interfacing physicality on one hand and spirituality on the other. Thus physicality is bridged to our soul connection with divinity.

Consciousness is a spiritual process, a divine spark that distinguishes us from all other life forms. Our spiritual power enables us to control conditions and to determine what manner of life we lead. It allows us to decide our destiny and bring it to fruition.

As proposed at the start of this chapter, we now have a new platform for exercising our choices to ensure life's fulfillment. It is an indisputable foundation upon which we all can rely. It sends fear and all its entrapments packing with all who would steal our rights and freedoms.

Can this platform be reinforced?

Oh yes! You have seen nothing yet!

Conscious Ascendance

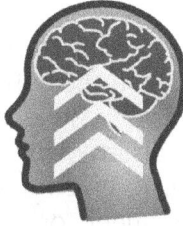

2. The foundations of thought

This chapter presents new foundations for consciousness, although they have have long existed. Later chapters will consolidate that platform. Health is the natural condition of Mankind. Nature constantly strives to uphold life while preventing any disease or disability. Perfection is the first state of our being, therefore. The divine mind creates only perfect things, of which we each are one expression. Only perfection should manifest, its divinity witnessed through health, mental agility and robust efficacy.

For these purposes, God gives us the power to work independently from Him. While our immune system is responsible for bodily corrections that escape our attention, our mental and emotional wellbeing invokes that we reject harmful or destructive notions or ideologies in like manner. The more we affirm mental and bodily health, the more our joy and happiness result. Health declines rapidly when lazy, apathetic or destructive thoughts take charge.

We are in charge of our lives through our free choices. Thereafter our subconscious mind is tasked with upholding our life. Thus we each have the innate power to decree our health through conscious thought and due diligence.

Disease sets in if our conscious choices oppose that mission. Conflict is a disease. It follows that the perfect adjustment of our mental abilities depends on our ability to harmonise our thoughts with the life-sustaining principles driving our subconscious mind. We each suffer in some form or to some degree to the extent that we fail. Moreover, such sufferance prevents or inhibits our repairing those orderly processes.

Conscious Ascendance

People fall prey to illness because their subconscious mind previously accepted that sickness or susceptibility to ill health is inevitable. Thus a mental picture of disease forms in the subconscious mind as a coming future event, whereby it accepts disease as our wilful choice. Because we know nothing of this potential disaster, very seldom do we form a picture of vibrant health to replace it. If, given that condition, we then expose ourselves to a toxic environment or ingest toxic substances, the subconscious mind will conclude that disease is now our present moment choice. Thus our choice to act now matches our previously accepted values. In effect, we have united negative mental values with debilitating or destructive material values, producing a negative outcome. Many will say that evil or negative energy has caused this result. But no, energy is not the cause. Life inhibiting 'values' are the root cause, materially, mentally, or both.

If, on the contrary, we consciously implant the idea of health in our subconscious mind, such that it repels disease, and we do all to uphold that choice, then a healthy outcome results.

We should never say, "I do not want disease or illness." That spells disaster. Why? Because our subconscious mind works only in the positive realm. As a result, it hears only, "I want disease or illness."

Success comes from impressing the subconscious mind with the value and virtue of vibrant health. For example, "my desire is health, fitness and ability." Likewise, if you say, "I do not want to be fat," it only hears "I want to be fat." It is far better to say, "I will be trim, taut and healthy." To affirm good health, replace all heath desires like I want, with 'I will.'

Remember that your subconscious is tasked to maintain your well-being and cannot do otherwise. The positive realm is its domain entirely. One sure way to impress the subconscious is to form a mental picture. If an organ is weak and fails to function as it should, we should visualise ourselves doing what we would do when in perfect health. The subconscious mind wants to learn about your passion for life and good health. It wants your body to rebuild according to your deep conviction and passion for health and success. That may take time, but your consistent passion for life and appropriate material action will speed the result.

For example, you may say to yourself something like this —

God is the source of all there is. I am one with the life of God. As God manifests perfection, so my health is perfected. I hold that image as my impassioned view of radiant health, and that picture is mine to complete. Health is my will, now and hereafter. My plea is that my subconscious buddy reforms my body in exact duplication of the perfect image held in the divine mind.

Read that through once more. Methodically translate those words into a vivid picture of health. Make it glow with your passion and enthusiasm. Make it rich, essential, and vital.

Are you all done? Well done! Now resolve to stay away from all that is unhealthy, including bogus thoughts and propaganda. If not, you will have convinced your subconscious mind that lying and cheating are of great value to you, whereby it will automatically re-prioritise your values. Then you're back to 'negativity,' and all its debilitating or destructive consequences. That is how the natural governing laws of our bodies work.

Fear holds us from success. Effectively it is the mental or emotional equivalent of disease. It carries mental poverty in its path, as a fear or severely anxious horror we experience as a physical limitation that stops us in our tracks. Mentally, we are arrested and deprived of that which we desire.

Yet, as discussed above for disease, we can acknowledge that Man is one with God and that God is Mans supply. We are thereby enabled to conquer fear in much the same manner.

We have access to all things needed, but because they are in the abstract, we must call them into manifestation. To that end, we must also recognise that to use the power God has placed within us, we must summons that power through our passion for life, albeit expressed as 'value.' I speak of 'life values,' or spiritual values, that may also be called virtues. Life values are our access code, given to us so that we may create the things we desire.

Fear blocks or hinders the divine response, but it is not an adverse power in real terms. Power is creative. Force is destructive. We may falsely refer to the lack of purposeful power as negative power or negative energy, but it remains that absence is not presence.

Fortunately, the Divine mind is all the power there is. Fear is our (mental) divorce from our inherent power; its denial or rejection. Fear arises from not knowing the power that you have. It comes from not knowing how to tap the divine process through your subconscious power of access.

That process is near the same as described for overcoming any disease. Remember, it is not the ridding of doubt or fear. Negativity plays no part. That, as explained, is fully self-defeating. The secret is to construct a definite and positive concept of what we want, which is the same process God himself used in creating the universe. It is positive visualisation. It is holding it in our minds eye, so to speak, which, as you will soon learn, is the vocabulary of our subconscious mind. Visualising benefits resulting from manifested desires amplifies our passion for life. Power is released when the subconscious mind recognises that our conscious mind joins it in complete harmony.

The visualisation process requires concentration but for no more than a minute. Why so short? Because dwelling on your desire for too long may cause your subconscious to read that you have doubts or some disbelief in it happening, meaning that you still fear.

The secret, therefore, is to visualise your desires with joy and its benefits. Then your expressed happiness cancels all doubts and fears automatically. Thus relieved of all limitations, the gate opens to manifesting your desires, positive evidence that the method works to perfection.

That idea will progressively develop over many explanations that follow. As later shown, material resources, products, and physical gains are tools (or agents) of spiritual accomplishment. They are not materialistic satisfactions or empire building.

Our bodies exhibit a certain natural orderliness and maintenance of that orderliness. The immune system, for example, facilitates cooperation and prevents infractions. Our speech also confirms harmonious order. For example, our lips, tongue, throat, jaw, larynx, and diaphragm all work together in near-perfect synchrony when speaking. Uttering the most simple phrases engages a most complex orderliness having remarkable accuracy. Better still, our free will is the master conductor of this symphony.

Now look further. Our endocrine system is a chemical messenger system utilising hormones. The hypothalamus in the brain is the neural control centre. A group of glands secrete hormones directly into the circulatory system to regulate the function of distant target organs. Feedback loops modulate hormone release to maintain homeostasis, also known as bodily order. This loop is of profound importance because the sequential endocrine process mimics our conscious process, later explained in detail.

I'll jump the gun for a minute to show how you can take charge. Our thoughts are wilfully intentioned because they are not automatic. The secret is requesting that your subconscious accept your desires. You do so not to remember but so that you do not need to remember. That automation is your Divine gift of mental efficiency. Understand it, and you will grasp the fullness of your conscious power as never told before!

Progress in life requires a degree of understanding developed along mental and spiritual lines. For this purpose, intellect is the faculty of reasoning and comprehension, especially concerning abstract matters.

Chapter 2

Today, vocabulary has become pliable, often bent or disguised to suit a particular purpose. Text messages and political correctness qualify as chief offenders. Many of the following concepts have precise meanings, and because many more are unknown, it is suggested that you bookmark this page/chapter for later reference and resolute understanding. Let's begin with two mental tools that are pure blessings.

- **Intelligence** is the intellectual ability to recognise self-evident truths.
- **Reason** is the mental ability to logically think through connected steps in search of truth that is not self-evident. Reason allows us to change attitudes, traditions, and institutions and to convert beliefs into knowledge, all within the realm of free will and self-determination.

Hereafter, different intellectual properties facilitate the critical thinking process, as follows —

- **Intellect** is the faculty of reasoning and objective comprehension, especially concerning abstract matters, particularly as distinct from feeling or wishing. Intellect is our capacity for knowledge and understanding. It allows us to learn, think and reason, to build our knowledge and comprehension.
- **Discernment** is the mental process of discriminatory investigation leading to understanding. It usefully separates beliefs from truths, illusions from reality, pretenses from facts, foolishness from wisdom, and ignorance from knowledge.
- **Thinking** is the choice to comprehend what exists, theories included, and project ideas into the future.
- **Logic** is the art of non-contradictory identification.
- **Rational thought** is the learned process of logic and reason to advance knowledge and wisdom.
- **Intellectual discernment** is the key to self-mastery, the tool of rational enquiry based on clarity and integrity of thought.

Perhaps you are asking why 'values' were omitted from that list. It is because values are the biggest and the most precious factor of all. If you've not guessed already, this whole book is about values. They empower the subconscious mind.

Sadly, our human sciences, psychologists, philosophers, psychiatrists or social scientists seldom venture this path, if ever. That is why conscious ignorance is so prevalent.

Just as the subconscious mind is a part abstraction of Source, so values are an abstracted element of the subconscious. Values are the source from which your subconscious is empowered to act — its fuel if you like. Its astounding ability to oversee all that you do, jointly with its ability to monitor and adjust progress is exactly what permits your material and spiritual goals to manifest jointly.

The fact we are not taught how quantitative brain processes unite with qualitative experiences, is a monumental tragedy. Nature's greatest gift is denied. But no more! The good news is that because we determine what values apply to our actions, so we author our feelings. They in turn oblige that we consciously back-engineer our feelings to objectively identify their source values. Thus we may retain them, revise them, or change our future behaviour.

There's the clue. 'Full consciousness' now answers what science has not yet discovered. Our quantitative brain processes are definitively united with qualitative experiences, and are thereby inseparable.

"The essence of the independent mind lies not in what it thinks, but in how it thinks." —Christopher Hitchens [7]

Values that empower the subconscious mind were not on that list because their importance demanded this book. Neuroscience, psychologists, philosophers, psychiatrists, and social scientists seldom venture this path, if at all.

Just as the subconscious mind is an abstracted part of Source, life values are the (abstract) element of the subconscious mind, which empower it to act and oversee all you do so that your material and spiritual goals manifest simultaneously.

Not being taught how quantitative brain processes unite with qualitative experiences is a monumental tragedy, explained by the fact that we author our feelings by (prior) determining what values apply to our actions. Therefore, we should consciously trace our feelings to their source values, then choose to retain or revise our values or change our future behaviour.

That short description of the role played by values answers what science has never discovered. Quantitative brain processes are definitively united with qualitative experiences and are thereby inseparable.

Thinking is not automated, nor is it mandatory. We are free to think or to avoid that effort. Thinking requires we choose to employ the focused awareness of our mind. Because we are not free to evade the consequences of that choice, let us examine the most pertinent properties of thought.

'Analytical thinking' differs from 'critical thinking,' but much confusion exists concerning each and their differences. The primary difference lies in the process.

Chapter 2

The process of 'analytic thinking' is to abstractly separate constituent parts from the whole, and then study those parts and their respective relationships with others. It is to break down complex information, one step at a time to form an overall conclusion, an answer, or a solution. Different points of view are investigated to discover cause and effect, and often to create it.

Critical thinking, in contrast, is the ability and wilful intention to think clearly and rationally. It is our choice to engage in reflective and independent thinking. Critical thinking skills enable us to—

- firmly grasp and understand the logical connections between ideas;
- identify issues or matters, thus able to argue merits and values, construct hypotheses and evaluate possibilities and benefits;
- detect and evaluate inconsistencies and common mistakes in reasoning;
- solve problems systematically and congruently, i.e., factually;
- determine the relevance, importance and application of ideas;
- properly examine and evaluate different criteria to justify our beliefs and values.

A critical thinker does not decide whether an event, a thing or a situation is right or wrong. Critical thinking is not the province of forming an opinion or belief but rather the process of discovering facts and ideas that inform, whereby what is (i.e., reality) is the final arbiter, not one's interpretation or belief. New information will then consolidate our comprehensive knowledge database.

Critical thinking is not the accumulation of information. Neither is it necessary to have a good memory and an arsenal of facts. A critical thinker deduces what is relevant and truthful and adds that information to that already known. Critical thinking uses valid information to solve problems, rejects what is not including beliefs, and seeks relevant information from other sources.

Critical thinking is a learning process, an essential part of creativity. It plays a vital role in cooperative reasoning and constructive efforts. It helps us acquire knowledge, strengthen our position, build pride from our effort and vitalise our self-esteem. It also assists in exposing fallacies and false reasoning.

"Critical thinking is self-guided, self-disciplined thinking which attempts to reason at the highest level of quality in a fair-minded way. People who think critically consistently attempt to live rationally, reasonably, empathically. They are keenly aware of the inherently flawed nature of human thinking when left unchecked. They strive to diminish the power of their egocentric and socio-centric tendencies. Use of the intellectual tools of concepts and

principles enable them to analyse, assess, and improve their thinking.
They work diligently to develop the intellectual virtues of intellectual integrity, intellectual humility, intellectual civility, intellectual empathy, intellectual sense of justice and confidence in reason. They realise that no matter how skilled they are as thinkers, they can always improve their reasoning abilities and they will at times fall prey to mistakes in reasoning, human irrationality, prejudices, biases, distortions, uncritically accepted social rules and taboos, self-interest, and vested interest. They strive to improve the world in whatever ways they can and contribute to a more rational, civilised society." —Linda Elder [8]

Without free will, we cannot function at all! With no cognitive faculty, we all would struggle through life with less than the (automated) perceptual nature of animals, and no such thing as Man would exist! We must choose to activate reason, necessarily, and, silly as it might seem, unless and until we do, we have no reason to initiate anything.

Free will allows us to think and reason, to inquire, research, discover, and evaluate difficulties and benefits. It opens or closes the gate to all ideas, truths, postulates, beliefs, wishes, whims, propaganda, and indoctrinations. Free choice is the conscious process of establishing values and benefits that advance our life and rejecting those that do not.

Free will is not a simple yes/no switch, therefore. It is a value-assessment tool first and foremost. It enables us to establish values and benefits, to reject what does not advance our life. The more we value, the higher our committed intention to attain it.

Free will is also the gatekeeper of our subconscious mind. It is the minder of self-respect and self-responsibility. Aside from instinctual, life-saving reflex actions, free will oversees all material, ethical, moral and spiritual outcomes. That said, it cannot alter its process or the laws of its nature.

We may abuse these virtues and our minds. We can refuse to think. We can accept erroneous faiths and superstitions as knowledge, but not with impunity, I hasten to add. Free will is not a free license. It carries enormous responsibility, as later described.

To full understand 'full consciousness,' we must divorce our mental processes from the content that is processed, much as we separate computer hardware from software. Thus we can be subjective insofar as free will is concerned and at the same time, deal with our mental processes objectively and scientifically insofar as upholding life is concerned.

Diagram 4 shows the full conscious process as a value transfer wave.

Chapter 2

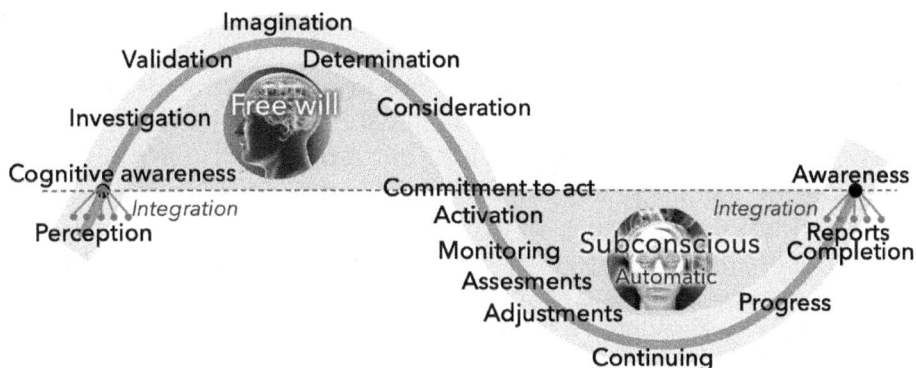

Imagination
Validation   Determination
Investigation   Free will   Consideration
Cognitive awareness   Awareness
Integration   Commitment to act   Integration
Perception   Activation   Reports
                        Monitoring   Subconscious   Completion
                        Assesments   Automatic
                        Adjustments   Progress
                                Continuing

4. The Value Transfer Wave

The process will later be expanded upon but for the moment, focus on its waveform simplicity. Our cognitive free will mind is above the horizontal line. The subconscious mind is below.

Perception, shown at the bottom left, is the subconscious faculty that integrates multiple sensory data, such as lines, colours, planes and textures. It forms an image of a surfboard, a birthday party, or a circumstance such as two smashed cars in an auto accident. In other words, 'perception' converts an unrecognisable jumble of multiple sensory stimuli into a and identifiable 'something' or an 'event.'

'Cognitive awareness' is the end product of that perception process. Awareness does not trigger an automatic response, as happens for animals. Instead, it prompts us to discover, to learn how, where, when and why. In other words, the conscious process shifts from subconscious perception to (cognitive) free will enquiry. At that point, the subconscious process effectively stops work, whereby our discoveries eventually prompt us to make choices leading to action.

Thus (cognitive) 'awareness,' commonly believed to be 'consciousness,' is only a tiny part of the process. It is little more than a trigger to learn more. Our awareness does not explain what thing, event or circumstance the subconscious mind delivered to our attention. Instead, we are alerted to its existence or an idea, so we can question, learn, and profit our lives. Free will then works freely and independently.

So our cognitive thinking develops an understanding of the thing, event, or circumstance. It has complete freedom to explore every avenue in search of truthfulness. In short, we enquire, investigate and learn, eventually choosing and committing to an action of some kind.

At this midpoint in diagram 4, the subconscious mind resumes work, and the conscious mind stops work. According to previously learned behaviours, the subconscious mind engages the autonomic nervous system to motor-activate our cells and muscles. It monitors our progress, thereby identifying and making corrections to complete the desired task.

Lastly, it ascertains the outcome of our efforts and presents two reports. First, it makes us cognitively aware of our progress via our perception. Secondly, it identifies success or failure and reports to our sentient consciousness through what we experience as 'feelings.'

The conscious process is now complete concerning that particular action. Our cognitive mind is now back at the place where it began, save that we now have additional knowledge from which to work. That looped process continues several times each day, while some cycles may take several days or even years to complete.

One cannot explain full consciousness any simpler. It is a fully unified process, charged by what we have accepted as valued truth, deliberately or have assimilated by default. It is doubtful that you will find that description in any textbook or website concerning consciousness. Yet, its understanding is fundamental to the success of your life, to every positive and spiritual emotion you could ever experience!

The subconscious mind sustains the whole of our life, including all our mental processes. Thus, ninety percent of our long-term happiness is not mere thoughts but, more importantly, what values our thoughts embrace, and our valued reason for engaging them. Ordinarily, this means our subconscious mind works in the spiritual realm while our cognitive mind plays with physicality. Physicality and spirituality are unified thereby.

Free will, and the process of thinking, are two different things. Freedom to think requires we not surrender the sovereignty of our mind. Thinking requires using our mind to answer fundamental questions such as, what is it? What is something's nature, purpose or function? What constitutes the postulation or idea of which I'm consciously aware? Valid answers to these questions will depend on—

- How intently and honestly we focus on discovering answers.
- The amount of information we can process at one time. (Our brain has a finite capacity — see 'concepts' below).
- Whether we validate information to discover its truth or falsity, and both fall within the ethics category.
- Whether we are prepared to correct any thinking errors. That returns us to point number one.

Our free choice is not only to reason but also to determine what manner of reasoning we will use. (Deductive or Inductive; Subjective or Objective?)

Free will is self-respect and self-responsibility in its most total sense, its

Chapter 2

ethical use being one of life's most critical assignments. Creator has facilitated free choice so that every conceivable nuance of thought is available to every man, woman and child. Nothing we choose can change the natural laws of our thought processes. It must be that way. Our thought process must be guaranteed protection. Unless our choices are protected, free will is uselessly redundant.

That protection allows us to change the content of our thought process. Our thoughts are free to roam the universe unconstrained. So it is that we can reverse our choices (change our minds) in milliseconds. We do this regularly to fine-tune our desires and our progress.

Threats, coercion and punishment may cause us to make different choices, but such is not and cannot be our free will acceptance. All forms of compulsion and initiated force trespass our free will. Additionally, severe mind control methods will employ torture and trauma to access our subconscious mind. More subtle ways may use media, music, entertainment, propaganda, unfounded beliefs, bogus philosophies, religious persuasions, censorship, and so forth. These villainous dealings have the potential to sabotage or assault the value database in our subconscious minds without our knowledge. By using that 'under the radar' means, nefarious results occur without our acceptance or permission. Torture or traumas may violently or criminally force our submission, but submitting to 'force' is not free consent. Nothing is lawfully enabled to override our free will consent.

Volition is the faculty or power of choosing to engage one's will — one's free will — one's choice. It is the conscious freedom to think and reason, to inquire, research and discover to evaluate difficulties and benefits. Truth is absolute. Truth is discoverable, and so is reality.

Ayn Rand pointed out that reality is absolute, existence also, and so is a speck of dust and human life. Therefore, whether we live or die is absolute. The problem, she continued, is being taught to *"hedge on any principle, compromise on any value, and take the middle of any road."* To accept supernatural absolutes when so introduced obliges us to reject nature as absolute, and that acceptance becomes our moral code.

The truth of our human nature and the laws that govern our faculties innately exist. They are immutable and intangible, but the truth or falsity of what mental content is processed is for each man and woman's free will to discover. Our nature pleads that we find out the truth and employ it in the service of our lives.

Free will means our freedom to 'will' an action. A conscious, calm, resolved determination expresses our 'will.'

'Free' means unrestrained. It is our unrestricted ability to uphold and sustain our life respectfully within the equal rights of all others. That imparts respect and responsibility.

'Will' means our determination and passion for succeeding. It is the express intention to pursue our enquiries and decisions, to benefit and prosper, despite all temptations or demands to the contrary.

'Power' is the subconscious mind's ability to initiate, direct, execute, monitor, and complete our intention(s). Our subconscious mind fulfills our choices.

'Willpower' is our conscious will to succeed, plus the subconscious mind's empowered capacity to make it happen.

Both minds are involved in exercising our willpower, and that combination is crucial. It means that will is of our conscious mind, while power is the subconscious mind's ability to initiate, direct, execute, monitor, and complete our intended tasks. Full consciousness is two-way mind communication.

Logical reasoning, being the art of non-contradictory identification, does not rule out our consideration of feelings, as later discussed, but it does reject feelings as tools of cognition, discernment or decision making.

The question, 'what is it,' implies an impeccably honest answer; else, any enquiry is fraudulent. Establishing 'truth' requires the use of logic because contradictions cannot exist. Neither an atom nor the entire universe can contradict its own identity. No part can contradict the whole of which it is part. The stabilising power of 'logic' allows us to analyse and validate information free from deceptions.

New knowledge or understanding must integrate without contradiction into the total sum of one's (truth-based) knowledge; without is to confess an error in one's thinking. Refusal to resolve a paradox or contradiction is the deliberate choice to surrender one's mind, an attempt to evict oneself from the realm of reality. Logical analysis alerts us to more fundamental questions necessary to ask and answer.

Rationality is forthright. It is our recognising that existence exists and that our mind is our only judge of values and one's guide to actions. Reason itself is an absolute that permits no compromise. To ignore that understanding is to switch from validating our conscious process to faking reality. As Rand pointed out, *to short-circuit and destroy the mind through acceptance of a mystical invention is to wish for the destruction of existence, which, appropriately, annihilates one's consciousness.*

Rational thinking is the deliberate choice to understand existent things, including theories and hypotheses. A theory is an abstraction based on actual reality. Tangible evidence of its (absolute) founding truth is verifiable through the laws of identity and causality (later discussed). Without concrete identification, there can be no theory because there is nothing for our conscious mind to process.

Reason allows us to change attitudes, traditions, and institutions and to convert beliefs into knowledge, all within the realm of free will and self-determination. It allows us to adapt ideas and material existence to life-sustaining purposes. Life is the reason we have values. Reasoning relates to 'integrity' that connects to 'courage.'

The natural law of right reason states: *"reasoning discovers truths that are not self-evident."* Accordingly, our reasoning is the testing point of all values based on the 'supreme value' of 'life.' If we are to live as Creator intentioned, we must accept 'life', dare to attest to our values, and have the will and fortitude to enact them. Thus reason is the only tool we have to redeem ourselves from the hock shop of irrational thinking.

"We live in a world where unfortunately the distinction between true and false appears to become increasingly blurred by manipulation of facts, by exploitation of uncritical minds, and by the pollution of the language." —Arne Tisselus

Those words bring to mind that many writers seem all too willing to jump to conclusions, especially if that helps make their case. Often they will cite how someone got an inspiration or revelation concerning some matter or idea that seems to be quite profound or came to realise little-known helpful information. Because such things 'seem' to be beyond the ordinary, they will be reported as proof of divine inspiration, intuit understanding of 'higher consciousness.' Many people portend clear and unmistakable evidence exists that the 'age of reason' has passed. Man is now shifting into the drawing of a new consciousness. Many other forms of equally vague verbiage or new age phraseology describe such occurrences simply because it sounds plausible, even though consciousness is not understood to begin.

Dare one question how any of these matters concern interaction between one's conscious and subconscious mind, and a storm of howling derision will descend. *"How can you think that way,"* is a typical response, as though 'thought' really was the basis of their question. "How can one be so blind to Divine Inspiration," others may question?

Answers to such questions lie in knowing how our conscious process works. With that understanding, it may well be that one's 'revelation' is indeed divine inspiration or intuit comprehension. But, conversely, one's 'revelation' may well be invented verbiage or new age jargon.

Our reasoning is far greater than we give it credit. Knowing how consciousness works is monumental. Intellectual mastery is the key to a future of freedom. Nothing less will suffice. Undoubtedly, today's masters of tyranny understand this and have for centuries, but they will forbid you that truth forever, or else their empire of rule collapses overnight.

Ayn Rand clarifies that reason is the enemy or authoritarian rule. Authoritarians know they must rule your mind for you to be conquered and made submissive. They know that your feelings, wishes or your instincts are largely irrelevant.

Knowledge keeps us from buying fiction and fraud. Wisdom warns of false beliefs and basic fallacies that often underpin organised society and its supposed branches of knowledge. There are levels of lies, of course. But the more logical your investigations, the greater your confidence and power to resolve that which eludes you.

The integrity of thought requires that we place nothing above the integrity of our mental functioning. With an unwavering goal and logic as our method and using the judgment of our mind as our guiding absolute, success is achievable and rewarding. In this sense, we each are on our own. What we consider factual or truthful ultimately determines our values concerning our acceptance. Both are primary to thought and, therefore, our actions and behaviours.

People who regard compliance with the directives of others as a moral imperative are trapped. Those people who accept sacrifice as a primary duty, or self-abasement as a virtue, are prevented from thinking. Their minds are a servant of others' edicts. Those people are not free.

Nothing serves our thought, knowledge, ethics, or morality when other people set the terms of our independent minds.

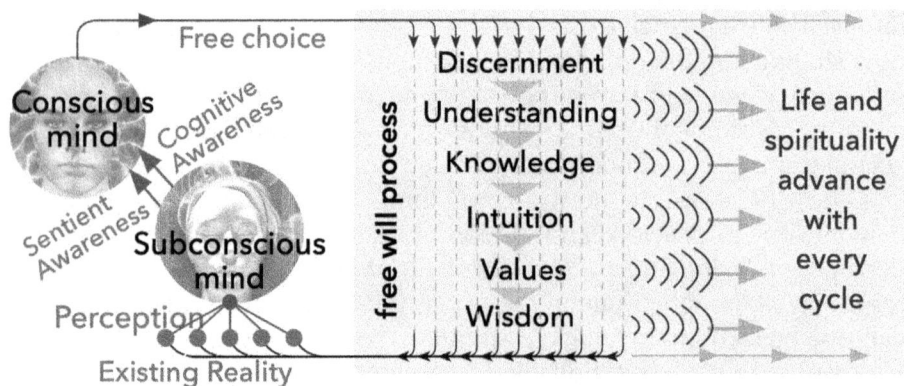

5. The full conscious process is a repeating cycle

You've seen how the value transfer wave works. Diagram 5 presents the same principle as a clockwise (repeating) loop. It shows how simple the conscious process is and how it works.

Chapter 2

Perception triggers cognitive awareness and prompts free will enquiry. We advance by engaging discernment, understanding and knowledge, and intuition, perhaps. Values kick start our actions leading to material outcomes and our feelings. Because the loop repeats for every new action, our mental, emotional and spiritual abilities grow and mature progressively. Each repetition allows for further information via our five senses, while feelings and conscience prompt our learning.

As diagram 5 shows, we are each living, sentient, volitionally conscious beings, complete and unified in all respects. Beautiful simplicity lies in the process repeating over and over throughout our lives. Value choices are the key to success! Complete orderliness and structure evidence natural law.

Your subconscious is the medium whereby everything relating to your needs can be provided or brought into manifestation. Your conscious mind is the determining factor in that creative process. It synchronises the power of your two minds through values, based on your life as the supreme value! Our solution to personal and societal problems lies in our ability to think things through, reason and logically accept what profits our lives, and reject what is unworkable or biased.

But sadly, in today's age, we are all held in check, propagandised to defect from our power. Denied any knowledge of what our control truly is, we're left to assume it does not exist. So we turn to the state for assistance. Propagandists hear our plea and hammer their case relentlessly. They tell us our allegiance to family, group, community and society. Never do they or will they promote individual sovereignty or your dynamic ability to create and venture into the unknown. That message would destroy their rule over our lives. Consequently, you must sacrifice your independence and individuality to the 'collective.'

As civilisation erodes and decays, intellectually robust individuals refuse to surrender. They find new frontiers. They understand that power comes from three sources.

- Their ability to apply logic to events and information, to reason from A to B to C, to analyse, deduce, evaluate and act on that wisdom.

- Their imagination is the capacity to conceive of inventions that would not otherwise exist.

- By exercising our Creator's gift of visualisation and imagination, they upload their values and choices into the image vocabulary of their subconscious mind.

- These rugged individualists also know that exercising their creative power to fulfil what they deeply desire has the effect of spilling over and positively affecting others in a way that will remind them of their power and lift them.

Still, we can learn more.

- Our free will 'process' (hardware) is constrained, but our mental 'content' (software) is unrestrained!
- Life immeasurably suffers when robbed of our subconscious life-sustaining ability.
- Free will's unchangeable process thereby protects the fixed subconscious process.
- Our subconscious mind cannot discern, evaluate, decide, judge, or create because that would countermand free will.
- Because of subconscious automation, the subconscious mind's processes cannot be overridden or countermanded via the conscious mind.
- Our subconscious mind is not open to external influence, save what we freely permit.
- Unless consciously arrested, undue influence will raid, rob, or violate our whole mental process. (That arrest is automated by intentionally uploading our value preferences to the subconscious mind.)
- The subconscious mind cannot discern, evaluate, judge, or create because that would overrule our free will choices and undermine our cognitive abilities.
- Necessarily, therefore, our subconscious mind protects our free will.

That means, in sociological terms, no individual may violate the life of another. That 'natural law of no trespass,' is encrypted in our biology and it cannot be erased.

Life values are crucial! I speak of spiritual values that serve your life, not your bank account. Ayn Rand made it very clear—

- *Life is what makes the concept of value possible, and,*
- *Life is what makes values necessary.*

When both minds are on the same page, glowing harmony results, and that gift from your Creator is priceless. It is the recipe for absolute joy. Programming our minds with our values causes confusion, anxiety, and stress to vanish. So we have more creative energy to press our free choices even further! Altogether, our whole conscious process is an astonishing masterpiece of nature that no artificial intelligence can match. Because we live, nothing artificial can perform that task or ever will!

The whole purpose of consciousness is to objectively sustain and uphold life, like all our bodily cells and organ systems. Consciousness is life-related, therefore. It is not matter related as science believes. Life objectivity renders human consciousness a science, equal to our biology.

Chapter 3

Whereas our immune system rids toxins and disease first-hand, detrimental mental effects like anxiety, stress, and mental trauma do not cleanse automatically. That would violate our free will and deny our chosen values. Instead, the cognitive mind is alerted to overcome this problem through choice. We experience success and distress via our feelings and emotions, which prompt free will to discover and activate a remedy. Thus free will prevails, and corrections result.

Therefore, what appears to be the mental equivalent of our immune system is *no less than the Creator's gift of an 'automated value-mentoring system,'* but that is not taught today!

- **At the personal level,** 'full consciousness' puts our most fervent desires on auto-pilot. Mental strain is reduced to near nil, while emotional joy excels.
- **At the social level,** 'full consciousness' offers twenty natural laws. These provide every ethic that society needs, from comforts, through security and protection, to natural justice.

That recognition now permits full consciousness to be defined.

Definition of Full consciousness

Consciousness is the systemic process of life-value transfer between the conscious and subconscious minds, interfacing physicality and spirituality.

Consciousness, now defined for the first time, means the real gem in this chapter is our blessing of a mentoring system that invigorates the conscious process and maintains its vitality. Now it is essential to grasp how our two minds work in concert. The next chapter begins its description.

Conscious Ascendance

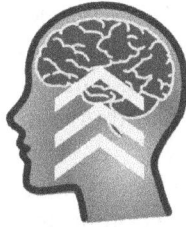

Chapter 3

3. The Conscious and Subconscious Minds

Whereas I have already defined the entire conscious process, I will now explain how that definition can be so concise yet fully comprehensive.

The secret is consciously and consistently using the integrated sum of knowledge. That does not imply a finite measure. It means applying one's present understanding irrespective of one's level of education. Both a young child and a wise old sage can use the complete knowledge they each have. Full consciousness is not the raising of it, the increasing of it, or some new vibration. It is instead our knowing how and why our two minds communicate and consciously applying that understanding for our benefit.

People want political and societal change, but no alternative offers to cancel the status quo. We've no choice, it seems, but to fall back on beliefs and political persuasions that have failed us for centuries. Technology will never correct that circumstance, however. Neither will artificial intelligence do anything but consolidate present ignorance. Centuries of bogus philosophies will not change overnight; thus, hypnotised social conditioning is near impossible to escape.

Knowledge is the only correction. But, without a healthy reappraisal of consciousness, nothing will rid our destructive patterns and thrust us into a healthy state of collaboration with each other and our ecosystems. Only that will remove oligarchic oppressors from power to allow the creation of healthy, harmonious, symbiotic societies in their place. Until then, ignorance fuels our minds, and we suffer unknowingly.

Conscious Ascendance

We've two choices. We can allow socialist and communist doctrines to extinguish societies as present behavioral consequences dictate they will. Or, we can discover our true nature as volitionally conscious living beings, cultivate that change in others and our societies, and thrive like never before!

Success means learning what consciousness is, how it works, and how we differ from animals. Thriving demands we discover and understand the governing laws of our nature, enabling us to rise far above today's severely arrested mentality. That will lift humanity into the glory of its birthright.

Two matters emerge, and the second overcomes the first.

1. Humanity has relentlessly pursued technology while abandoning consciousness, psychology and spirituality.

2. Although blessed with light-speed faculties so complex they almost defy description, still we can write our subconscious programs as infants do without language, math or science.

The senseless tragedy is that we've not recognised consciousness's simplicity or spiritually empowering nature, and we've paid a hefty price. Having never discovered the importance of spiritual purpose, we've sacrificed it to a currency of materialism, greed and plunder. Two prime factors are responsible.

*   **Philosophical materialism** is the view that non-physical things do not exist. All talk of 'spirit' or 'spirituality' is considered senseless mysticism. People are nothing more than matter in motion, whereby physical nature triumphs. The theory completely defeats itself because it belies the non-physical nature of thought from which it arises.

*   **Philosophical idealism** is almost the opposite yet is equally nonsensical. It holds that everything is an idea, energy, or consciousness, whereby there is no such thing as matter, physical objects, or bodies. Physicality is a hologram, an illusion since everything is energy or frequency. This theory also defeats itself because no expression is possible without the physicality of vocal cords, pens, or a keyboard. Our ears, eyes, and brains must materially exist before anyone can hear or read such claims.

Ayn Rand summed the absurdity of materialism and idealism when she said—

"A body without a soul is a corpse, a soul without a body is a ghost."

Others argue that the ultimate goal of spirituality is to transcend the self. Self is an illusion. People say they cannot find the 'self', the 'I,' and the 'ego.' Forget your body and brain — consciousness is not your 'self.' It just emanates from your body and brain. Neither is there a thinker because thoughts emanate from consciousness (aka awareness). This argument is also self-defeating. It denies the very being to whom spirituality matters, namely one's self.

Mental illusions and delusions have succeeded in depleting our mental and spiritual capacity. Bogus doctrines and erroneous philosophies have corrupted the subjects of consciousness and spirituality so profoundly that few people understand their inner realm—thus chaos and trauma reign. No one cheats on nature. We cheat ourselves. Nature ensures we reap what we sow, always.

Spiritual achievement begins with uploading chosen values to our subconscious database so that they will manifest our desires. After that, full consciousness is an interactive and energetic process of value enactment that interfaces physicality and our soul.

In simple terms, values are inherent in our commitments, whether we know of them or not. They are transmitted between our two minds much as blood is oxygenated and circulated via our cardio-vascular system. We're blessed with a perfect model of mental efficiency once we learn how to use it. First, word concepts and principles facilitate mental efficiency. Second, values enable subconscious efficiency that integrates vast sums of data in a millisecond. In short—

Our cognitive mind uses (word) 'concepts and principles to integrate vast sums of information.

Our subconscious mind uses its (integrative) 'perceptive' ability to package and transmit vast amounts of information.

'Integration' is the key word in both cases. But unfortunately, those vital distinctions are neglected today. Awareness, perception, and understanding have different meanings, but mental efficiency is grossly impaired when frequently interchanged as though equal contributors. Unsurprisingly we are rendered docile, to be herded like cattle and ruled as enslaved people.

It gets worse. 'Knowledge' may be claimed with no necessity to validate it. As a result, self-deception arises, and the problem magnifies. Beliefs may then be considered knowledge. Likewise, we may regard feelings as understanding an event or circumstance, thus dismissing the root cause. This merry dance to cognitive dissonance and emotional distress means we never suspect inadvertent or deliberate sabotage of our whole conscious process.

Not cheating yourself, not being apathetic, and not dodging what might seem to be onerous overcomes many problems. Success is full of intellectual diligence, fortitude, and integrity, all in one parcel. The opposite polarity is mental abandonment, desertion, neglect, and betrayal of one's true self.

Conscious Ascendance

'Awareness' is the conscious recognition of an 'existent' thing, event, circumstance or theory. We become aware of some object, event or action, or that some idea or knowledge exists. Our subconscious perceptive faculty condenses multitudes of data into a tight package and delivers that as a 'product' to our conscious awareness. Nothing is explained concerning its makeup, however. For example, an infant does not know whether a spherical object is a ball, a sphere, a bomb, or a balloon. It does not understand their differences. We must learn if we are to benefit. In summary;

- **Perception** is an 'integrative process of the subconscious mind.' Compiling multiple data into singular (abstracted) entities or events enables our cognitive mind to handle masses of information without mental stress.
- **Perceived information** is raw, authentic and accurate. We have no (free will) say over what the subconscious mind offers.
- **'Conscious awareness'** of an object or event offers no understanding of the essential information. We might instantly recognise it from what we have previously learned. Otherwise, we must choose to understand what it is or what it means.

To attribute conscious awareness as being equal to cognitive understanding is probably the most debilitating short circuit of one's mental faculties possible.

Concepts and principles help us embrace the big picture and reduce mental stress. They carry vast amounts of information in one or two words. For example, the word 'airplane' contains all the information about every plane ever built and every new airplane. The information is complete because all essentials are abstracted. Ayn Rand offered valuable insight regarding concepts. She defined them as *"a mental integration of two or more units isolated by abstraction but united through a specific definition."*

Concepts are named to become words. Language and communication derive from this ability. 'Concepts' retain the essential 'constituents' of (their) origins. For example, the word 'book' refers to a bound stack of pages. This concept applies to books with music or pictures, whether soft or hardcover, reference books, and children's books.

'Conceptualising' is drawing inferences, making deductions, reaching conclusions, asking new questions, and discovering their answers. Knowledge expands into an ever-growing sum. By organising perceptual material into concepts, thence into more expansive and comprehensive concepts, we can grasp, retain, identify, and integrate vast amounts of knowledge far beyond the immediate concretes of any given moment.

Chapter 3

Similar data from different sources are abstracted into a new frame of reference and given a name to form a new concept. Thus we can include all essentials whilst seemingly dealing with one word or a few. E.G. garden, vegetable garden, or garden hose.

Concepts greatly assist in solving mind-numbing complexities. They allow us to consider alternatives rapidly to evaluate, judge and decide upon actions instantly. Our mental abilities flourish. Efficiency improves, and stress fades.

Concepts enable higher-level thinking — where one idea springs from another resulting in a ladder of 'concepts.' For example, the concept of a car rests on transport and both rest on the idea of mobility. So principles are formed, these being fundamental truths or propositions that abstractly serve as the basis for future reasoning. Thinking in 'principles' is among the most significant abilities of our intellectual consciousness.

Organising perceptual material into concepts, thence into more comprehensive concepts and principles, enables us to grasp, retain, identify and integrate an unlimited amount of knowledge extending far beyond present moment realisation's.

Conversely, arbitrary concepts are a waste of time and effort because nothing is tangibly or cognitively 'essential,' for example, attempting to conceptualise wishes to form a belief.

Word concepts transform the basic 'arithmetic' of conscious awareness into an algebra of conscious understanding. Ayn Rand.[1] explained that the basic principle of concept-formation is the equivalent of the basic principle of algebra. Where algebraic symbols must be given some numerical value but may signify a particular value, omitted concept measurements must exist in some quantity or any quantity. She concluded *"conceptual awareness is the algebra of cognition."*

For example, the word 'table' is a concept denoting a working platform, having legs, height, material and colour as constituents, but with no measurements of those constituents, such as three legs or four, low or medium height. The fact that measurements must exist in some quantity but may exist in any amount is akin to the basic principle of algebra, as Rand described in the quotation above. Effectively, therefore, 'conceptual awareness' is the algebra of cognition.

As with awareness, concepts do not necessarily inform constituent properties, such as origin, importance, material properties, durability or use. The word 'book' tells nothing but a bound stack of pages. But that same integrative (not reductive) ability is precisely how our (subconscious) perceptive faculty works to perfection. That incredible ability powers six of our nine higher faculties simultaneously, as later explained. Consider the subject of our comprehension.

Conscious Ascendance

Knowledge is acquaintance with facts, truths, or principles, and where understanding results from study or investigation. The intellect's capacity to retain knowledge is called 'intellectual memory.'

Full consciousness means consciously and consistently using the integrated sum of knowledge acquired from exercising our choice. 'Fullness' does not imply a finite measure. It means wilfully applying what we know regardless of how much we know.

This list shows how our two minds function, as revealed through observational science and deductive reasoning, not neuroscience.

- Awareness is a function of our cognitive (or conscious) mind, our brain. Its task is thinking and decision-making according to our free choices.

- Our automated subconscious mind is below (sub) our awareness. Its 'operating software' utilises the values we choose from our enquiries. The subconscious mind carries them out, meaning it enacts and oversees our voluntary choices, then adjudicates an emotional response according to our selected values on completion.

- Our subconscious mind also works involuntarily. It monitors all bodily functions and adjusts our heart and breathing rate according to our activities. It releases chemicals into our system, such as adrenaline. In other words, it maintains our bodily systems in an orderly manner so that everything functions optimally for our most significant benefit.

- The subconscious mind's sole purpose is upholding and sustaining our life. It cannot overrule our free will; otherwise, no free will would exist.

- Psycho-epistemology is a branch of philosophy that studies how material and spiritual values transfer between our conscious and subconscious minds. Physicality interfaces at the conscious level, and spirituality interfaces at the subconscious level.

- Consciousness is our creative life force, therefore. It is an operating system that spiritually upholds our lives according to our (value) choices.

- Free will is in charge of the whole process, like the conductor of a symphony orchestra.

- Biologically, our bodily organs thrive or suffer depending on what nutrients or toxins we decide to eat, drink, or inhale. The same applies psychologically, according to our chosen mental or spiritual values.

- Life is the supreme value because, without life, nothing is of value. We are obliged to author our 'values' so that our free will is not corrupted and remains free. We face the consequences of choosing or not choosing and the value or non-value inherent in our choices.

- Values that uphold life are the prime concern of our conscious process. Ideally, they will harmonise with the life-sustaining values inherent in our automated subconscious mind. Our two minds are then on the same page, working in harmony.

Caution is vital. The subconscious mind will default if we do not specifically and deliberately choose life-upholding values. It will assimilate other values from past actions or activities without our knowledge. That circumstance is a recipe for disaster, but it is our choice nonetheless.

In sum, values enrich our material choices and goals. Perception informs our progress. Additionally, feelings and emotions tell of our spiritual (value) progress. In all, physical matter is merely a toolbox for our spiritual growth.

Philosophy	Rationale	Method
Metaphysics		
Existence	What is there?	Reality, identity, causality
Epistemology		
Knowledge	How do I know?	Senses, reason, logic, discerment
Ethics		
Thought/Values	How should I think & live?	Rational self interest
Morality		
Action/Respect	How should I act & treat others?	Respect, integrity, cooperation
Law		
Force/Justice	Legitimate force/ natural law	Restraint, justness, natural justice
Aesthetics		
Art	Happiness	Romantic inspiration, sprituality

6. Objective consciousness in philosophic terms

In table 6, the first column defines the branches of philosophy. Each is further explained in the two remaining columns.

'Metaphysics' is the branch of philosophy that deals with the first principles of things, including abstract concepts such as being, knowing, identity, time, and space. As Ayn Rand described it, "Metaphysics identifies the nature of the universe as a whole." Thus we can learn about our world, dimensions, solid entities, facts versus illusory fragments, miracles and natural laws. And importantly, whether our perceptions inform us of a compressible reality or some unreal appearance that renders us helpless.

Feelings refer to our varying emotions, not our natural or normal mental attributes. The subconscious mind is one with the conscious mind, yet its functions are distinctly different. Here is the philosophical key to understanding how they communicate and share values.

Epistemology is the theory of knowledge, especially concerning its methods, validity, scope, and the distinction between justified knowledge versus beliefs and opinions.

Psycho-epistemology studies our cognitive processes as concerns value interaction between the conscious mind and the automatic functions of the subconscious. Novelist/philosopher Ayn Rand coined the term. This science pertains not just to the content of one's ideas but also to interactions between the conscious and subconscious minds.

Tragically, few people address this branch of philosophy. For example, no one teaches that different functioning processes of the subconscious mind sandwich our free will.

Different natural laws exist, but no one teaches how this tapestry of efficiency and protection unites all our higher faculties. Likewise, no one teaches 'assistance' and 'protection' are woven into every aspect of our physical, mental, emotional, and spiritual life.

None of these matters exists in isolation. Neither of our faculties deals in fiction, fantasies or energies, save what we permit through free will. But unfortunately, human sciences have failed to discover the harmonious totality of our mental processes.

The brain is physical, and the mind is non-physical, yet they interface. The mind and the spirit can receive information from the Source, which means from God. As the instrument through which the divine has chosen to function, our subconscious mind is the only medium through which we can establish contact with the Source. Likewise, our conscious (or cognitive) mind is the only medium through which we can influence our subconscious mind.

Some people refer to the subconscious as our 'subjective mind,' but sadly, that description is very misleading. Dictionaries describe 'subjective' as *"based on or influenced by personal feelings, tastes, or opinions."* Once grasped that our subconscious mind is the generator of our feelings based on our chosen values, that dictionary description is shown back to front. Furthermore, we must reckon our tastes and opinions through free choice. They are the 'subject' of our conscious mind, not that of our subconscious mind. Life is the sole object of subconscious attention, all its efforts and power objectively directed to that end.

Given the astounding abilities of the subconscious mind far exceed our conscious skills, it is above and not below. However, our subconscious mind remains a portion of God's spirit or the essential mind. Therefore, although its great expertise elevates it above our cognitive capabilities, it remains below God's critical mind; thus, the 'sub' prefix is most fitting.

Chapter 3

Throughout history, religious and spiritual teachers have attempted to identify and label this more significant part of ourselves using various labels. These include the Higher Self, the Oversoul, Christ Consciousness, Higher Consciousness and Oneness. The name is unimportant, provided we understand its place and its role. However, unresolved names easily give rise to terms such as universal consciousness, group consciousness, or unity consciousness, as though all of our conscious abilities are communal or universal, not individual. Fortunately, once we grasp 'Source 'is a (universal) repository of abstractions and is not the individuated means of addressing that repository, our consciousness is decisively individual, not universal.

The subconscious mind makes up an estimated ninety-two percent of the total. Our conscious mind comprises the remaining eight percent. Our subconscious mind functions absent orders of any kind, nor can it evaluate, adjudicate, or decide. Neither can its automated processes be overridden or countermanded. Instead, its operations are inviolate and automatic. Consequently, it issues no orders, and it accepts none.

The term' subconscious mind' refers to the functionality of all mental, emotional, and spiritual processes that occur outside of our conscious awareness. It operates the physical body utilising the least effort through repeating patterns. It remembers everything, including operations, experiences and values, assisted through its use of metaphors, imagery, and symbols. The subconscious takes direction from the conscious mind, refusing all negativity. It cannot overrule free will; thus, our values amass to become our soul in totality.

The term 'subconscious mind' addresses the functionality of all mental, emotional, and spiritual processes that occur outside our conscious awareness and our recognition. Since the word 'unconscious' means without consciousness, I've not used it. Likewise, I have rejected the term 'superconscious' simply because subconscious functioning is already superlative, to the point of no challenge.

As mentioned, our subconscious entirely relies on values as the source of feelings and emotions. So what happens should we fail to supply it with our chosen values and passion for life? Does it switch itself off? No, and neither can it. It simply utilises values inherent in past actions and behaviours, which, of course, we chose. Thus free will is always honoured.

Its most notable distinction aside from automation is that it employs an image-based vocabulary instead of a word-concept vocabulary. The subconscious image vocabulary is powerful and fast, primarily since 'a picture paints a thousand words.'

Conscious Ascendance

Our whole conscious process is the bridge between physicality and spirituality. Many people believe that the subconscious mind is the 'soul.' To explain, we choose values that our subconscious mind stores in our memory database. According to our actions and behaviours, these values later manifest as feelings and emotions. Thus our values are (abstractly) stored in the subconscious database. Emotions are reports concerning our 'values' relative to present moment activities.

Our values, as abstractions, sum to being our soul as we have made it. The portion of the mind of God that we know as our subconscious returns upon bodily death, whilst our 'value-made' soul lives on.

Then shall the dust return to the earth as it was: and the spirit shall return unto God who gave it. —Ecclesiastes 12:7 —King James Version (KJV 1900)

The subconscious mind accepts our choices as that which we prize. It has no ability to decree otherwise. That would overrule our free will choices and undermine our cognitive skills. Thus blessings or disasters are ours to choose, precisely because free will has complete autonomy.

We should note that criminal mind control programs can overtly traumatise free will into submission, thus influencing or controlling our actions. Notwithstanding, coercion is not our free will agreement! It trespasses our free choice.

When we choose (consent) to watch television programs,' we inadvertently give our subconscious mind permission to accept any or all subliminal values and ideas contained therein. (The word 'program' is not accidental.) However, if we have chosen different (overriding) values, as discussed later, contrary values embedded in TV programs will be automatically rejected.

The subconscious image vocabulary does not distinguish between real and imagined, as psychologists have verified through laboratory experiments. Our task is to learn the difference between the (conscious) alphabetic and (subconscious) pictographic vocabularies. The first must learn to reason. The second compares images to discover similarities or discrepancies to form and deliver emotional reports, called feelings.

The subconscious mind can perform trillions of operations simultaneously. For example, we sweat when we are hot, digest our food, fight foreign bodies, and release insulin effortlessly without conscious thought. The subconscious mind constantly communicates with all the cells and organs in our body, and they, in turn, communicate with the subconscious mind.

The subconscious mind must monitor all body organs and systems and our progress via the five senses so our muscles and body functions are

Chapter 3

correctly adjusted. Its focussed intention to succeed is millisecond bound to mind-numbing precision.

Witness, for example, the most sensitive and delicate finger movements of a watch repairer or heart surgeon. Just one (wrong) twitch of a muscle nerve and their most delicate operation fails. This example shows that the subconscious mind is bound to administer our choices. It is also finitely bound to monitor our actions, nerve by nerve, cell by cell, millisecond by millisecond. All this information processes through our subconscious mind at lightning speed so that our muscle efforts are instantly and precisely adjusted as the task progresses.

Now translate that example into dealing with split-second (hand and feet) driving complexities to avoid a potential car accident. Simultaneously, the subconscious mind directs our eye movements, heart rate, breathing, adrenaline release, and every muscle action required with split-second, mind-numbing precision. It even amasses emotions, ready to release a dozen expletives when the car has safely stopped.

Vast sums of information are processed with blistering speed and flawless precision to satisfy our desires. Y our subconscious mind powers your body through every minute of every day to meet your choices. Although you are not consciously aware of any of it, you entirely command it. Choose differently at any time, and action ceases or changes.

In sum, the subconscious mind has two control tasks—

Involuntary Control: From the stream of constantly changing information arriving from one's five senses, even while sleeping, the subconscious mind automatically controls all intuitive functions 24/7/52 for decades without sleep. Simultaneously, it monitors and regulates all internal body functions, lungs, heartbeat, blood pH, etc. It also produces emotions in the form of feelings.

Voluntary Control: Subconscious mind accepts our free will instructions to act (e.g., talk, listen, climb, eat, drive, dance, etc.), whence it monitors and controls all necessary muscle functions as previously discussed. This ability shows that Creator has employed similar governance principles, biologically and psychologically. In other words, natural laws that govern our functioning exist on the material, conscious and subconscious planes. Should we have expected anything different from one Creator?

Human sciences should adequately explain these processes, relationships and functions, but sadly they do not.

Because the conscious mind does not fully develop until about the age of fifteen or more, we do not have full access to this knowledge filter during our early formative years. The result is that we may accumulate many garbage values in our subconscious mind, about which we know nothing, despite them being counterproductive to our health, peace of mind, productivity and happiness.

Characteristic	Conscious Mind	Subconscious mind
Size	Small 8%	Large 92%
Communications	Words / Concepts	Images & Visualisations
Time	Past, present, future	Now
Will power	Will	Power
Driver	Free Will	Automated
Functions	One at time	Trillions simultaneously

7. Conscious mind compared with the subconscious mind

This chart shows the fundamental differences between our conscious and subconscious minds. Most importantly, the conscious mind filters the input to the subconscious mind. While the subconscious mind is receptive to all that our senses recognise, our conscious mind correctly determines what we most prize. Free will acts as that filter. Whatsoever is not intentionally filtered out is subconsciously accepted as having our approval or consent. It is thereby *'accepted for value.'*

That is essential because the subconscious mind cannot work in a vacuum, just as an empty stomach cannot process food. Throughout all of its respective faculties, life-sustaining values are its measure and its tools. We cannot alter its process, but we can change the (value) content in its database, thus producing different outcomes.

We are obliged to choose what we will prize or nominate to be of value, materially, intellectually, emotionally and spiritually. The subconscious mind then accepts our choices regardless of truth or falsity. Therefore, we must implant our most cherished life values into its database. (Refer to Life-Values.)

Once done, extraordinary synergistic power develops because your minds are in complete harmony! Frequencies match, and emotional satisfaction results from success. Feelings source from your values and goals. Alternatively, if you do not so choose, your two minds will likely conflict. Emotional stress and trauma most likely result.

Because our two minds use different vocabularies, data passing from the conscious mind to the subconscious mind must be transmitted using its language, or else it will not register. For example, we form images in our conscious mind for transmission. The subconscious mind employs its perceptive faculty for the same purpose.

Chapter 3

Some important points are worth noting. If our subconscious mind were not open to conscious influence, our chosen values would mean nothing. Our free will choices would be insufficient, ineffective or useless. Conversely, our subconscious mind refuses all (mental) harm save that which free will admits. Therefore, we must exercise care in choosing wisely. If we permit our subconscious mind to accept detrimental or destructive values, its life-sustaining ability suffers drastically. In short, our two minds protect each other, yet we are in charge of both superbly.

Severe mind control methods employ tortures and trauma to cancel free will refusal, thus gaining access to the subconscious mind. Less extreme forms may use media, music, entertainment, propaganda, unfounded beliefs, bogus philosophies, sexual persuasions, religious theologies, censorship, etc. We are the gatekeeper, notwithstanding.

Part One briefly described Perception and diagram 8 shows the process. Perception is defined as the organisation, identification, and interpretation of sensory information, to understand it and our environment.

Our being aware does not explain how sensory data presents in an

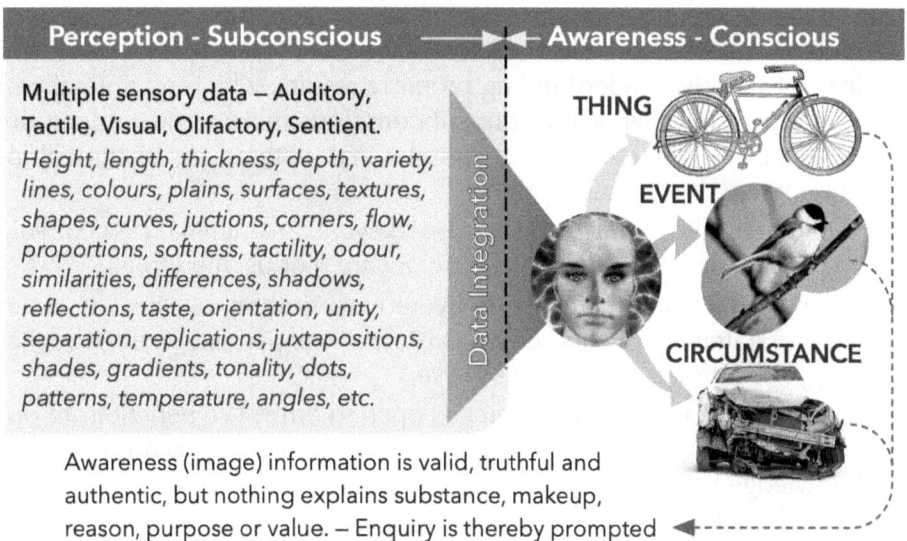

Perception - Subconscious	⟶ ⟵ Awareness - Conscious

Multiple sensory data – Auditory, Tactile, Visual, Olifactory, Sentient.
Height, length, thickness, depth, variety, lines, colours, plains, surfaces, textures, shapes, curves, juctions, corners, flow, proportions, softness, tactility, odour, similarities, differences, shadows, reflections, taste, orientation, unity, separation, replications, juxtapositions, shades, gradients, tonality, dots, patterns, temperature, angles, etc.

Data Integration

THING

EVENT

CIRCUMSTANCE

Awareness (image) information is valid, truthful and authentic, but nothing explains substance, makeup, reason, purpose or value. – Enquiry is thereby prompted

8. Subconscious perception delivers conscious awareness

integrated form. Neither does our awareness of something explain its properties or makeup. It is possible, for example, to walk into a factory or science laboratory and become consciously aware of many different objects. Yet, we do not know what they are, what material they're from, or what purpose they serve. Nonetheless, we see complete integrated forms or objects, not a haphazard assortment of sensory stimuli. Thus we are prompted to question and learn from our perceptions and feelings.

When we speak of perceiving something, what we're saying is that we're consciously aware of that thing. We are aware of the result of the automated perceptive process, and are now conscious of a particular entity or event. It registers as 'organised,' as a unitary thing, which is identifiable and can be named accordingly—for example, a pin, a car smash, or a fence. Many components unite as one picture of awareness.

Nothing is explained to us or interpreted unless we know from past learning or experience. We are made aware of some 'thing,' but that 'thing' is not explained, despite its coherent presentation.

Clear understanding becomes even more critical.

- Animal awareness results from its perception of something but has no cognitive understanding, precisely because animals lack that mental faculty. That is because Creator chose to have the animal respond automatically to what it perceives. An automated response is in-built because that is the particular form of animal protection and survival.

- We are differently equipped. No automatic responsive action happens with us as it does for animals. Instead, we must enquire, investigate and learn. Cognitive understanding properly results, which no animal can ever grasp. In other words, our subconscious mind stops working the moment we become aware, despite that nothing is 'identified' or 'interpreted' by our perception.

Said differently, for the same witnessed event, an animal is perceptively aware, while we are made consciously aware. For us, therefore—

- Perception is automatically delivered as truthful because it is an (image) statement of concretised existence. (All perception must be that way, else animals would not survive.)

- Human conscious understanding is open to error. We benefit from our willed authentic investigation or suffer otherwise because neither knowledge nor our responses are automatic.

Do the actions of our five senses cut us off from reality? Early philosophers did not know how the 'means' delivered 'results.' Previously they had concluded that perception is correspondent to the observer. Indeed, Sigmund Freud contended that our minds possess innate bias. However, it took time for skeptics and those who sought to defend the validity of the mind to appreciate that the mechanics of perception only determines the 'form' of one's awareness, not what the 'constituent objects' are or their properties.

Chapter 3

In sum, perception imparts no knowledge. It simply triggers our free will to enquire and learn. The way we perceive, visually, as in form, shape, size and colours, for example, is the image product of our senses. We perceive the object in objective reality, although our perception is pure imagery. That's great news because it explains how our (subconscious) image vocabulary transmits data to our cognitive word vocabulary.

Our five senses do not cut us off from reality; instead, they bring absolute truth to the point where our reasoning mind can properly and affirmatively deal with it. For example, we learn what makes welding two pieces of metal possible but not two pieces of wood.

Although perception delivers a legitimate expression of reality, the danger remains. We can misread our perceptions, misconceive their purpose, and misconstrue vital information. We can flavour what we perceive through bogus beliefs. We can doctor the evidence, correlate our misconceptions with other misinformation, and thereby butcher our findings, actions, and feelings.

Perceived facts emphasise that although we are free to choose subjective content, our conscious processes are entirely objective. They treat truth and lies equally. The essential information is authentic and accurate but only in (abstracted) vision form. We have no say over what offers, although we might instantly recognise it from that learned already. Nevertheless, unless we choose to learn and profit, we likely fail through ignorance.

This chapter has helped unveil the big picture of full consciousness; no need to become cognitive whiz-kids to succeed. More importantly, success is more deeply concerned with the values we choose, apply and practice, this being a way to express our passion for life. We cannot overemphasise that success. It remains to show how we choose values and how they can be impressed on our subconscious minds.

Conscious Ascendance

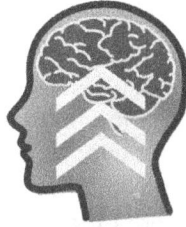

Chapter 4

4. Mastering the subconscious mind

Most people regard 'consciousness' as 'awareness' and nothing more. That inexorable lack of understanding deprives most people of any ability to capitalise their mental, emotional and spiritual skills. Thus it is exceedingly valuable to develop a more robust and encompassing understanding, particularly concerning the role of values in the subconscious process and how to master them for efficacy, efficiency and profound happiness. Only then can the astonishing power of our subconscious mind be employed.

Our subconscious mind cannot differentiate between real and imagined, as laboratory experiments verified long ago. It relies on sensory input and thereby responds to what is real and imaginary without distinction. We are obliged to know the difference.

The notion that our subconscious mind will defeat our cognitive minds because it is bigger and more powerful is false. There is no conflict since our chosen values fuel our subconscious process. Moreover, when our two minds harmoniously synchronise, 'single-minded' willpower bursts forth. Your subconscious mind becomes your genie, an exceedingly powerful partner. Once you become accomplished, you can converse with it, freely explain your values and desires, and express gratitude for its remarkable ability to deliver.

Thus given our sanction and blessing and our passion for life, it has the power to change habits and reverse destructive thinking patterns. Improve our physical and emotional health, regulate our involuntary functions, manifest our desires and even search beyond the limits of our conscious mind. Our conscious mind initiates and enlivens that incredible power. Indeed, free will conducts the whole conscious process.

Our subconscious partner has no power of self-expression. God has decreed that it solely responds to the free choices of our conscious mind. Thus our subconscious mind is never compelled, never ruled. It refuses any 'authority' from our conscious mind. It accepts no orders, and it issues none. It is not consciously commanded or enslaved. Its task of fulfilling our desires is of our 'will,' our passion for success, never of our 'command.'

We choose values to solicit or petition its assistance as our mental partner — our buddy.

The divine mind has ensured that we each possess unlimited power. We each can cause this power to manifest or experience anything we desire. The more acutely spiritual our values are, and the more pertinent they are to our desires, and the more our influence in response is incredible.

The operative word is 'desire,' precisely because no 'command' or 'order' is permissible. Our task, therefore, is to impress our desires on the subconscious mind by expressing our passion for life. It responds affirmatively when our spiritual choices harmonise perfectly with its task of upholding and sustaining our life. It engages when our chosen values correspond with 'life as the supreme value.' Harmony of mind excels. Discord does the act opposite.

That perfectly explains why we have a subconscious mind. We each are God's idea, whence our conscious mind is in charge, much like an orchestra conductor. Our subconscious is that orchestra effectively, but it has no orchestral score to follow and no power to choose. It is in the abstract, devoid of free will. Fortunately, our conscious mind has the freedom and our 'will.' Thus it writes the musical score in 'value' terms, and by exercising passionate will, it conducts the orchestra of life.

The word 'passion' conveys eagerness, an excited, animated, spirited, vigorous, strong, and willing desire. It is your 'will' to thrive and flourish as Creator intended that you should.

Our conscious mind initiates the (orchestra conducting) power of self-expression or desire. The subconscious responds, sequentially honouring and completing the (value transfer) process of full consciousness.

The unalienable power and God-given right to freely use our subconscious mind to attract to ourselves the things necessary for our happiness and success is assured. But our specific knowledge of success results from developing a conscious conviction of our innate creative power and then learning how to use it. The more accomplished we

Chapter 4

become, the greater our confidence and certainty.

Sadly, many people are infused with hope that things will turn out to an advantage, and they cling to 'hope.' They believe that outcomes are beyond their influence. No doubt you've heard comments like, "I guess that is what 'The Universe' wanted for me." However, hope has nothing to do with the outcome. The universe is not separate from us. Our being is an integral part of it; thus, experiences are created jointly according to our free choices.

The subconscious mind engenders that we consciously use 'positives,' not hopes or proclamations concerning the riddance of 'negatives.' It has no favour for hopes, wishes or mysticisms, strictly because life is absolute.

Logically, the same choices apply to overcoming lack. Lack in our life is effectively a negation. It amounts to denying that what we seek is possible, attainable, or even that it exists. We are thereby unable to attract to ourselves what we most desire. Nevertheless, the very thought of 'lack' implants it as a desirous goal in our subconscious mind, as a value. So it accepts our choice without question and honourably works to that end.

More generally, if an individual thinks that something will happen to him, very often because it recently did, he usually attracts that thing to himself again, whether it be advantageous or detrimental, good or bad.

'Synchronicities' in which values, desires, occurrences and manifestations magically seem to coincide are explained. They, too, are authored via choice and subconsciously resourced.

'Force' is generally considered self-expended energy to change an external thing or another individual. 'Power' is different. It is energy amassed within oneself, for oneself. The word power usually applies to government control over others, but such enactments are 'force.'

While the familiar concept of power is physical, power, in reality, is the product of one's mind. And that in all its different phases is God.

Concentrated thought is exceedingly more powerful than an idle thought. Our ideas must be of sufficient (value) intensity to register a definite impression upon the subconscious mind. Concentration generally achieves this intensity or passion; stillness and quietude assist greatly.

Such is not 'meditation,' I hasten to add. It is one's wilful, cogent deliberation. An intensity of thought concerns strength, fortitude and forcefulness very little. Instead, the word 'intensity' describes our prized measure of life and the values that our thoughts and actions contribute to life. Our cognitive or conscious mind contributes 'life values' to our subconscious mind. In other words, we offer our choices to that part of the spirit of God placed within each of us to live independently from God.

Life as the supreme value is spiritual in that sense. On the other hand, our conscious mind is free to roam the material cosmos; thus, it may choose whatever it pleases to be of a life-sustaining value. It may be ethical or unethical in its deliberations, just or unjust. It may lie to itself or uphold the truth. So we determine what we consider to be material values and spiritual values.

Consciously or unconsciously, our values are garnered by the subconscious mind as it enacts our desires. If these values coincide with that part of the spirit of God inherent in our subconscious mind, joyous emotions result from our actions; if not, debilitating emotions result. Our feelings are non-material; hence they are not vibrations, even though they may set our hearts racing. They are spiritual value reports concerning life-sustaining values versus life-depleting values.

Ordinarily, for any action we undertake, the material outcome differs from what existed initially, but our (spiritual) values remain the same. This understanding imparts that we learn what life values are, how to implant them in our subconscious, and how to profit from the feeling reports we receive. Using that means we can access whatever we seek. Thus we can benefit handsomely in health, wealth, happiness or illumination of any kind whatsoever.

Vibrations and frequencies are for scientists to figure out. That aside, 'life values' can be treated as the root source of our feelings and emotions, all frequencies and vibrations entirely incidental. By dealing with the spiritual cause, material effects will take care of themselves.

If you are familiar with photographs developed in a dark room in the good old days, the following explanation will strike chords of familiarity. Our conscious mind is the camera lens. It registers your goals and values on the photographic film of your subconscious mind. The Source, being abstract, represents the liquid chemicals used for development. Our desires manifest through actions like a printed 'development' of that negative image. Light and dark are now correctly rendered. The more acutely focussed and intentional your desires using visualisation, the more perfect your picture and the more successful its materialisation.

Consider a different metaphor. The reason for having no lights in a cinema is that "black' cannot be projected on a screen, since black is the absence of light. The degree of blackness (or greyness) on a cinema screen depends on how much black (no light) the cinema auditorium has. That is why the inside of the camera admits no light but what the lens allows. Light is life; hence your (mind) pictured visualisation must be impassioned with the light of life. Every extraneous matter is like light leaking into a cinema or a camera's body. The more leaked light, the more your visualised picture is degraded.

Do you now see why your subconscious mind works entirely in the positive realm? To do otherwise is to fail. Image clarity does not require

Chapter 4

every detail. For example, if your express desire is an overseas vacation, you may express and even name the particular country. But you should omit details like mode of travel, accommodation, length of stay, and activities unless an express activity is your whole reason for visiting. Think along the lines of algebraic concept formation, wherein some travel and accommodation will be called for but need not be specified initially. That achieves two goals. First, it makes your visualisation more focused on your trip eventuating. Second, Source is not confined, restrained or prescribed. With no specified limitations, success is more confident because its avenue of address is much broader.

We have two options when it comes to values. We can consciously choose them and deliberately upload them to our subconscious minds. Alternatively, we can allow the subconscious mind to assimilate them through our actions. Preferentially, we should' will' our subconscious mind to fervently employ our deliberately chosen values. No command is needed, and neither can any be accepted. Instead, the subconscious mind responds joyously when our 'will' harmonises with its Divine commission. Emotions and feelings later report whether or not our values have been satisfied and to what degree. That report prompts us to consider whether to pursue that particular value, alter it or cancel it. So the sequential process is repeated.

Once grasped that the subconscious mind strictly follows the (value-directed) 'will' of the conscious mind, it becomes clear that emotions derive from our values, not vice versa. Tragically, when our values unknowingly assimilate, we've no control over the emotional consequences.

Some say that the 'mental atmosphere' we hold produces a specific reaction, such as sorrow, joy, misery, happiness, love or disgust. Think about that. The term 'mental atmosphere' is best described as a lingering emotional state of being, subconsciously generated from our' values.' But it is not that state that produces a specific reaction. That state or condition is a reaction itself. Once more, cause and effect are irreversible.

People commonly speak of energies and vibrations as causal factors, which disastrously conceals that conscious (process) values are spiritual.

Cause and effect reverse. Both values and their lack, such as reliance on hope, will produce a mental state or vibration. An expectation is a mystical wish, not a purposeful 'will' that one's goals will assuredly eventuate.

Therefore, it behoves to separate our projected values from the feelings we receive. We can then trace (experienced) feelings (the effect) back to one or more values (the cause).

Conscious Ascendance

Fervent desire attached to a particular value packs a potent subconscious power. Once that is experienced several times, there is no turning back. Each new success builds on the last. Purposeful values assume preeminence and act like your teacher. Positive emotions and material benefits greatly help refine your focus and commitment. Wishes, hopes, beliefs, feelings and wishful vibrations no longer appeal. They have no 'power.' Your prized values do.

The 'subconscious mind' should not be confused with the 'subconscious' discussed in psychology. Neither should it be allied with the term 'unconscious.' Instead, our subconscious mind is that more significant part of ourselves always connected to the 'Source,' to the infinite mind of God.

Dictionaries define 'source' as a place, person, or thing from which something originates or is obtained. Alternatively, the site something comes from, starts at, or the cause of something. So it follows that if the subconscious mind is our allocated portion of the essential mind of God, then that is the Source of its power. So we may use phraseology such as 'I am connecting with Source' or 'tapping into Source.'

Moreover, using the term 'Source' instead of a denominational phrase such as 'God' eliminates religious connotations while definitively pointing to life's origins. The Source is the initiator of everything, which supplies information through divine guidance, intuition, and inspiration, as later discussed. In that sense, it is where everything starts and the cause of everything.

There is another aspect at play. Rupert Sheldrake is a very well-known author and in his book 'Morphic Resonance,' he describes recently observed molecular changes in xylitol that effectively create a new morphology. Moreover, once this happened in one laboratory, all the other xylitol everywhere else changed also. All of it simultaneously began forming into this unique morphology. Around the world, xylitol would never go back to its liquid form. Can you explain that? Modern science cannot explain it. Physics and chemistry have given up trying.

What explains it is that these molecules instantly communicate through a system called morphic resonance. Recently, a science journal reported this happening to all kinds of molecules, not just xylitol but also ampicillin, an antibiotic, and other sugar molecules.

Keep in mind that when scientists observe molecules, elements, and chemicals, they are witnessing expressions of the mind of God. So how do these molecules know how to replicate the changes made in like molecules and effect this change simultaneously? They know because they are getting information from a morphic database. That database is the Source. It might also be called God's cloud storage system.

In other words, these molecules are downloading information from the Source. We can leave science to figure out that process if ever it can. Meanwhile, our sole interest is knowing how to access the Source through our subconscious mind. If 'intuition' and 'imagination' spring to mind, you are a winner!

Let's pursue this idea further. Is Source a deep and inclusive part of our subconscious, or is it additional, even remote? Differently, is it possible that we can find the 'Source' within ourselves when we seek wisdom, guidance, and spiritual accomplishment? The answer is straightforward. Subconscious is our connection to Source, to that portion of self-knowingness of the spirit. The link is inherent and immutable. Think of Source as a giant mass of light, having potential in the form of energy. A part breaks away from this mass and becomes 'you.' You expend this (spiritual) potential as you go on your journey through life, and one day, you return to this light mass. You return to Source, which, truth be known, was with you all the way.

Our subconscious mind is a divine communication system conducted by chosen life values. They fire your subconscious, and that spark connects you to 'Source.' Therefore, you cannot be separated from Source because your subconscious is a part of it.

The connection to this deep spiritual essence is profound. Intuition projects spiritual values on your 'awareness' that beseech and entreat your cognitive mind to party. So you develop ethics and morality, inner wisdom, and divine guidance. As these inspired thoughts propagate, you grasp your mission, vision, and reason for being. Progressively it dawns on you that your life is entirely spiritual and that physicality is merely the toolbox for exercising spirituality. That again confirms that your spirituality directly connects with the Source.

Sadly we have little understanding that God's supreme power is ever present, all-wise, all-powerful, all-loving, all-protecting, all-providing, and all this power is ever at our disposal when we call upon it. We are taught instead to look upon God as some vague, incomprehensible mystery being or an intangible something in some far-off realm.

Yet Divinity is an essential part of our very essence. Our task is to learn of our oneness with the Source of our being, realising God's desire that we develop the ability to control and master our life without interference. Importantly, we should remember that the Divine mind does not resist our desires, even those unworthy or debilitating. Our choices and our value choices are always honoured.

That does not mean that God has set us adrift. On the contrary, the conscious process fully protects our free will. This inherent guidance comes in two forms later discussed. First, in brief, our feelings report on our value-based progress, which facilitates amendments or remedies. Second, twenty natural laws govern the consequences of our actions. Thus we are blessed with two reporting systems never described before. Neither prescribes our activities, so free will is fully protected.

Once understood that we each possess a power higher than our human power alone, ever at our disposal, it becomes evident that both reporting systems testify divine assistance. First, we have free rein to exercise our creativity in the most comprehensive manner possible, following which comprehensive reports called feelings to let us fine-tune our progress. As a result, our mental efficiency multiples astoundingly! What better could we ask?

Understanding endowed Divinity imparts feelings of security and unshakeable confidence to all individuals who choose to enact their divine powers. Many believe "faith in God combined with the earnest efforts of an individual will bring success at all times." Your blessed assistance is far more than mere faith, however. It is your absolute knowing of Divinity and sharing creatively in its successful manifestations.

Success comes with effort. To benefit, we must develop our innate abilities, consistently using all of our endowed faculties. This power is in the abstract, however. It can only emerge in reality through engaging with our values. Although we are alone in our choices, we can learn of our divine power with friends and family.

Doubt or fear, or even entertaining such thoughts, is expressing uncertainty concerning an outcome. Our purposes fail because the subconscious has received no definite impression concerning what we desire. We've shut the door and thwarted the outcome we desire.

Fear and doubt are confusions in the mind, very easily assimilated subconsciously. All connection to Source is severed thereby. The eventual outcome is lack or disorder of some kind. That is precisely how natural law (natural orderliness) governs the consequences of our actions — but more about that subject later.

Undoubtedly, 'faith' contributes to the subconscious working in positive alignment with Divine power and Source. However, faith is more a glowing trust in eventual success, not a conviction of success. Faith is too open, both as a concept and in practice. It leaves room for doubt. Conversely, our finite 'knowing' cancels all uncertainty. It stabilises our thoughts, reinforcing our reliance upon divine power and protection.

To believe in the fruitfulness of prayer is to believe in the efficacy of subconscious supplication. It is to believe in 'will,' as opposed to belief. Will is the determination to succeed, all the while 'knowing' that 'value input' must produce 'value output,' no doubts entertained whatsoever. That casts prayer in a new light entirely. It establishes the certainty of subconscious supplication.

All negativity is cancelled thereby, not by attempting to activate its riddance but by our willed replacement with positive values that benefit life itself. 'Life values' supercharge our subconscious mind. They cement our subconscious link to Source abstractions awaiting manifestation. Nothing less suffices. Nothing more is needed.

Contact with Source is maintained as long as we continue to hold life values sacrosanct. So long as we knowingly trust in divine power, our desires manifest in some manner. The more perfectly our desires conceptualise and are passionately valued, the more their manifestation perfects. Fear, doubt, confusion and failure are out of the question. Accordingly, life values spiritually enrich our material desires.

To be ever vigilant, diligent, committed, and honest in our appraisals, all of which impart obligations, sounds like hard work, if not mental overload. So, what happened to the idea that our complete conscious process models efficiency and efficacy. That begs another question. How can we substantially reduce our workload yet still obtain the desired benefits?

The answer is simple and delightful! Our subconscious mind is fully automated. Uploading values such as vigilance, honesty, diligence, and commitment to our subconscious mind, allow them to run on autopilot. Our connection to divine power and Source abstractions (awaiting manifestation) functions with total efficiency and efficacy, with no additional effort required. Humanity has never understood this beautiful, fast track to triumphant joy. No one teaches it.

Think about it. Life values listed in the paragraph above are abstractions themselves. We can't b buy them at a store or online. Now recall that Source is a warehouse of 'abstractions,' and join the dots. Your (uploaded) abstractions meet face to face with Source abstractions. Their connection is immediate, profound, and immutable. Not only your values automatically share across all your endeavours, but also your power. For example, the value of diligence applies to lawn mowing, driving, cooking, making a car, and teaching.

When feelings remind you of your values and virtues for reassessment or confirmation, your workload reduces considerably. Your efficiency multiplies further. Mistakes and errors fade into non-significance.

How then are life values uploaded to the subconscious mind? My answer to that question is a simple three-part, three-minute process applied to each value.' This process is near identical to that described for ensuring good health and as described for removing fear and doubt. It requires focus and concentration. But, as before, it should not be laboured since perceived doubts and confusion can easily prevent the desired outcome.

The tool is imagination and visualisation, 'imagery' being the vocabulary of the subconscious mind. First, picture what you want in your mind's eye. Is it an item of jewelry, a vacation cruise, money to clear a debt or a mortgage? Is it a new house, specialised education, romance, or a move to country living? Identify what you seek very clearly, with no attachments or embellishments.

Now you can begin the three-step visualisation process, each step taking no longer than one minute.

1. Visualise preparing to receive what you desire. What steps will clear the way for its arrival? Picture what things might have to be resolved or overcome first? Visualise that your ability to access Source is absolute and that you are genuinely connected. Visualise any preparatory steps and that you are excitedly doing them.

2. Visualise receiving what you seek. Picture your excitement and joy. Visualise unpacking your gift and setting it up. Picture your excitement in sharing with your partner and family. Picture yourself joyously expressing gratitude for the means that enables your desires to realise.

3. Now picture all the benefits and how your life will be more prosperous; your enjoyment richer. Picture more lavish comforts and security, greater efficiency, less work, and more time for relaxation and calmness. Picture rejoicing that you have triumphed over all doubt and all fear and have advanced as you envisaged.

Now relax. Please do not overdo it. Yes, those pictures will take several minutes to register in your subconscious mind. But, as time passes, rejoice that the more passionately you impress your desires as having life-sustaining (abstract) value or virtue, the more effectively your pictures will take hold.

You can repeat this program, of course, maybe a day or two later, but do not overdo it again. Results may take minutes, days or weeks, but that is no reason for doubt. Instead, focus on your values more so than the material acquisition. Prize those values. Picture vigilance, commitment, honesty, and diligence. Does respect play a part? Picture its importance and how it relates to your desires.

The Source receives your visualised impression of values. It will respond because it is the more significant part of the subconscious. That explains why you should be clear about what you want. Any vagaries, discrepancies, incompleteness and uncertainty will fail your desires. They are failures exactly. When nothing specific is defined, nothing will result.

Those people who know the value of what they want will succeed because they have a life-assisting reason for it. No conflict exists between the value they seek and its material expression. On the contrary, their exactness and life-passion for it will accomplish exactly what they desire, in material and value terms.

Understand that at no time have you commanded your subconscious mind to do anything. You've informed it of your impassioned 'will,' with a complete understanding of its commitment to honouring your desires. Any commands you issue to your subconscious will deny its connection with the Source. Your mission will fail.

Your visualised pictures will frequently pop into focus from memory. That reinforces that your 'will-pictures' are now impressed upon the Source through your subconscious mind. They will hold until your desires are fully realised and delivered into your physical possession.

Additionally, you may say to yourself something like this–

I am in touch with all the power that exists. I have willed that my subconscious partner accesses Divine power's ability to materially provide my desire [to— for—]. Thus willed, I express gratitude that my valued desires in abstraction will now manifest materially.

Do not concern yourself with how your desires will manifest. Instead, do those things that you identified as clearing the way. They reinforce your 'will' considerably. Remember that your subconscious absorbs every move through your five senses, so help it join the dots through your actions. The Divine mind knows the balance necessary for complete fulfillment.

To idly sit while imagining your prize will not bring it to you. Your idea will achieve nothing alone. That is wishing. A strong motivation of what will bring value to your life must permeate your desires. Picture this to the exclusion of everything else. Synergistic harmony develops when the idea of success is consciously established with conviction and impressed on your subconscious mind. Failure is rendered impossible. The very notion of success imparts the essential elements of success. It will attract whatever is necessary to your life cause.

If you have additional plans concerning an ambition to succeed in another line of endeavour, they too may be visualised. You may omit the specifics if you've no unique talent or have not received specialist training. For example, one individual may seek excellence in portrait painting or photography, even though not attempted before. Equally, one may strive only to excel in 'artistry' while only accomplished in portraiture presently. How will such petition manifest? Will it be commercial logo design, sculpture, or landscape photography? All are different forms of 'artistry.' Particular specialisation may come years later following specialist visualisation. You are the architect of your life. Never forget it.

In only the last twenty or twenty-five years, science recognises that our brain has far greater capabilities than have ever been credited. Our mind, conscious, subconscious and emotional interactions and associations have only recently emerged.

"It's certainly true that humans are capable of thinking in [that] deliberative way. But neuroscience research tells us that much of the brain is constructed to support "automatic" processes — which are faster than conscious deliberations and which occur with little or no awareness or feeling of effort.

Research also tells us that our behaviour is under the pervasive and often unrecognised influence of "affective" (emotion) systems that are absolutely essential for daily functioning.

So our behaviour emerges from the interplay between controlled (conscious) and automatic systems on the one hand, and between cognitive (reason) and affective (emotion) systems on the other."
—Sydney Morning Herald [9]

That quotation supports all discussions thus far. The following chapters will build out that picture so that no doubts will remain in your mind. There is no need to wait, however. You have the formula to manifest your earnest desires, leaving past wishes in the dust. Begin with something small and benignly innocent, such as waking yourself at a specified time, to the exclusion of an alarm clock or bedside radio.

Use the same three x one-minute program. If it fails the first time, then repeat. Soon you will grow into making subconscious requests a habit, all to your great joy. In a short time, you will learn how to do as I do for my daily cat-nap. At (say) 2.15 pm, I request a 45-minute cat nap and to awaken at 3 pm. Do the math, and you'll see that I must fall asleep within seconds and be awakened at 3 pm exactly. Regardless of a different start time or duration, that technique works every time.

Chalk up some successes like this, and not only will you have learned how to master your mind, you can tap into the source of the only power that exists, all to your great joy and betterment. With your more robust understanding of values, and your ability to master them for efficacy and efficiency, it is time to delve deeper into the conscious process. Programming abstract spiritual values like discernment, respect and tolerance are vital. Infants show us how, which means you have already proven beyond doubt your ability to excel.

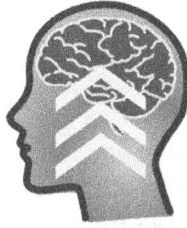

Chapter 5

5. Values and Mind Communication

Because life values are new to almost everyone, it is essential to learn what they are and their role in the entire conscious process. Infant children point the way. This chapter introduces Life values and then describes how they benefit us materially, mentally, emotionally and spiritually.

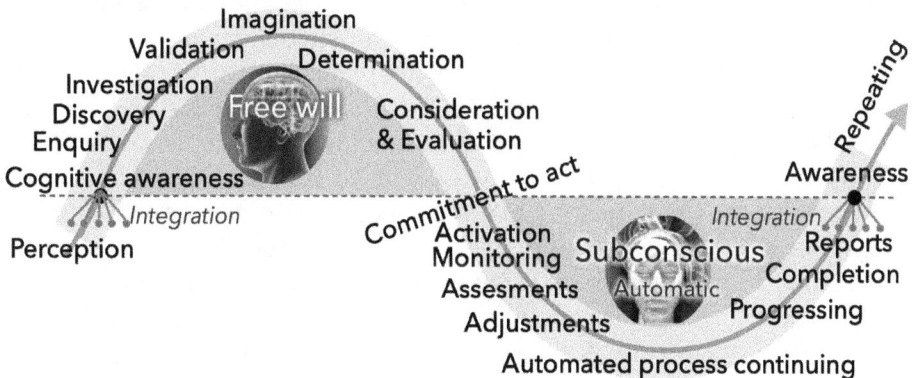

Imagination
Validation   Determination
Investigation
Discovery   Free will   Consideration
Enquiry   & Evaluation
Cognitive awareness   Awareness
Repeating
Integration   Commitment to act
Perception   Activation   Integration
Monitoring   Subconscious   Reports
Assesments   Automatic   Completion
Adjustments   Progressing
Automated process continuing

9. The Value Transfer Wave (VTW)

Diagram (9) shows the value transfer wave with more detail than in Diagram 4 in Chapter 2. More information will later reveal. This diagram embraces our (wave crest) conscious mind and (wave trough) subconscious mind. Data switches across the horizontal line from one mind to the other, meaning from one vocabulary to the other.

Conscious Ascendance

Information passes from left to right through these phases in turn. Awareness is common to both left and right-hand sides, meaning that if the right side of the wave flips over to the left, a Value Transfer 'loop' results. Thus full consciousness is a recurring loop process shown by diagram 5 in Chapter 2. That diagram briefly explained the conscious process for adults, not infants and children.

First, consider that the subconscious mind delivers two reports to conscious awareness at the wave end. First, we perceive what our particular task or activity has achieved. Secondly, we experience sentient feelings concerning success or failure.

The subconscious mind takes account of every ambition, analysis, desire, thought, value, imagination, goal, validation, commitment, and action in forming those reports. It correlates this data with every adjustment, correction and confirmation made during the process. The sentient information report is complete; nonetheless, it remains an abstracted summation of all intent, values and manifestation. Unless we instinctively know and understand our feelings, we must learn more through enquiries investigations. That's what we do with (initial) material perceptions, you'll recall.

We must include infant learning in our study of consciousness; else, it is not valid. That poses a vital question. How can infant children advance when they have no cognitive ability? After all, they've no innate ideas, no science, no math, no language, and no knowledge. They cannot question their feelings and discover what values worked well or what failed.

Go back to diagram 9 (last page) and picture a low, curved shortcut line from 'cognitive awareness' at the left, through free will to the 'commitment to acting' in the middle. This short circuit will show a bypass of eight cognitive functions. That is how infant children advance. Their minds jump straight from their 'awareness' to subconscious 'enactment' via free will choice. It must be that way because they have minimal or no cognitive ability. This mental bypass is crucially important.

An infant who cannot yet crawl becomes aware of a place beyond reach. Their conscious mind curiously asks, "what is it?" It must get to that place to satisfy curiosity and the desire to explore. They want to explore, investigate, see, touch, feel, or taste, and so keep longingly looking at that place. Watch how infant children stretch out an arm and wriggle their fingers as though pointing. The subconscious mind picks up this image signal through perception, and, being tasked to advance life, it responds by activating muscles to satisfy the infant's desire to visit and explore.

It assimilates and combines all the data involved in accomplishing this goal. It integrates the idea of movement with the necessary muscle actions to get to that place. This information includes the intention, the envisaged value or benefit, what muscles are involved, and what body adjustments are necessary and need monitoring. Every nerve and cell in the body is monitored, and progress is observable through the five senses.

Despite learning to crawl may take several attempts, the infant's free will pleads with the subconscious mind to continue. Progress duly compares with the (expressed) value of arriving at that place, resulting in a feeling of joy, or sorrow, according to success or failure. All the while, the infant knows absolutely nothing about the conscious process taking place. Notwithstanding, the subconscious mind memorises the crawling motions, and practice makes perfect.

Understand what has happened. The mere act of looking intently at some place conveys a visual image to the subconscious mind of the desire to visit that place to explore and advance. Repeated staring and pointing to it emphasises the infant's passion. That is sufficient because the language of the subconscious mind is images. If the mission succeeds, a feeling of joy will result; and if not, the infant feels disappointment or failure of a kind. With no words to describe that failing, it cries. Distress results from failing to achieve their desired value. The infant will ultimately succeed with good health and opportunity, resulting in a joyous feeling of delight.

Their achievement is beyond measure. This tender infant engaged its subconscious mind without words or concepts, without any conscious understanding, and with no mentoring or outside influence whatsoever. It expressed a sincere desire to advance and thrive. Exercising free choice, it willed to be in that place, which gave subconscious mind a (valued) life reason to go there. All the while, the infant knew nothing about how the conscious process works.

This whole process is so simple and so logical. It works perfectly because no diversions or perversion of truth such as propaganda or false ideologies can interfere.

The infant's perceptive faculty triggers direct action via free choice. Success results, despite complete bypass of the cognitive process.

You've now been introduced to the Creator's gift of 'The Natural Law of Allowance.' It allows infants and young children to choose their actions and experience the emotions of success or failure while growing their cognitive abilities and building their understanding. The subconscious mind powers the infant's abilities and delivers emotional reports of satisfaction or disappointment.

Given all five senses function in normal health, emotions begin as soon as externalities are available to an infant's senses. Primary emotions manifest when infants are fed, comforted, or sleep deprived, best described as pleasure or pain, joy or sorrow. In addition, they testify that the subconscious mind monitors and reports life's progress, setbacks or limitations.

This experiential window of opportunity permits and encourages conscious enquiry and learning, thus exercising value-based choices. It also enables our understanding and mental maturity to become habituated through our preferences over our entire lifespan. As a result, higher percentiles of truth are amassed in our memories and intuit database at our own pace, all of which fosters reliability and certainty with the least effort. This law allows you to be all you choose to be, as you will, at your pace, and for mental efficiency to build over time.

Although the discoveries and actions of young children yield different emotions, and despite some disappointments, their life is predominantly one of excitement and revelations. Each hour and day presents an exciting new vision of reality, life, and vibrantly new possibilities.

Out in the woods or playground, the actions of young children also yield emotions. These are pertinently instructive because life's experiences are authentic. Their feelings directly inform what they are motivated to do and report their accomplishments, vastly different from passively watching others act on a television screen.

Outdoor kids are 'self-creators.' They are not passive responders witnessing some storytellers' invented emotions. Completely divorced from make-believe influences, they learn that future choices originate from past emotional responses. They understand the cause of failures and successes first-hand. Progressively, they comprehend the value of rational thought before acting out their choices and that their actions and words generate feelings and learning experiences. Experience is the most excellent teacher.

Babysitter television offers nothing of the kind. It offers new images, but because young children have not developed cognitive discernment, visual TV images stimulate their motivations, not real-life circumstances. Television rivets the child's attention, demanding subjective focus and concentration. It switches their mind from exciting experiences and discoveries to passive absorption of other people's actions and emotions.

Young children's indoctrination is very easy, even intentional. Producers know very well that reason and explanations will kill rapt attention, so they focus on the excitement and drama of counterposed emotions. But unfortunately, because resultant emotions in their young audience do not spontaneously originate, as happens in a playground, the child is deprived of first-hand (creative) learning and thereby exposed to passive indoctrination.

Chapter 5

Values may be subconsciously implanted without the child or parents consciously knowing. Soapies and sitcoms influence adults similarly. Subliminal advertising adds harmful effects in addition. Technical trickery can embed images that bypass conscious recognition. This problem is severe. Viewing soap operas and the like effectively gives our subconscious mind consent to assimilate the portrayed values. As a result, we are blind to depicted values and mental diversions, indoctrinations, fictional notions, censorship, and much more. All of that, not forgetting parental proclamations such as 'you must learn to conform,' are sufficient to suffocate full conscious development. All of it exacts a devastating toll that humanity scarcely recognises, if ever.

Give me the child until he is seven and I'll give you the man —St. Francis Xavier (1506-1552)

Indeed! St. Francis fully understood the influence of a child's mind, especially when poisoned with regular doses of dogma. The child grows up with toxic beliefs and debilitating theories planted in their innocent, unsuspecting, unquestioning, subconscious minds.

Secular philosophy still clings to Emmanuel Kant, Rene Descartes, Sigmund Freud, and many disciples who extol the same principles. The Keynesian economic theory that today props up fiat money systems and fraudulent banking practices also relies on ideas planted in subconscious minds, seldom questioned or challenged, much less rejected.

Do you now see what most academics have never understood? Parents see and applaud their infant's first crawl from one place to another. They excitedly text family and friends, saying, 'junior has learned to crawl.' The real news, however, is that junior (visually) programmed their subconscious mind with life-supporting values, including enquiry, commitment, diligence and passion for succeeding. As a result, the subconscious mind learned how to crawl. Junior masterminded the subconscious learning process through free will. That is what truly happened.

This achievement is far more significant than the mere act of moving from one location to another. The infant experienced the world of spiritual values, but sadly, no education curricula teach what took place, nor its profound spiritual significance. The subconscious mind honoured the (infant) chosen values expressed through visualisation, not words. Emotional joy resulted from exercising those values, but no one explains that the infant's progress was more spiritual than material.

Have you noticed in the value Transfer Wave diagram (9) that our free will (cognitive mind) mind is (sequentially) sandwiched between the subconscious functions of 'perception' and 'activation?' Think about that discovery. It means that our free will conducts our whole conscious process. Thus anyone who refuses your free will denies your right to life. They are outlaws indulging in criminal behaviour.

This 'free will sandwich' also smashes the notion of mind/body duality. The (believed) soul/body dichotomy (mind versus heart) is also false. Why? Because material values and spiritual values are processed simultaneously. Each is dependent on the other.

Our ego functions automatically to all intent and purpose; nevertheless, we author its content and hence the feelings we receive. This understanding highlights the difference between egotism and egoism.

'Egoism' refers to self-esteem, self-importance, self-worth, self-respect, self-image and self-confidence. All are worthy attributes from one's attention to their well-being and responsible happiness.

'Egotism' is almost the exact opposite. It refers to the fact of being excessively conceited or absorbed in oneself. It means arrogance, egocentricity, egomania, self-obsession, narcissism, unwarranted self-adulation, vanity and conceit. These attest to falsity, a false belief in oneself usually arising from contemptuous disregard for most all other people. In all, egotism is the hallmark of a 'second-hander,' not a creator.

Yet again, the notion that consciousness is mere awareness is proven false. Instead, our free will choices conduct one complete process driving material, mental, emotional and spiritual sustenance. Once grasped that physicality is Creator's toolbox for living a spiritual life, human consciousness appears very different from anything ever taught.

- Our conscious process is endowed, and this 'hardware' is unalterable.
- We, each, are the free will author of its content, meaning that we write the 'software.'
- Our free will, aka 'volitional consciousness,' separates us from all other life forms.
- We are spiritual beings living a spiritual life, albeit in a material realm.

Tragically, neuroscience finds no need to separate our conscious mind from its subconscious counterpart. Body and mind are all there is. It follows that with no inter-mind communication, no spiritually valued purpose presents for our consideration. Consequently, we have no hint of what mental, emotional, and spiritual achievements are possible to us. Thus deprived, we're victims of all who would capitalise on our ignorance for their benefit and our sufferance. Denied knowing our extraordinary powers of consciousness and resultant unawareness of that impairment, most people, exist without really living.

'Life values,' as a term, refers to exactly what empowers our spiritual wellbeing and accomplishments. Each has differing degrees of spiritual

Chapter 5

expression. Truth and honesty are good examples. We exercise honesty in dealing with ourselves and others, while the truth is the bottom line of honesty. Thus life values vary according to the passion for life we give them. After that, they flow like a stream, coursing their way over and around obstacles like an unstoppable power.

Perhaps you have now glimpsed that values fall into three categories.

- **Material values** such as a house, car, recreation, vacation and wardrobe are all no-brainers.
- **Satisfaction or destination values** are those we seek to achieve for our emotional or spiritual satisfaction. Examples include happiness, joy, pleasure, contentment, peace and fulfillment, all absent mental stress and strain.
- **Life values** are spiritual values or virtues that help us reach those satisfactions. They aid our journey in life on a day-to-day basis. Diligence, resilience, respect and honesty are prime examples.

It should be evident that life values put our conscious mind on the same page as our subconscious mind. Take diligence as an example. How could your subconscious mind function properly if it threw attentiveness and assertiveness to the wind? How could a surgical operation succeed without meticulously monitoring and controlling the surgeon's hand and fingers muscles? Her subconscious mind must exercise diligence throughout a six-hour procedure. It must also respect the surgeon's wellbeing, in addition to respecting the life of her patient. What about the word commitment? Is that not a pertinent value as it concerns all parties involved? In that example, diligence, respect and commitment all work cooperatively. Life values are spiritual guidance, therefore, demonstrably assisting our material, mental, emotional and spiritual growth.

Ayn Rand beautifully described three cardinal values for the realisation of our lives. 'Reason' as our only tool of knowledge. 'Purpose' as our choice of happiness satisfied by reason. 'Self-esteem' as certain knowing that we are competent to think, thus worthy of joy, meaning worthy of living. Now you've seven life values on your list, I trust.

Life depends on a process of self-sustaining and self-generated action. Consider productive work as what we do to sustain and advance our lives. As the central purpose of a rational life, it is the core value that integrates and determines the hierarchy of all others.

The concept of 'life' answers the question: *'of value to whom and for what?'* No values are possible where no alternatives exist. Reference to the facts of reality and our lives is necessary to validate our choice of values. As mentioned, we may choose to make life our central purpose or stumble through existence, hoping for more success than distress. Rand emphasises my thoughts precisely.

Conscious Ascendance

A central purpose enables us to focus all the concerns of our life into one concerted package. We can prioritise and rank our values according to their importance. The efficiency of that order saves us from pointless inner conflicts and permits us to enjoy life in any field of endeavour we choose.

Conversely, confusion and chaos result from having no purpose. Knowing nothing of values means we've no means to referee or judge what is essential and what is not. As a result, these people drift like corks in the ocean, helplessly at the mercy of any chance stimulus, direction by others, or momentary whim. They struggle to find enjoyment, deprived of what makes happiness possible.

Why should life be so complicated? Is purpose impossible? Not at all, since we all act with sense and drive every day. Life or death necessitates we choose what to eat, what to drink, and what air quality we breathe. None of those choices affects how our cardio-vascular system works or how our immune, respiratory, circulatory, or skeletal systems work. Nonetheless, every cell in our body depends on the 'value' of what we eat, drink, and inhale. So it becomes necessary to pursue values that sustain and uphold our lives and develop a mental, emotional, and spiritual purpose.

Values outside of life are nonsense. If one chooses only to exist, no fundamental values are possible, no code of ethics makes sense, and no moral actions are necessary. The same applies to the (value) quality of thought, including the validity of all information, beliefs, superstitions, and ideologies. Life determines what values it requires. We are obliged to learn of them and profit accordingly.

This importance is far greater than anything presently taught in religion, philosophy, psychology, or human science. Taught that we cannot control our subconscious mind, which is true, most people are stopped in their tracks. Taught they cannot control its process, they can never assuredly influence what content it processes. Yet mental content is of the same importance as nutritious food that aids bodily health. Life makes values possible and makes them necessary.

The subconscious mind cannot choose your values because that would override and cancel your free will. It must rely on what spiritual value you decide to place on your actions. No one but you can provide this life-value information.

We are blessed with harmony and positive emotions when our two minds share the same values. We thrive to our best potential. Everything is in order, meaning all accords with 'natural law.' Conversely, conflicting values produce discordance, stress and conflicts. As a result, we experience (so-called) negative emotions like anxiety, stress and trauma.

Chapter 5

Material values such as a house, car, money or vacation are related to spiritual values, but seldom are we taught to think in those terms. We should consider profit over any loss, of course. 'Profit,' as a concept, seems perfectly in tune with the subconscious intent of sustaining our life. But our thoughts are not actions.

If, for example, we choose to 'profit' our business by offering increased customer benefits, likely we will strive to increase the value that customers receive. What value exactly? Will it be bigger, stronger, more attractive or less costly? Or, not forsaking such goals, will we also foster staff cooperation, respect, truth and commitment, and emphasise that we share those core values with our customers. We should because those spiritual values assist in delivering increased consumer benefits profiting our business. They are 'life values' since they help our journey in life, just as they assist the functioning of our subconscious mind.

Spiritual values cannot be bought, traded, taxed, gifted, or bequeathed. Yet, if we employ these values, our subconscious mind will soak them up like a sponge. First, actions speak louder than words. Second, as described in the surgeon example, values like diligence, respect, fortitude and patience are imperative to our lives.

Can we crush competitors to profit our business? By what means? If we indulge in deceit, lies, or disinformation, our subconscious mind will soak up such behaviours as our most prized values. Guess who suffers? Employers, suppliers, employees, and customers.

At every turn, we must master life values and empower our minds. Failure is our choice also. However, that understanding is a mental make-over for most people, although a worthy change. It remains that—

> "There will be no shake-up (let alone revolution) in ethics unless emotion drives the reasoning, just as well as vice versa. [Notice in that sentence how our two minds mutually respect each other.] [But] beliefs can be specified and managed whereas we can't define, explain, nor predict emotions: we can propositions; but we know next to nothing about emotions. No psychologist of which I am aware has a comprehensive theory of emotions which I find emotionally satisfying (i.e., persuasive to me).
> I propose that adding value be the one norm, or operating principle that we need to have to incentivise and to motivate us in the ethical direction." —Marvin C. Katz, Ph.D.[10]

Neither had I seen emotions explained in a manner that satisfied their purpose, or import. Little if any is written concerning how values spark emotions, or of our ability to program our subconscious mind.

Katz continues—

Conscious Ascendance

How does one achieve this added value? One must be aware of him/herself and be detached from the negative thoughts, impulses, and negative conditioning from external sources. Therefore, one needs to know how to work on him/herself. Maybe the next step is to put together some ways in which people can practice working on their being—.—Marvin C. Katz, Ph.D.

That last sentence describes this book. Working on oneself to add values is the means to master emotions and live a joyous, emotional, and spiritual life because your empowerment and joy are at stake.

Virtues attach to a material value most often. For example, 'I will study diligently.' Here, 'knowledge' is a material gain, while 'diligence' expresses the willingness to ensure that it is pertinent, valuable and supportive of life. In other words, one studiously seeks to become knowledgeable.

Such values and devotion to life's blessings and joys allow the development of a personal code of ethics. The great news is that, given sufficient thought to your choices, you'll find little more than fifteen primary values. Why so few? Because life values apply to intention and commitment.

Learn and employ the basics, and you've mastered life itself. For example, how many different activities, situations, or people in your life will benefit because you 'respect' them? Will you profit in return? Some values on your chosen list will have subset values, of course. If you choose the same values already resident in your subconscious process, no conflict between your two minds can exist. Absolute joy results because both value sets synchronise.

Spiritual values fuel the automated programs that power ninety-two percent of our lives. They enrich your material pursuits as your subconscious mind automatically cares for your biology. The word 'spirit' refers to the human spirit or soul in general. Our will to live is our soul in action; hence values that uphold life are spiritual. Thus we are the makers of our souls.

We've all heard the statement, "actions speak louder than words." As a result, our subconscious mind gets a grandstand picture of what we value through perceptual observation of our chosen actions. It discerns our passion for those values from the intensity or passion for life expressed while performing them. As prior mentioned, the subconscious mind automatically uses values from past actions unless we deliberately upload overriding values. Those default sources stem from childhood and many other sources, including propaganda, employment, social activities, political correctness, career upsets, broken marriages, social media, false ideologies, etcetera. The list is endless.

Chapter 5

Unless checked, the subconscious mind assimilates those values and retains them in its memory database even though we know nothing of them. We do not know what they are, which have a high or low priority, yet these values are the source of our feelings. We've no remedy, hence the grief-stricken complaint, *"My emotions rule me."*

Whether our values are chosen or are default assimilated from past actions, we originated or voluntarily accepted those values. That means our conscious mind authors (originates) our emotions, not our heart (or emotional mind) as countless people believe. Are you beginning to see why? Denied learning what consciousness is or how it works, we naturally tend to gravitate to what motivated or satisfied us during childhood. It is easy to believe *"it worked then, so it must work now."* But no, it's not that simple. Such responses depend on the belief in heart-based emotions, which is only partially true. Later, the story explains how the cause switches for effect. 'Beliefs' arise out of such misunderstanding whereby ignorance multiplies unchecked.

Detrimental values almost invariably lead to life-harming actions and practices, including mental traumas. Lies, false beliefs, erroneous ideologies, or soul-destructive theologies, when indulged, are readily accepted as one's values unless categorically asserted otherwise. Emotional consequences, erroneously known as negative emotions, then result in the corresponding measure.

A burglar places a high value on freedom of choice, tax avoidance, not having to be employed, and so forth. He substitutes the plunder of value, which he regards as legitimate achievement, in place of creating or producing values. Material values thereby substitute for spiritual values. Most often, burglars choose to escape from the nature of life and from natural laws that impel productive effort. They seek a mental cop-out, deriving emotional satisfaction from looting in place of creating spiritual values. (Taxation is of the same ilk.) Thieves must use their minds nevertheless. Success entirely depends on it. They prepare every move with meticulous precision, or they fail.

Such people and all those who thrive on value-theft have no idea they are second-handers dependent on other people's values. Material values are their only measure and concern. Tragically, many others exploit this ignorance and thrive on it. Corporate governments write voluminous tax codes to protect their thieving. Indeed, every wicked, criminal victimisation in history rests on the premise of stolen values, which is blatant theft! You produce; we rob!

That drains our time, energy, motivation, and resources. Little by little, our surrender of life's values due to ignorance is the unrecognised surrender of our life. Nature takes its course based on our choices as 'natural law' decrees.

Often, maturing adolescent minds are denied their free choice. Teenagers generally want to accept life's responsibilities, grow, and mature. They want to spread their wings and learn more, but tensions, trauma and fisticuffs with parents often result when their will is refused. The prime source of this anguish is that neither teenagers nor their parents are taught anything about the changeover from subconscious motivation to intellectual motivation, later discussed.

Teenagers have no wish to rebel. Indeed they inwardly plead for maturity and to use their minds and accept responsibility as Creator intended. They crave engaging in life's fulfillment. They recognise creative urgings but cannot express any as they should because they've not learned how their minds are maturing. Neither can their parents understand, for the same reason.

Often, the door to free will and independence slams shut in their face. Authoritative domination and control refuse their attempts to engage full consciousness and exercise independence. Neither parents nor their offspring has any understanding of what is transpiring. Thus ignorance prevails, friction amplifies, and stress multiplies. Mental abandonment often takes root. Drugs, sex, music and group activities offer relief but no remedy.

Deliberate or accidental short-circuiting of our mind amounts to complete reliance on the automated subconscious mind, just as animals function. However, we cannot exist in this state of animality because we are not so equipped. We can ignore reality but cannot escape the consequences of that choice.

If we blank out our minds and thus wilfully suspend our consciousness, we punish ourselves. As Ayn Rand describes, our refusal to think is not blindness. Our refusal to see and to know is not ignorance. All too often, it is deliberate un-focusing of one's mind to escape the responsibility of living. All such attempts to short circuit knowledge will inevitably cause mental or emotional distress. We reap what we sow. People who rely on (nature's) bridging pathway provided for children, thus pretending they can thrive in adulthood, will suffer. Wishful thinking, mysticism, and subjectivism are good examples of blissfully attempting to bypass conscious understanding.

Fortunately, most of us developed and learned to consciously rely on enquiry, investigation, and critical thought throughout our childhood— the more personal and value-charged our thinking, the more our life blossoms.

Chapter 5

As a lesson in free will expression, our gifted opportunity to progress at our own pace is perhaps the most beautiful natural law Creator ever bestowed. No (purported) law we've invented can match what the Law of Allowance offers. Better still, it allows learning and mental maturity to grow and become habituated through choice for our entire life.

Do not fall for the commonly used adage, *'this is my truth.'* Life is truth, and it is absolute. Values support your passage through life, and their validity is crucial to life. Whatever does not uphold your life has no value. Pretenses must be rejected, including propaganda, make-believe theories, and misconceived ideologies.

The natural laws of 'identity' and 'causality' (later discussed) help to identify spiritual values based on your nature. Every favourable value decision confirms your agreement that life is of paramount importance. The result is peace, harmony, gratitude, love, abundance, and a joyful life beyond compare.

Later, a technique may be used to implant spiritual values in our subconscious minds to refuse all bogus values. That is how you master your mind. Of course, many people will complain bitterly, saying, for example, *"You mean I've got to mentally ascribe a life value for every damn thing I do, every second of the day? You're kidding, I hope!"*

No, save about every three to six months because deliberately uploaded values are fully automated. Every emotion reminds you of your chosen values. They may only need revision as frequently as you upgrade your computer software. The reason is that life values are more an enduring attitude, an underlying yet addressable subconscious program, based on spiritually sustaining one's life.

For example, at some point between exploring and choosing an action, we usually consider how we will benefit. Almost invariably, the value will be material in nature, e.g., a new dress, food on the table, a vacation, or learning from a talk.

Now consider what spiritual values may be involved.

- Will you settle for a new dress because it looks pretty and is priced right, or will you insist that it portrays your passion and excitement for life?

- Will any food suffice, or will you insist on nutritious food because your health is at stake?

- Will you take a vacation because it's that time of year, or are you determined to re-vitalise yourself through excitement, relaxation and meditation?

- Will you attend a talk out of casual interest, or will you determine to listen intently, thus learn and profit your life?

Conscious Ascendance

Do you see what effect this value-based approach might have? The subconscious mind upholds your life in nature. So it questions — *'are you on the same page, or not?'*

The second option in those examples testifies to your spiritual approach to life. The material element is purely a vehicle to exercise your values.

Think what values would underscore reason, purpose and self-esteem. The answer is in your biology and its proper functioning. The word is 'nutrition', which signifies 'value' absolutely.

Our physiology also depends on exercise, hygiene, and relaxation, not forgetting sleep. What word describes all of those? None do, so let's try a different tack. What spiritual value or spiritual expression addresses all those priorities? Several come to mind, like integrity, diligence, and respect. If you agree, pick up a pen and begin writing your list of life values right now. (There is a page for this purpose in the Appendix).

Upon which do your mental powers rely on? Does your mind need cognitive 'nutrition'? Yes, because it came from the same Creator. So what spiritual values or spiritual words address its priorities. That's easy; knowledge, truth, honesty, rationality, efficiency, independence and integrity, leap off the page!

Consider more life-value suggestions like those in this table and those listed previously.

Write your own list - 15- 18 max.			
Truth	Discernment	Diligence	Responsibility
Respect	Justness	Knowledge	Thoughtfulness
Honesty	Leadership	Reason	
Purpose	Rationality	Vigilance	

10. A starter list of life-values

Gratitude, love and compassion are missing since they represent destination values to which most people aspire. Use a Thesaurus to look up any or all of those values, plus any that you can think of. You'll soon see that some values I've listed are subsets of another. For example, is 'fairness' a subset of 'justness'? You can build your list vertically, with subset values horizontally, like this—

- Integrity: Truth, honesty, dedication, ++ ??
- Rationality: Discipline, thoughtfulness, responsibility, ++?
- Reason: Knowledge, discernment, etcetera.

Chapter 5

The first three bullet values in that list are exactly what your subconscious mind employs. For example, try driving a car without discipline. Arrange your chosen values as your list takes shape. Remove any duplicated values. You'll soon see how little more than fifteen life values assume priority and how all subset values fall below. Remove any leaches. Please keep it simple. Stay focussed on matters that vitalise your mental activities, just like you would choose nutritious foods for bodily health.

All feelings and emotions derive from our values. Leave them to chance, or permit other people to seed their values into our subconscious mind, and we've no idea what our feelings are reporting.

Feelings bring respective values to our present moment awareness. Thus we have an opportunity to update our values or alter our future behaviour. Feelings and emotions are the Creator's gift of an automated mentoring system. You learned that in school, right? No! Nothing concerning one of the most profound gifts we could ever receive! Using that gift facilitates your dynamic power of full consciousness.

Spirituality cannot be an illusion; else, you would not be the part of the Source, which you already are. Since spiritual values connect the physicality of your being to your spirituality, it is worth developing both in unity. Then you are complete, independent, self-confident, a sovereign being.

It is not easy to let go of attachments, especially the ego. The secret is to build what works, not demolish what does not. We often seek to know our brothers and sisters to enjoy mutual experiences. We seek a shared understanding and emotionally benefit from joint encounters. Also, to learn what we might expect from others in the future. We strive to know their moods, or 'vibrations' to use today's buzzword. The problem is that relying on others for life satisfaction leaves us dependent on what they depend. A mere acquaintance may evolve into a deeper relationship, whereby the mood of that relationship or emotional investment in that individual becomes value-fixed. That is not bad necessarily. Let me clarify a vital distinction. Love results from shared values, which is as it should be. But 'shared values' are most decidedly not 'dependent values' as in one person being dependent on the other. Shared values are originated or determined individually, whereas dependent people plagiarise other people's values.

It is easy to become dependent, thus reliant on moods or so-called 'energies.' Then others prescribe your life while you've little or no knowledge of what values their subconscious mind draws on. How can this stifling condition be overcome? Just choose what you value, then exercise and manifest it. Emotions then become your broadcasting channel, not your reception channel. You are free. You've cancelled your dependency on others. Your values are yours, and you manage them. That done, now you master your life, which brings it into spiritual providence. You have enacted your nature in accord with the spiritual power of Source.

Shine a light on your values; others will recognise their Source as divine. Energies and vibrations will fade into insignificance; illusions and pretenses likewise. Never lose sight of how infants show the importance of using 'journey' values to reach their goals. Success is inevitable because our subconscious relies on the same value structure. It remains to learn how we can ensure this meeting of the minds, even though this chapter is one of the most important in this book.

Infancy shows the importance of life values and the subconscious vocabulary. The Value Transfer wave shows how they commute between our two minds and how their role is crucial to success. Spirituality assumes prominence. Because life is the supreme value, consciousness is now equally as objective as the science of biology. Practise what you have learned. List your most prized life values as described. Employ them as described in the following chapters and become free from conscious ignorance forever.

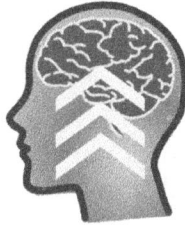

Chapter 6

6. Programming the subconscious mind

Values are consciously chosen and uploaded to the subconscious mind or subconsciously assimilated. This chapter describes how you can program your subconscious mind and take charge of your life. Then you can learn from your feelings and emotions to your great advantage.

If perhaps you think that ascribing a spiritual value to every choice you make is an arduous task, think again! Undoing mental and emotional damage is far more troublesome. Divergent values produce stress and conflict. Corresponding values deliver harmony and happiness.

Uploading your (fifteen or thereabouts) value choices to your subconscious mind is or should be a 'one-off' task, save for revising what you prize from time to time—once done, your spiritual passion for life is partnered with mental automation that sustains it. No chore exists once your values are prioritised and automated. You will tap into a power likely you never knew existed! 'Health' and 'mental efficiency' will serve all your undertakings without added work.

None of this is to teach the subconscious mind its job. The object is to consciously affirm that a wholesome and productive life is your choice so that your two minds can work in synergistic harmony and without conflict. What follows is no mind game for idle or amusing indulgence. A robust fullness of your life is at stake or great disappointment. Please read, then study what follows. Then, beginning with simple choices, practise the method suggested and prove to yourself that it works.

Some people advocate using mantras and repetition to program the subconscious mind. That is how we learn the alphabet and times table in school. It works as we know, but that is mere repetition for memory's sake. Repeating words or phrases over and over may convey insincerity and pose grave risks.

It is better to take charge with certainty. Putting values on autopilot removes any need to be reminded; hence your workload is significantly reduced and errors minimised if not cancelled entirely. Auto-activated values render mental efficiency and efficacy precisely. Additionally, the subconscious mind shuns all hesitations, discrepancies, confusions, doubts, beliefs, or reservations concerning 'what is most valued.' Hopes, wishes or cravings fade into insignificance when success results from passioned intention and commitment to live to the fullest.

Our human sciences have yet to grasp the vital importance of our sensory capacity to form images and, indeed, the proper role of imagination. For example, infants show us that visual images convey one's desired value. That lesson teaches that visualisation and imagination are adult tools for painting value images on the canvas of our subconscious mind.

Here is a simple mind programming exercise concerning health. It follows the same protocols previously described for fear but is now a formula you can follow for many different desires. Study this carefully and understand its subtle nuances. They will become critical when uploading spiritual values, as later described.

First, describe your goals in a short sentence. For example—

'I want to improve my health by enjoying 20-minutes of exercise each morning.'

Think what that conveys. More than simply exercising, you want to enjoy it. Implicitly, you want benefits and feelings of joy and good health. All of these sustain your life and make it worth living. Notice the deliberate intention; namely, I 'want' to do it. Observe the time slot as being each morning, not just every day.

You can employ this method for anything you choose. It might take a few attempts to specify your goals. Nevertheless, everything should speak of your consciously assertive intention. Passion, earnest desire, and the will to uphold life grab the attention of your subconscious mind, as happened when you learned to crawl. Was your subconscious mind impressed then? You bet it was!

Orally state your goal, then write it. Look at it. Per my example, study the three core elements. 1) willed intention to act. 2) passion for life. 3) acting that part. Those three elements should be present in all future value assignments because they confirm your purposeful intention to engage with your subconscious mind. It drives your enactments, after all.

Chapter 6

Each of those attributes should be within your written goal. If not, then add whatever is missing. For example, I want to achieve— (specify exactly what). My particular reasons are— (to establish the life value it will bring you). I'm committed to this achievement and my life's betterment. (Show desire, passion and commitment.)

Here is the method in brief. — Using my example above—

1. **First,** visualise preparing to do what you've chosen so that your desires result.

2. **Second,** genuinely and truthfully picture doing what you intend. Visualise enacting it.

3. **Third**, visualise the many benefits of putting that value into practice.

Do not take longer than one minute for each of the three visualisations. Keep it short and stay entirely focused. Thirty-seconds may be sufficient.

If you cannot complete each task in one minute, revise your presentation and begin the next day again. The subconscious mind wants succinctly assertive information. Lengthy descriptions imply laboured thought, incompleteness, or a lack of sincerity.

1st Minute– Visualise preparing

Your goal is critical. The more concise, the more it defines your valued reason, the greater will be its acceptance.

If you are not passionately assertive, convincing or decisive, your subconscious mind will accept 'indecision is your most prized value.' Because it has no interest in wishes, every distraction or uncertainty will fail your goals. Every hope that the subconscious mind might work will block it. Doubts, cancel your request without question.

During the first minute, orally state your goal and picture it in your mind's eye as we say. Visualising preparing, perhaps accepting morning exercise as a joyful wake-up call with time to mentally prepare for the day ahead. Picture your subconscious mind becoming excited about some valued choices coming to it. You are priming its readiness and your readiness to explain your desires in picture form, as lively and exciting. Picture your subconscious awakening to something vibrant and joyful, something to enjoy regularly. Picture your subconscious curiosity begging, *"Please show me more."* Spend no more than one minute.

2nd Minute - Visualise acting your goal – your actions

During the second minute, mentally picture yourself doing what your goal expresses. That will transfer your plan to your subconscious mind's (image) vocabulary. In my previous example, the infant could not ask to be 'there,' so it looked there repeatedly, which pictorially impressed 'there' on the subconscious mind, thus the infant's desire to go 'there.' The subconscious mind grasped the infant's passioned intent from its continuing visualisation.

Picture yourself doing what you've expressed you will do. Be legitimate, genuine and truthful. Visualise enjoying what you intend. For example, picture yourself waking at 5.45 am, as birds sing outside your window, then dressing to go walking on the beach or in the park. Picture this preparation as fun and excitement. Visualise removing your shoes, the festive touch of cool sand under your feet, and the feeling of nature coursing through your body as you deeply inhale fresh morning air. Picture enjoying a warm glow of satisfaction as refreshing water washes over your feet or body. Envisage reveling in nature; all cares gone. View improved health flowing through every part of your body. Picture it all as actually happening. Relish feelings of happy emotions, and feel a spring in your steps.

Stop after one minute. Please do not overdo it. Be convincing, never pleading.

You are presenting the subconscious mind with a painted picture of passioned intent, using your brush strokes of clarity. You're showing your picture image and impressing it upon its library of images, brimming with passioned intention to do it. This intent confirms your will, and the subconscious mind has the power to deliver. Thus, full conscious cooperation will progressively become the benchmark in your life, soon to become habitual.

3rd Minute - Picture positive benefits and satisfaction.

Picture your goal as accomplished. Visualise triumphant success as illustrated in my example. Picture health amassing in your body, driving all negativity out, just as your subconscious mind does. Picture gradual improvements in your life, such as your loathing of junk food. Picture warm emotions, affirmations that your goal supremely corresponds with the fullness of your life and that your subconscious mentor agrees. Picture improved health assisting everything you do, listening, laughing, teaching, driving, sex, cooking. Picture rejoicing. Express thanks to your subconscious partner for its assistance in achieving your prized goal.

That's it! Your first (three-step x one minute) program is all done, save for its enactment. Have no doubts that what you've willed will happen, absolutely none! Your subconscious mind has the power, and you've given it your passionate blessing to achieve all that you've pictured in your conscious mind.

All of those steps are together what trigger your subconscious mind to concur and oblige!

Chapter 6

Start work on your glorious future life today. Choose simple values initially. Do what you've programmed, and establish success. Once you have used this technique several times and been rewarded, no matter how simple your valued request, you will have no doubt that life-values are nutritious food for your subconscious mind.

Choosing valued goals will soon become second nature. Any fear of independence will vanish. Your confidence will grow, and your self-esteem. You'll be humbly proud of your achievements and be emotionally rewarded. Your focus in life will shift. You'll see that spiritual values enhance material gains, not the other way around.

When you passionately and joyfully picture values and intently prize them, your subconscious mind will prioritise them above all. As a result, old values will fade into oblivion.

It's a cost-free exercise. No psychotherapy is needed. Develop the habit of expressing gratitude each time your subconscious mind reminds you of a particular value in life. Foster this back-and-forth dialogue with your buddy.

Ascribing spiritual values is not an arduous task. Undoing mental and emotional damage is much more troublesome since unknown values offer no clues regarding what might be changed. Pretenses will be rejected, including propaganda, make-believe theories, and ideologies. Does a particular idea relate to existent reality or not. To whom or what does it offer value? Remember also that your mind interfaces physicality through your five senses, primarily via perception. 'Length' and 'rotation' are not physical, yet both depend on physicality. Ideas not grounded in causal reality cannot uphold the truth of your life.

Question your beliefs because they lack definitive substance. Such are not values at all! You can study them diligently and prudently, also respecting who offered them. But without the same (positive) assuredness that powers your subconscious mind, conflicting values and 'non-values' will produce turmoil.

Once you have programmed your subconscious mind as described above, it is essential to detach from your images. Let them go. Let your higher self do its job. It knows, with the certainty you delivered. Hope plays no part. The longer you hang on to those visualisations, the less your passion for them is convincing. So let go, fully knowing that your desires will indeed manifest.

Now do what you've vowed you would do. Take action to cement your values in your subconscious mind. Do what you promised. Per my example, exercise every morning without fail; adverse weather is the exception. Reinforce your drive for life in the manner you promised yourself. Integrity is vital because when our expressed goals match our actions, our subconscious mind fits one to the other. Its ability to accurately integrate and assimilate information is astounding.

Once you accomplish this, even if only in a small way, you will realise and understand how your two minds communicate. Your silent partner is no longer silent. You can orally speak to your subconscious because hearing is one of your five senses. With some initial practice, it will be your habit to embellish your words with pictures of what you desire. For example, you can say, "Hey buddy, please wake me at 5 am," whilst you picture a clock face showing five am.' It will wake you right on the second! Marry the clock face to your words, and you will benefit.

Make connections regularly. Say words like, *"I'm seeking your help."* Or, *"With my earnest desire, we will do this. I'm committed to this achievement and my life's betterment."* Use your words. Do not tell yourself, *"I can do this."* That puts your subconscious mind on the sideline. Say instead, *"We will do this,"* or *"I love your assistance."* Or, *"Let's go, partner."*

Unless we definitively assert our desires and why, most importantly, the subconscious mind will not prioritise them above the values it has garnered from past actions. Those default values will remain. It takes courage to pursue your goals and dreams. Importantly, you need to overcome your fear of failure or doubts. Assertiveness concerning what you prize will do just that.

Here is beauty and simplicity; once specific value choices become your life-sustaining ethic, their regular practice becomes a cultivated habit. You win by visualising your goals, which reinforce when you activate them. They become habituated, not through repetition, but because both of your minds synchronise in harmony. Decisive actions lock your values in place. They, in turn, loop to cultivate more decisive actions.

What happens if you do not enact your values? You can cheat your cognitive self. You can lie to yourself, and your subconscious mind will accept all such deceptions as truth. If you do not practice the value you have promised to enact, your subconscious mind will conclude that lying, cheating, falsity and lack of integrity are what you truly value. Your previously specified goal will have backfired because you enacted its converse outcome. Either way, the truth is inescapable. You proved you could program your subconscious mind when you learned to crawl. You did it, remember?

Conflicting values result in conflicting emotions. If what you value conflicts with your actions, stressful feelings will occur. That's your alarm

Chapter 6

bell. To choose one path and live another is to pretend that different values will harmonise. They cannot and will not. Stress results. Discord develops. Anxiety increases because you've cheated yourself. Always express the 'positive,' and, most importantly, express gratitude for its delivery.

Life values are the key to harmony. Your life is worth it, so become the best version of yourself.

Programming abstract values

The same three-step (3x1) technique applies to abstract values such as respect, honesty, and integrity. First, find different circumstances in which one value fits all. Second, visualise situations and events where particular value concepts apply. 'Respect,' for example, applies to one's own life, partner or family, employer and other people. 'Will' allows us to hear other people speak. It applies to work, sport, marriage, financial matters, and every aspect of life and dealings with others.

Consider forthcoming situations where a particular value is of prime, for example, a weekly business meeting. Use the same three-step method described above, each taking one minute or less.

1. First, visualise preparing to practice your particular value in advance.

2. Second, genuinely and truthfully picture yourself putting that value into practice.

3. Third, vibrantly picture all the benefits that might result, as though you have already achieved what you seek. Feel your picture, as you would feel it when done.

That's it! Visualise preparation, then your enactment, and finally, picture and feel its benefits as though they already occurred. That done, you must take action to cement your values in your subconscious mind. Please do what you have visualised when that opportunity presents itself. You may have to wait a few days for that imagined situation to eventuate, but strive to reinforce your passion for that value as soon as possible. If you do not practice your chosen value, it will not lock in or become habituated. As before, fail what you promised yourself and that failure will become your prized value because you enacted it. Millions of people do this and wonder why they are emotionally torn.

Find circumstances where you can actively indulge the values you have uploaded. Two or three experiences are usually sufficient to cement your deal. After that, your subconscious mind will habituate those values, and they are automated. Evolve this new version of yourself, and you will splendidly achieve your goals.

Conscious Ascendance

Recall the surgeon example given previously. Precise, minuscule, millisecond adjustments perfect the desired goals. (One slip, and the patient dies.) What better example of diligence or commitment and even respect is there? Those values became so impressed on the subconscious mind during medical training that they automatically apply to all following surgeries.

Spiritual values apply to all physical undertakings. For example, diligence applies automatically to board meetings, also showering, abseiling, lawn mowing, public speaking and cake baking. Physical life is spiritually enriched across the board, automatically, consistently, and without stress.

The 4P program - Practise to Prove – Polish to Perfect.

Once having Practised the technique, and Proven it, now Polish and Perfect it. I call that the 4P program. Practice to Prove and Polish to Perfect. Your subconscious mind will soon grasp and establish as (predominant) values those which you most fervently practice. Chalk up two or three successes using the three-step program, and you'll know that your life values prevail, excluding all posed by pretenders or imposters. Choosing valued goals will become second nature. Any fear of independence you may have had will have long vanished. You will have 'proven' the technique.

When you begin to experience a warm glow in your heart each time you are reminded of a particular value in life, express gratitude to your subconscious mind. Agree that when something hinders your goal, and you feel it, commonly called a negative emotion, what you experience is still positive news, despite the debilitating circumstance that initiated it. Learn from it. That's why your subconscious mind delivered it.

Develop and nurture conversational communion between your two minds, as two loving partners do, each independent of mind but alike in purpose, direction and value. Read your feelings, and respond to your subconscious mind. Polish this back and forth communion until it glows within you. The subconscious mind deals in the positive vein. It hears your gripes and your grizzles, but it will not act to change that value until you freely commit to replacing it.

Practice these suggestions, and you will 'polish' the subconscious mind programming technique. Be very thankful. Learn to treat mistakes as a positive lesson. Become excited through your achievements and enamored to seek more from the same method. Be very grateful for what you've mastered and that you did it. Be delighted you are spending less than ten percent of the mental energy most folk waste undoing emotional stress, chaos, trauma, and confusion they suffer.

Chapter 6

As later described, deconstructing your feelings will become a breeze. The more accomplished you become, the more this beautiful, gracious and straightforward exchange is polished! It has no equal! Never let go of this masterful blessing in your life.

Your two minds are in complete unison and harmony. Their mission is now 'perfected.' That is what you desired. Your success is their passion, and they have the blessed ability to deliver. Feel their warmth and beauty deep within your heart. Understand your love of spirit and its love for you. It is you. Lovingly grasp hold of spiritually experiencing your whole self. Be mindful of your absolute completeness and wholesome, beautiful, unique, spiritual individuality. Love that your minds know what you are and how you function. Be graciously and humbly thankful, knowing that you are the master of your destiny and maker of your soul. Be abundantly glad! Offer thanks to your Creator with sincere and loving reverence.

Practice these exercises, and you will 'perfect' the technique. The 4P program will become automated under your watchful free mind as the master conductor.

Self-mastery accords all other people the same opportunity. Self-mastery, in this sense, is a moral discipline because where the rights of all other singular beings are respected, no one can offend another through any application of his own. The principle of 'suffering no unnecessary offense because one is careful to give none' extends to us. How our two minds communicate and the stupendous importance of value transfer is crucial to mastering consciousness and our sovereignty.

Does it seem right that such manners and respect could substitute for what we call law? Would such etiquette or ethics possibly benefit society and preclude conflicts? Could 'orderliness' of this calibre resolve or even nullify any need for today's so-called laws? Could this ethic stretch further than they can even reach? Yes, indeed; nature has bestowed every individual with complete orderliness sufficient to translate into all societies without amendment or addition. That is the subject for another book, however.

From a psychological point of view, emotions are considered a complex state of feeling. Many people, including researchers and philosophers, believe emotions result from physical and psychological changes that influence our thinking and behaviour. But do they? Some say that emotions such as love, affection, happiness, surprise, anger, and fear are pre-programmed, innate, and universal. Is that true?

What if our feelings report on the values we hold, including whether our values are upheld or challenged?

Conscious Ascendance

Before answering that question, we should first ask why we have emotions? What is the express purpose of feelings? Philosophers, psychologists, and researchers have put forward different theories that attempt to explain them, and these theories divide into three categories:

1. Physiological theories propose that physical body responses are responsible for our emotions.

2. Neurological theories argue that brain activity leads to emotional responses.

3. Cognitive theories suggest that our thoughts and other mental actions play a vital role in forming emotions.

In all probability, those theories could fill pages, but let's ask one vital question. What role does the subconscious mind play, particularly regarding values we may choose? It seems very clear from everything discussed so far that while those theories hint at some truths, they fall far short of identifying the real cause and purpose of feelings and emotions.

I submit that feelings report whether our life is on track with our desires and values or, instead, is amiss in one or more respects. For example, if we get a gut ache or toothache, we feel poorly, and our mood suffers as a result. On the other hand, if we have eaten well, we feel physically and emotionally satisfied. Now translate those outcomes into the mental realm.

Our pleasure-pain mechanism automatically indicates our body's welfare or injury. Our consciousness performs likewise but instead registers our two primary emotions of joy or suffering. Emotions result from our value judgments. They inform us what is working for or against us. Our feelings are lightning calculators showing the sum of our profit or loss.

Notably, the physical pleasure-pain mechanism of our body is automatic and innate. We've no say in what it informs. Feelings and emotions are similarly intuitive in delivery terms, but our values determine their content. We determine the value standard by which they function. The crunch line is that no automatic values are possible because we've no intuitive knowledge or understanding. With no automated values, there can be no inbuilt values, no innate ideas, no in-built value judgments and no inherent morality.

Digressing momentarily, that given description is crucial since it reverses the underlying premise of natural law theory. Feelings are much like perceptions, therefore. We are alerted to a particular circumstance or situation but given no explanation; we must learn. What is it? From what is it made? Is it living or inert, etcetera?

Chapter 6

Feelings are sentient and pose different questions concerning whether our values are on course. Emotions are not physical or tangible but can physically affect our body, such as raising our hackles. The degree to which we prize something will affect the intensity of the feeling we receive. This intensity may include the amount of effort we have invested. We feel joyous emotion if a particular value is applauded or rewarded. If the exact value is challenged or denied, we may feel sorrowful, upset, or angry.

Feelings come with no names. Instead, we name feelings according to whether it distracts, irritates, annoys, or angers us. The same applies to the intensity of positive emotions, such as amusement, interest, happiness, excitement, thrill, or being overjoyed. Altogether we have positive and (what we call) negative emotions, each having different intensities.

- **Positive emotions** confirm that our values are on course or not.
- **Negative emotions** demonstrate that our value goals are not succeeding or denied.

Yet, contrary to common belief, negative emotions are impossible. Every feeling delivers positive news. Being informed that our mission is falling off the rails allows us to trace the cause and fix the problem. That is good news. The particular circumstance may indeed be adverse. It may be hurtful or even harmful, but warning signals are positive news, our reason to take corrective action.

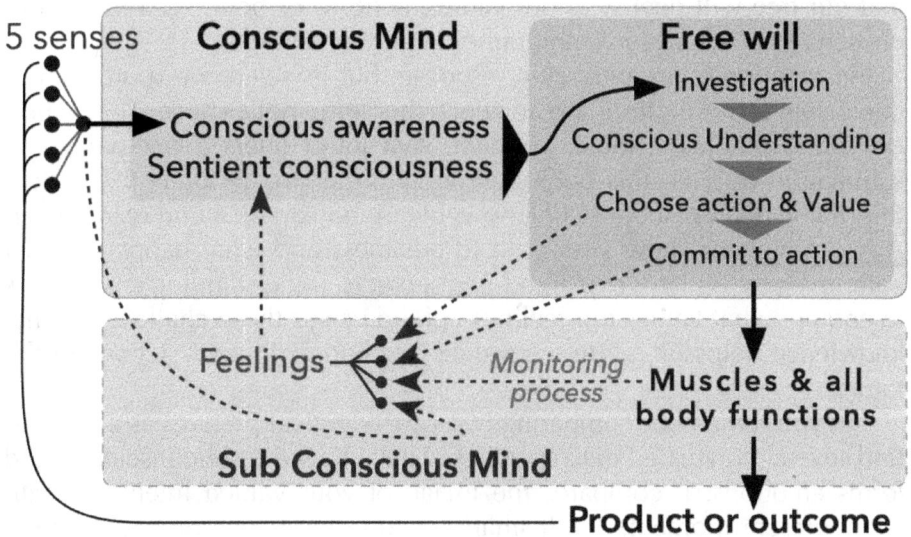

11. The four sources of feelings

Conscious Ascendance

Feelings may result from truth or fallacies, but our subconscious mind is always truthful. It matches a current event or circumstance with what we have chosen to value or permitted our conscious mind to accept as value. It must be that way because our subconscious mind is forbidden ability to judge or overrule any values we have chosen or permitted by default. The subconscious mind always works in the positive realm to highlight the values we each hold. Therefore, all emotions are positive, even those advising of unfavourable conditions.

Diagram 11 shows four (dotted) pathways from which feelings are formed. We are sentiently informed of how our values relate to our actions. Material success is a contributing factor constantly witnessed through our five senses in keeping with our material goal.

Although data comes from four different sources, every feeling is an abstraction offering no causal explanation. Nevertheless, it prompts our enquiry and the (process) cycle repeats.

Positive feelings occur when our actions match our values. Conversely, when our actions conflict with our values, we receive (so-called) negative emotions— our values are check-pointed thereby.

Feelings and emotions checkpoint our choices in value terms, remarkably similar to how our immune system works to rid our bodies of toxins and disease. Most importantly, detrimental effects like anxiety, stress, and mental trauma, cannot be automatically eradicated because that overrules our free choices. The alternative is simple. Feelings prompt that our free will deal with our values, actions, or both. As a result, our chosen remedies preserve and uphold free will entirely.

An emotion is an automatic response, but its reference source is our choice entirely. Emotions are an effect, therefore, not a cause. They report on values that we choose to enact. Ayn Rand offers a one-paragraph summation of what this book describes in the two chapters that follow this. If you decide not to read it now, please bookmark it and read it later. A few sentences show your path to greatness and what happens if that path reverses. As later explained, the secret to understanding emotions is to enquire what values our feelings uphold versus those challenged. That knowledge helps us revise our values or choose different actions in the future.

Do you remember comparing two near-identical pictures as a child to find several concealed discrepancies? That's how the subconscious mind forms emotions. It compares the image of your valued intentions with every present moment. As all smart kids do, it puts one picture over the other and holds both to the light so that differences appear in a flash. Perfect matches trigger feelings of success. Mismatches trigger feelings of dissatisfaction or hindrance. Several anomalies may cause different emotions, while emotional intensity often results from several corroborating value-matches (or mismatches) rather than one.

Our subconscious mind must use this image-matching process because it cannot enquire, choose, or judge. Images (its vocabulary) are the only resource it has for compiling feelings.

Love and fear are powerful emotions, so we respond almost instinctively. Consequently, many people believe that emotions rule our lives. We are told that love is a cocktail of chemicals, such as oxytocin secreted by the pituitary gland. It is easy, therefore, to believe we have no conscious control over fear, love, or any other powerful emotion. That is not true.

To deconstruct an emotion, first find the value it supports or challenges. For example, feelings that arise from falling into a stream while leaping over it seldom emerge from the mishap. The fall triggered the emotion, but the casualty does not explain our misfortune, annoyance, frustration, self-blame, or why those feelings differ. Our enquiries might point to wasted time, for example, ruined clothing, missing a bus to meet a friend, being late for an appointment, or a thousand other reasons. Distractions aside, the trustworthy source of our feeling results from identifying *what value-benefit should have resulted from successfully jumping the creek.*

People who conscientiously assign life values to their actions find it relatively easy to reverse engineer their emotions. They will ask—

- Which life value originated the feeling?
- Is it real or false?
- Should it be affirmed or altered?
- Or should I act differently in future?

Feelings always point to our values, whether we know of them or not. We should deal with the cause of an emotion else it serves no purpose. Changing our values or behaviour allows us to grow mentally, emotionally, and spiritually.

Unknown values deny appropriate responses. People who have not mastered values will seldom understand their emotions. Likely they won't know what a 'life-value' is. They won't understand how values are assigned to their subconscious mind, else acquired by default. Having learned the subconscious mind is impervious to control, which is true, they'll never consider how they might 'influence' it but never 'control' it. So they will not inquire further.

To determine our values is to define our feelings. Success advances or accelerates our progress in life. Failure curtails it.

Intense emotions can undermine a person's capacity for rational decision-making, even when the individual is aware of the need to make careful decisions— The authors draw on recent research that demonstrates that human decision-making is governed by two neural systems–the deliberative and the affective, or emotional. The latter, which the authors dub emote control, is much older, and served an adaptive role in early humans by helping them meet basic needs and identify and respond quickly to danger. As humans evolved, however, they developed the ability to consider the long-term consequences of their behaviour and to weigh the costs and benefits of their choices.

"Human behaviour is not under the sole control of emotion or deliberation but results from the interaction of these two processes," Loewenstein said. —John M. Grohol, Psy.D. [11]

Agreed. There is no clear-cut pathway to the origin of a feeling without first instilling life values into the subconscious mind. Without doing it, we cannot know whether a particular emotion is an appropriate response, a mistaken reprimand or accolade, or a vicious illusion resulting from years of self-deception.

People who short-circuit value considerations do not get off lightly. Our choice is simple. Either we deal with values up-front, or we must eventually wrestle with emotional stress and trauma with no remedial relief. The way natural laws govern behavioural consequences appears once again.

Many people will vehemently disagree, likely saying, *"I know instinctively whether I'm irritated, happy, delighted or ticked off. My feelings are real. They leave no doubt about how I feel! How can you say that I cannot know what I feel, when you can't even feel, what I feel?"*

Sadly, many believe that feelings arrive already named and explained and see no need to investigate the root cause. With conscious discovery short-circuited, they cannot profit from their emotions. In short, these people indulge in non-thinking, emotion-driven *'re–action'* instead of (cognitive) *'response-ability.'* To investigate a feeling is to seek its founding truth.

- **For positive feelings,** we should enquire what value our feeling supports.
- **For adverse circumstances**, ask what prized value is denied or arrested.

Drill down to the underlying premises of ideologies and beliefs. Ask, does this particular sentiment uphold and support my life, or not? What value does that premise offer? Is it founded in something wholesome, life-supporting, authentic and truthful, or not?

Answers will significantly assist in revising your values or point you to behaving differently in future. In summary—

- Life values are nutritious food for the subconscious mind and, when practised, quickly become second nature.
- Spiritual values enhance and enrich material gains, not vice versa.

Practice 'life-values' and old values fade into oblivion. No need exists for psychotherapy.

The method is simple and cost-free. Conversely, undoing mental and emotional damage is troublesome since unknown values offer no emotional or intellectual remedy.

Many, who consider investigating their feelings a demanding task, or imposition, will complain. Likely they will say, *"My feelings leave no doubt, about how I feel."* For these people, sadly, feelings are their explanations. They feel hurt and seek to escape via the quickest route possible, but they cannot cheat nature.

Introspection is the only way to reveal the objective truth behind our feelings. Each enquiry must seek the truth, for only that will indicate whether a particular emotion's (causal) founding value is true or false.

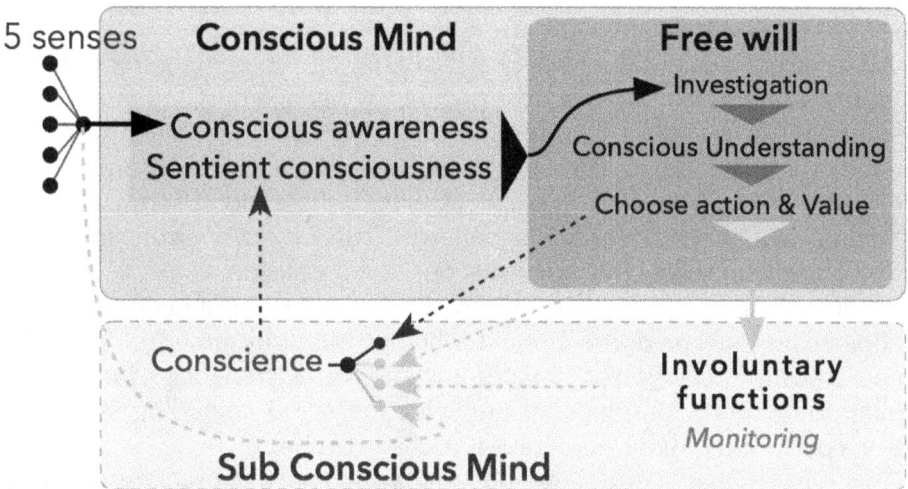

12. The source on Conscience

Having identified and dealt with what caused a feeling, it usually vanishes. Its purpose is complete, but still, it may commit to memory, thus serving 'intuition' in the future.

If all that sounds an arduous task, automate it. Impress fifteen or so values on your subconscious mind, and it's 'game over.' You are a winner!

Many people believe that conscience is a person's moral sense of right and wrong, a guide to their behaviour. But do we each have an inbuilt, unchangeable moral sense? Do we really, or do values trigger our conscience in the same way our feelings generate?

Diagram 12 shows that our subconscious mind assesses our value choices before taking action. 'Conscience alerts' are thence delivered to our sentient mind. This diagram is almost the same as diagram 11 concerning the source of feelings. But because no action has begun, three additional sources that trigger feelings do not yet exist. Accordingly, conscience reports only on our values, having respect for 'life' as the bottom line. Later, following our actions or behaviour, feelings are generated from all four sources, as previously shown in diagram 11 (P103).

Conclusions sum as follows—

- **Conscience** delivers 'value-reports' concerning a proposed event or action.
- **Feelings** provide 'value-reports' after an actual event or activity.

Note that pangs of conscience may occur in tandem with emotions. For example, one can be emotionally satisfied that an action has succeeded yet feel guilty for having done it.

Conscience uses our values to assist in distinguishing right from wrong. Values are ethically apprised respective of our intentions before being enacted. In sum, we have a life-sustaining ethic that automatically advises life's prospective advancements or regressions according to our values. Conscience shows we do not have a fixed, innate moral sense as many 'natural law theorists' ardently believe. That would overrule free will. Conscience preserves free will, thus our moral choice.

Our whole being is (auto) monitored every moment of every day. Free choices are accepted and upheld whether truthfully based or not. The conscious mind is alerted to value matches or discrepancies before and after our actions. All selections are value measured, including respect or disrespect for the rights of all others to their own life.

It follows that morals are the (free will) enacted practice of every individual's self-chosen ethics, or lack thereof, respective of their life.

This process and these faculties are a blessing indeed. They exist within every man, woman, and child. Automation enables us to ethically sustain the process of living, whether alone on a remote island or in society. Thus hails a complete overhaul and re-appraisal of conscience, the science and practice of ethics, morality, and all human and social sciences.

This importance points to a notable conclusion—

- **Conscience** alerts and reminds us of our chosen life values. *Conscience appraises our ethics.*
- **Emotions** alert us to actions that uphold (or trespass) our desired values.

Chapter 6

Emotions appraise our morality.

We are blessed by having two parallel systems, 'conscience mentoring' and 'emotional mentoring.' Ethics and morality are of our choosing, all escape efforts penalised. If you are now beginning to sense the makings of self-governance, you're a winner.

The common sense of conscience and emotions serving as our protector is straightforward and beautiful. Just as our body's immune system works to eradicate and clean out a harmful matter, our emotional faculties advocate mental and spiritual clean-outs or retentions.

As previously mentioned, what appears as the mental equivalent of our immune system, is no less than nature's gift of an (automated) 'value-mentoring system' that functions inwardly (thought before action) and publicly (morality in action).

Tragically, we are taught nothing about either, and the reason is straightforward. Material values have driven spiritual values to near extinction, and no one knows how to reclaim them. Sufferance exists as through normal, not abnormal as it truly is.

Our endocrine system (process) bears remarkable similarity to the conscious process, as previously described. It maintains homeostasis, which is our 'natural order.' Likewise, spiritual and material values regulate the body's motor functions. Feedback loops thereafter generate perceptions, conscience, and feelings, allowing us to preserve mental and spiritual homeostasis via our free will. That description is not in any textbook but should have been for centuries past.

Although defined in monetary terms, most people think abundance means 'an excess of something.' It may also be defined as 'the ability to do what you need to do when you need to do it.'

If that means having an abundant mindset, then a complete understanding of human consciousness delivers success. Program your subconscious mind as prior discussed, charge it with upholding your life to consistently meet your needs with the right timing, and you will have abundance.

The secret is to focus on your 'values.' Changing how you feel activates the feeling of being abundant all the time. Fear and doubt vanish as a direct result.

Russian Scientists have recently proven that DNA is programable. Convinced that nature was not dumb, they joined linguists and geneticists in a venture to explore the ninety percent of 'junk DNA.' Their findings and conclusions are revolutionary! Not only is our DNA responsible for the construction of our body, but it also serves as data storage and communication.

For example, they found that the alkaline of our DNA follows a regular grammar and has set rules just like our languages. Thus human languages are a reflection of our inherent DNA.

Modulating specific frequency patterns onto a laser ray influenced the DNA frequency and thus the genetic information itself. No DNA decoding was necessary, but these scientists emphasised that the frequencies must be correct, even using words and sentences of the human language, as was experimentally proven!
This scientifically explains why affirmations, autogenous training, hypnosis, meditation, prayer, and other forms of focus, can have such strong effects on humans and their bodies. The individual person must work on the inner processes and maturity in order to establish a conscious communication with the DNA. — Universal lighthouse radio [12]

Their two DNA discoveries seemingly speak of the same thing. However, the first argues broadcasted emotions, while the second argues 'group consciousness' results, albeit given the correct frequencies.

Think about that. If the correct frequencies amount to broadcasting life-sustaining emotions, then they are the god-like power spoken of, not group consciousness.

Therefore, our DNA seems more critical than has ever been credited. Suppose chemical changes occur in our bodies resulting from each emotion we experience. That encourages us to be mindful of our feelings, particularly their cause.

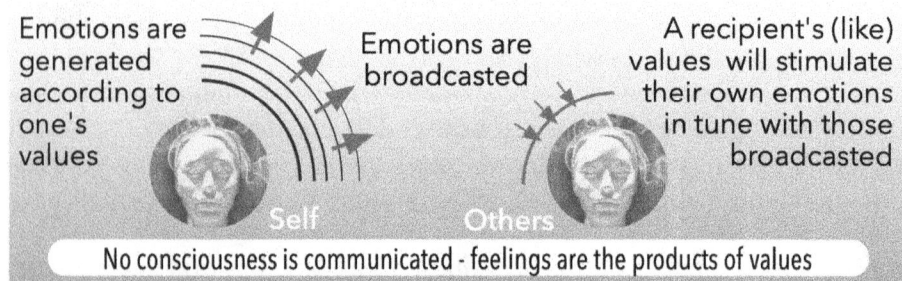

Emotions are generated according to one's values — Emotions are broadcasted — A recipient's (like) values will stimulate their own emotions in tune with those broadcasted

Self   Others

No consciousness is communicated - feelings are the products of values

13. Transmitted and received emotions

So let's view these findings based on 'values' being the causal source of our emotions. As already explained, feelings are the sentient (end) product of one complete conscious cycle. Given our feelings are broadcast, is the value source broadcast also? No, I submit. It is not. Our feelings' root (value) remains, as does our conscious process; but its product is the only thing broadcast.

Chapter 6

That means no shared or group consciousness is possible, but group awareness is. Diagram 13 tells the whole story.

People whose own values correspond with those broadcast by others will alone recognise the incoming signals. Since no values were transmitted, only their (emotional) product, the result is conclusive. Emotions are transmitted, not values or consciousness. Our receipt of broadcast emotions triggers our values; thus, we may experience near identical feelings. In other words, other people's (emotionally expressed) values stimulate matching emotions in ourselves, provided of course, that we share those same values.

Consequently, so-called 'group consciousness' is nothing but our becoming 'aware' of corresponding values that other people express. All participants are 'aware,' leading to the mistaken belief that awareness is consciousness.

It remains that if emotions affect our 'DNA following a regular grammar, having set rules,' then we are obliged to be mindful of values as the source of such changes. To re-quote the scientists above–

"The individual person must work on the inner processes and maturity in order to establish a conscious communication with the DNA."

Indeed we must, and for that reason exactly. Do you now see why certain people want to tamper with your DNA? Do you see a need for absolute protection?

Emotions such as great enlightenment, calm, joy, and contentment typify spiritual experiences broadcast into the universal quantum world beyond our bodies. So too, is our spirituality. That confirms that consciousness interfaces with spirituality.

This chapter has filled out the big picture of full consciousness. It has shown the crucial importance of life values and how important we must take charge of them and protect them. Life values and their management is of utmost importance to our mental, emotional and spiritual wellbeing.

Conscious Ascendance

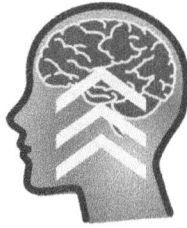

Chapter 7

7. The higher faculties, benefits, and sovereignty

Understanding how our higher (mental) faculties process our value choices in serving our desires and ambitions is prudent and very important. A deeper understanding will put all the puzzle pieces together in one tight parcel and show how each faculty strengthens the others. Therefore, although benefits almost become self-evident, I will enumerate them before showing how personal sovereignty results.

Is it any wonder conscious ignorance is rife today? To refuse 'conscious' study because academia deems it is not science, owing to free will, is like saying biology cannot be science because we can choose what to eat. That conclusion is senseless, whereby conscious ignorance marches on. It gets worse. Intelligence cannot be a science for the same reason, but stupidly, artificial intelligence apparently can. We can stupidly build a synthetic model of something we've never studied; and applauded for scientific know-how.

Communication between our two minds is unknown; thus, no sequential orderliness appears. No natural laws are present as a result. No value-based emotional feedback loop is observable, yet our bodily endocrine system uses a strikingly similar process. Either humanity is hopelessly inept, or those who know the truths of human consciousness conceal it from all others for nefarious purposes.

Regardless, nine higher faculties bless ourselves, fifty percent more than science recognises. Will, Imagination and Reason are of our free choice. Perception, Instinct, Intuition, Conscience, Memory and Emotions are all subconscious.

Conscious Ascendance

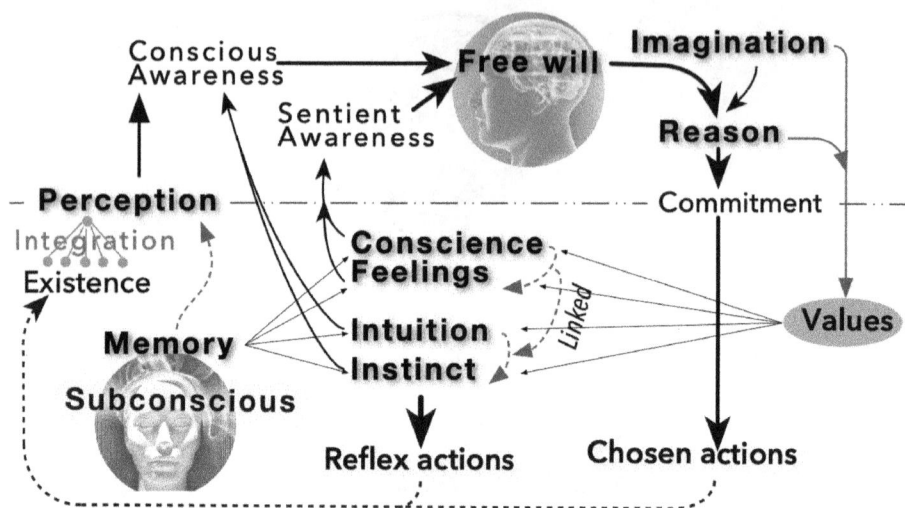

14. Relationships between the higher faculties

Diagram 14 shows the three higher (cognitive) faculties above the dash/dot horizontal line (through perception and commitment). Five subconscious faculties are below, plus perception is the connecting interface. Of these, two groups of linked pairs exist, themselves also linked. Values are not a higher faculty but power both couples in concert, assisted by our memory faculty. Perception, as previously described, is the integrating faculty that converts physical reality into awareness. All six subconscious faculties share this 'integrative ability,' which effectively unites all six faculties as though one.

As this astonishing marvel of intellectual engineering opens before your eyes, the more you will see its simplicity and the sheer beauty of its unification. Butcher or deny one part, and you've sacrificed all. Given that most people fully believe that consciousness means awareness (top left in the diagram) and nothing more, you will now sense the global tragedy of conscious ignorance.

Our cells, tissues, and organs all work in unison, and our subconscious genius does the same on the mental and spiritual level, as pictured in diagram 14. That helps explain how emotional and spiritual blessings manifest. Free will is seemingly apart, but not really because it conducts the whole spiritual symphony.

Imagination: Under our conductor's baton of free will lie the formidable cognitive powers of logic and Imagination. Logic is the grounding and stabilising of our reasoning ability, allowing us to analyse any situation or information and to grasp its validity or falsity beyond deception. Logic fixes our focus and encourages us to pursue all avenues, casting aside all distractions, diversions, contradictions and falsity.

Imagination is very different, expansive, and not delimiting. It opens our thoughts to opportunities and potentials. It facilitates forming new ideas or images of external objects not present to the senses. It imparts clarity to thoughts or ideas, enabling clear expression of an idea to oneself or others. Likewise, it assists in accomplishing a particular goal, or objective, while holding the image of its completion in view. It allows us to envisage our ideas as complete, to see them in the mind's eye, as vividly as if they already existed.

So we can soar on wings of enlightenment, to see our grandest vision for life and thus act for its fulfillment. We can project the future, aim for it, and fuel our desire to get there.

Better yet, Imagination has a far greater purpose. It allows us to visualise our values, receptive to the 'image vocabulary' of our subconscious mind. *Thus its real goal is to paint pictures of our values on the canvas of our subconscious minds.* Then our intuitive abilities are boosted far beyond anything we can conceive. Thus empowered, we can master our life and our emotions.

Imagination is our (free will) translation medium, from experience to a map of our glorious future, allowing us to envisage the most expansive possibilities and potentials. Imagination is the key to a free spirit that engages our potential as independent creators.

These explanations testify to two-way conversations between our two minds, known as 'psycho-epistemology.' The reason why free will is sandwiched between two subconscious processes becomes crystal clear.

Imagination also enlivens the brain's chemistry. When people feel whole, and spiritually in tune with themselves, they know that their two minds are in synchronous harmony. That is when dis-ease departs. Nature did not miss a single thing.

Memory is the subconscious process of storing and recalling information. It fuels our discoveries, imagination, intuition, instinct, conscience and emotions, recording our values, knowledge, beliefs, and experiences.

Extreme caution is necessary because we fuel its database. When sensory 'perception' is considered 'awareness', and thence understanding, the door slams shut on further enquiry. Spiritual values, thus rejected, is our sufferance.

Absent chosen values, default values take charge, and we lose control—our conscious process centres around unknown values. Effectively we are forced to exist in a state of (volition deprived) animality.

Conscious Ascendance

We respond to those default values as though nature itself, yet are not equipped to live in that state. Worse again, we've no knowledge a problem exists, nor do we know how to eliminate it.

Stress results from the subconscious process of drawing on life-depreciating values. Our feelings necessarily correspond. This deprived intellectual, emotional and spiritual state is the fundamental cause of most emotional stress, anxiety and trauma witnessed worldwide.

Permitting our subconscious mind to depend on (gathered) unknown values is a fast track to misery and trauma. When people say we must raise our consciousness or vibrations, they refer to this base state of consciousness. Consciousness is not the cause, however. Life-crippling values are!

Memory is sometimes attributed to some infinite, eternal mind, seemingly because neuroscience seems unable to find where it nests in the human body. Why do we invent such notions? Given that concepts such as velocity, rotation, inertia, and sequence inherently make an engine work as a function of design but are not tangible or material things, memory is a non-physical abstract functionality of the subconscious process. Whether in our DNA or not, it is 'abstract,' only manifesting as our conscious awareness, much as perception abstractly presents physicality to our (aware) attention.

Intuition: It is commonly believed today that intuition is the ability to acquire knowledge without proof, evidence, or conscious reasoning. This shortsighted notion suggests we can rely on intuit information as gospel truth. That sounds inviting yet it is likely not in our own best interests.

Intuition derives from our subconscious mind's ability to access a vast array of resources, including Source itself. For the sake of clarity, let's study the first phase of the value transfer wave in more detail, as shown in diagram 15.

Beginning at the bottom left, perception employs its powers of integration to make us aware. Thus we are prompted to discover what something is, how we might use it and what benefits might result. So begins a process of reasoning, enquiry, and discernment from which new thoughts emerge.

During our enquiries, pictures form in our minds concerning possibilities and potentials. All the while, the subconscious mind is looking over our shoulders. It sees what we see because images are its vocabulary. Memory also comes into play. It recalls pictures from your past and reads what you imagine will be your future. It also sees what you are doing in the present and has access to Source. It integrates previous conscious choices, persuasions, and values with our present values,

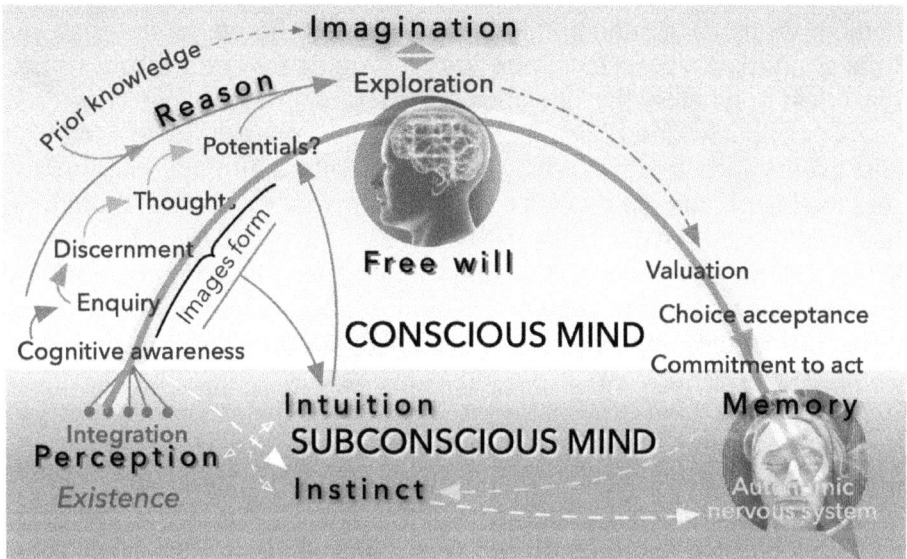

15. Intuition - as part of the Value Transfer Wave

thoughts and activity. Consequently, past, present and future are integrated to become the magical picture we call intuition.

In this abstracted form, much like perception works, a picture is brought to our conscious awareness as the magical realisation of a new idea. It seems esoteric because it derives from multiple sources beyond our cognitive understanding, much as 'perception' presents its material information in an abstract form. Nevertheless, this (abstract) image is pertinent to our present and future potential considerations.

This outcome squashes the irrational belief that intuition is some supernatural manifestation or magic wand creation. Instead, we see that intuition is the same value-matching tool that powers our conscience and feelings, albeit differently employed.

Intuitive information will automatically include some degree of purpose, reason, and value because of past thoughts and actions that trigger it. The potential to mislead begs that we learn whether past information was prior-investigated, evaluated, or authenticated. The extent to which intuit information is valuable will depend on previous determinations. If they confirmed truthfulness, and thus offered advancement, profit, learning, or spiritual awakening, then the same applies here, all else being equal. Current intuitions uphold present moment goals.

In short, new information prompts investigation, and authentication, while intuited information should adequately have been prior examined.

Conscious Ascendance

Remember that the subconscious mind cannot choose or prescribe our values. Instead, it accepts our wilfully uploaded or default values, regardless of whether they advance our life or depreciate it.

As previously described, the subconscious mind flawlessly matches past events and circumstances with present values and material goals. It sees the big picture. So it offers a snapshot of what we seek, as though we had leapfrogged the discovery path and reached its end. That is intuition. When our values support and uphold our life, intuit information will endorse our goals. But, equally, it will support bogus ideologies and erroneous beliefs that we have (vacantly) accepted as truths, thence accepted by our subconscious mind as our values.

The phrase, 'I knew it intuitively,' is fundamentally accurate, but let's be cautious. Intuit information may be truth driven. However, it may instead be founded in beliefs, propaganda, or indoctrinations, having little or no truthful foundation.

It follows that intuition is not some divine inspiration, sixth sense awakening, spiritual manifestation, angelic invocation, energy prompting, or mystical revelation. Or is it? If such-like are what some people hold to be truthful, then their intuitions will be founded on what they've accepted as valid, whether or not they are. If one's knowledge is objectively and factually based, intuition profitably advances one's life. Falsehoods regurgitated as truths will not.

Complete with spiritual overtones, intuition is a mental abstraction appearing to us as a hitherto unknown realisation. There is no magic, nor is there any guarantee that the values utilised by our intuition are life supportive. Intuition is the Creator's gift of automated mental efficiency in the form of insight. However, because values are its fuel in part, what we intuit must still be value assessed in life terms.

The common belief "intuition is the ability to acquire insight without proof, evidence, or conscious reasoning," is a recipe for disaster. On the contrary, scrutiny, reasoning, value selection and evidence are crucial to our success, and so too the laws of identity and casualty.

Fortunately, those who program their mind with values of their choice can far more assuredly rely on their intuition. They will be highly grateful for its ability to smash their mental workload to near nil.

So it emerges that our intuition is a more expansionary version of perception in that it accounts for our values in addition. The intuit image is an abstraction that poses a 'potential,' specifically relevant to present moment considerations.

It's all so utterly simple. Intuition assists in forming the values that empower our conscience and feelings. However, during our creative thought process, those integrative powers lie idle. In the interest of efficiency and efficacy, therefore, Creator chose to employ them. The result is intuition.

It gets better. First, we are blessed with an automated mentoring tool called emotions or feelings. Our second blessing is an automated mentoring tool called conscience. Thirdly, we are gifted an automatic (intuitive) search tool that works behind the scenes to enhance our mental abilities.

Now reverse that order, as it should properly be, and you will witness the most astonishing conclusions never before made public.

- **Intuition** prompts our thoughts *creatively*.
- **Conscience** value checks our ethics *constructively*.
- **Feelings and emotions** value-check our morality *protectively*.

Please study the structure you've just read. Read each bullet point as two separate columns. All use the same automated faculty of data integration, mastered by your free will — better yet, the whole creative and constructive process is ethically and morally protected. Accordingly, the core principle unites all three faculties as though one, and all use the same integrative function employed by perception.

I've shown how intuition and perception are functionally very much alike. Both have enormous power to integrate vast amounts of (otherwise inaccessible) data into a coherently tight package for our consideration. Still, there is more.

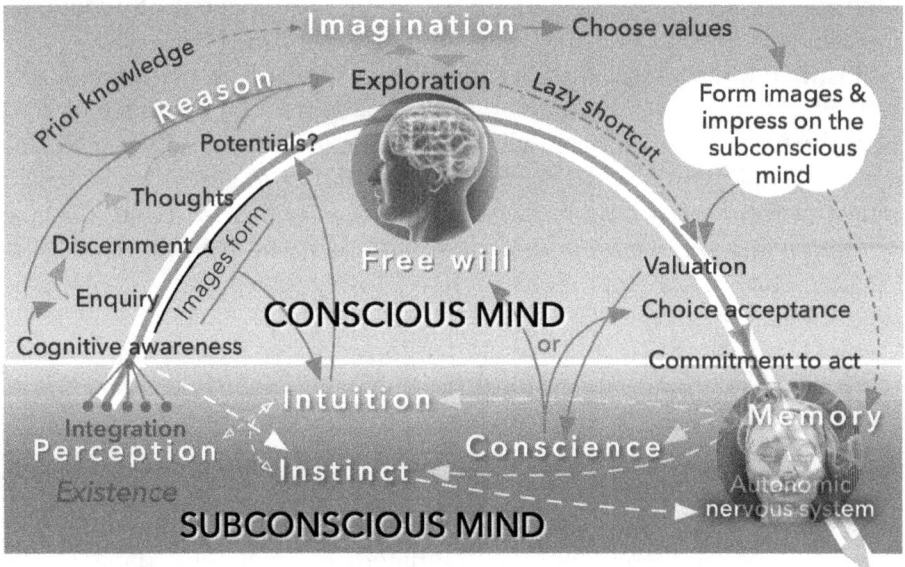

16 Conscience - part of the Value Transfer Wave

Conscious Ascendance

Diagram 16 adds the faculty of 'conscience' to the previous illustration (15) concerning intuition. For clarity, let us first consider imagination as the means of uploading values to the subconscious mind.

The top of the diagram shows that our 'explorations' trigger imagination. Imagination presents images of possibilities we had not previously considered, much as intuition does. In addition, it allows us to visualise what we envisage may be possible. In other words, imagination expedites images that our subconscious mind can read.

Regardless of whether we prioritise our values or take the lazy shortcut when we arrive at the point of 'valuation,' our values are available for our conscience faculty to read. Thus our conscience gets a complete picture of what we propose. So it performs an automatic value-check and reports accordingly. If our values coincide, our choice is readily accepted. But if not and our' conscience is 'pricked' alternatively, it is proper we should abandon our proposal and begin again.

That is the role of conscience and how it works. Thus another similarity appears in the conscious process, this time between our intuition and conscience. In short—

- **Intuition** delivers *value-based insight* before we act.
- **Conscience** gives *value appraisals* before we act.

Do you see the remarkable parallels running through our whole conscious process? Multiple checkpoints are a gracious blessing, yet conscience and intuition are effectively the same subconscious faculty. One announces where our values are headed. The other reports where our thought train leads.

Instinct: Reflex actions are instantaneous, like pulling one's hand from a flame. Diagram 16 illustrates that our perceptual faculty accepts data from the five senses and memory. It automatically activates life-preserving actions at lightning speed. Instinct or instinctual action thus described is a reflex action. For example, we instinctively brake to avoid our car slamming into another without thinking whether we should or not. We've already learned that conditions such as closing speed and close vehicle proximity are hazardous.

Most importantly, instinctual action does not bypass free will because our reflexes rely on previously learned behaviours. Thus our free choices are always honoured, even in split-second emergencies.

So another parallel emerges, this time between intuition and instinct. Instinct is an endowed faculty of self-protection and preservation. It bypasses all conscious thought processes that ordinarily take time. Our reflex actions are thereby limited to (immediate) impending danger, vital for self-preservation. In sum—

Chapter 7

- **Intuition** is an offer of information — to be considered and evaluated before acting.
- **Instinct** delivers instant action — bypassing all consideration and evaluation.

Effectively, instinct is the mental equivalent of our body's immune system. Both exist to arrest or correct errors. Now add 'feelings' to this mix since it exists to keep our spiritual values on track. Do you see how richly we are blessed? Some faculties aid efficiency and efficacy. Others protect and correct. All function automatically to sustain our life, while our free will mind provides physical, mental and spiritual values as fuel.

Now we can see how these vital faculties aid and support each other.

- **Conscience,** feelings and emotions are our mentor.
- **Imagination** translates values from word concepts into the subconscious vocabulary of images.
- **Intuition** taps unknown sources to offer valuable tips and information in keeping with our choices.
- **Instinct** protects against material accidents, much like the immune system protects our bodies.

Every one of our nine higher faculties plays a vital role in the value transfer loop. All are interconnected and interoperable thereby.

Our higher faculties thrive on spiritual values, of which free will is the author.

Yet another similarity emerges, this time between instinct and the 'law of allowance' gifted to infants. Both bypass the discovery process. Whereas emergencies offer no time for deliberations, infants have no cognitive base from which to make deliberations. As previously described, the subconscious mind must motivate an infant's actions. Resultant feelings of success or distress, and its memory of positive results, propel it to act in like manner in future. As the infant progressively learns from its actions, its cognitive mind and free will gradually take over from subconscious motivation.

The same is true of values. The more we learn about values and the more we action them, the greater our material, mental, emotional and spiritual rewards. The more we prioritise our value database, the greater our efficacy, efficiency and success.

Are you beginning to see how consciousness is a sequential process in more ways than that described by the Value Transfer Wave? Altogether it is a process of beautiful simplicity, efficiency and efficacy. Grasp how your various faculties are autonomous on the one hand but otherwise share processes in common. Moreover, this sequential flow of information is orderly, a common orderliness of function. From etymology, 'orderliness' is 'law,' hence 'natural law' derives from the orderly nature of your being. Finally, this revelation is awesome, because it produces a cooperative outcome with great virtuosity and power.

Do you glimpse what cut-throat competition in today's business world never sees? Do you sense that cooperative societies can thrive and prosper greatly based on some simple rules of your being that seven-year-old kids can grasp?

The great human tragedy is that many people believe (and teach even) that our heart-based spiritual self should adequately allow us to 'feel our way through life.' Sadly, they've not learned that free will conducts our spiritual self like an orchestra. Conscious ignorance has disallowed our knowing. Science has not understood these looped functions, nor their astounding similarity and interconnectedness. Consequently, we are deprived of our most blessed gifts and effectively denied all means of discovering them.

Considering the substantial similarity between perception, intuition and conscience, it is worth noting that during every passage of the Value Transfer wave, the border separating our conscious and subconscious has been traversed back and forth up to six times.

That has two-fold importance. It shows unequivocally that human consciousness is the exclusive property of each independent living being and cannot be communal. No group consciousness is possible. It also shows the source of conscious ignorance. When neuroscience, psychology and philosophy fail to distinguish our two minds as autonomous and that multitudinous (value) communication unites them across two vocabularies in support of life, we are left utterly helpless.

Moreover, suppose some intellectuals know this but deliberately hide it for totalitarian control and domination. In that case, we are dealing with the most widespread heinous crime against humankind in world history!

Perhaps you've already sensed that consciously formed word concepts are remarkably similar to subconscious images since both reduce data to manageable packages. Subconscious takes the prize, however, due to its breathtaking ability to garner multiple data from widespread sources with pinpoint accuracy at lightning speed. Now multiply that ability six-fold because the same expertise of 'integration,' used by perception, has the compound ability to integrate all six faculties simultaneously, with the same speed and accuracy! Our six higher subconscious faculties are fully united yet autonomous.

Think about that! Forget the senseless idea that consciousness is nothing but 'awareness' as we're taught. Look deeper, and you'll see that all six faculties are fully synergised.

Chapter 7

Synergy is the interaction or cooperation of two or more organisations, substances, or other agents to produce a combined effect greater than the sum of their separate effects.

Understand this astonishing 'miracle.' The incredible ability to perform

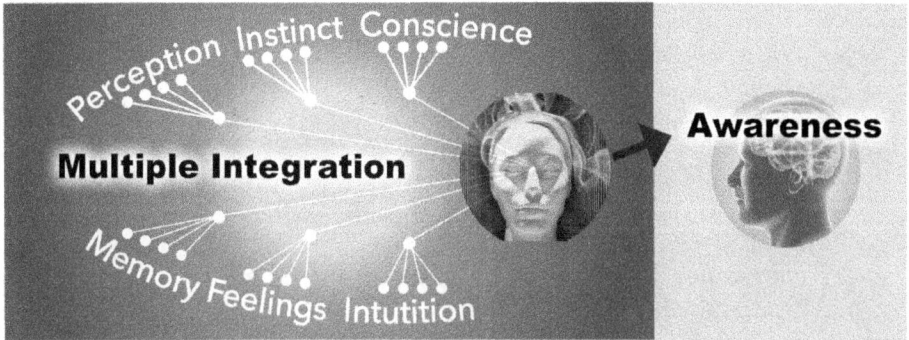

17. Compound integration – all six higher subconscious faculties

six different integration functions simultaneously with blistering speed, and unite them all into a manageable cognitive package, is a feat almost beyond comprehension! Every instrument of our being merges into an unsurpassed, orchestral masterpiece of creation, for which our free will is the conductor. 'Awareness,' as the receptor, is minuscule in comparison. Yet, because human sciences know nothing of this miracle, awareness remains insensibly considered as full consciousness, proof again of our tragic mental deprivation and conscious ignorance.

Now, however, our two minds are re-united. Of course, they never were separated. But now that you have grasped what no one has ever explained before, think what this mind-numbing synergy might be capable of producing!

Forget unexplained magic. You've automatic faculties, two each for protection, correction, and mental efficiency, all automated with lightning speed precision, all free will conducted and sandwiched inside a protective environment. They and our biological processes combine to deliver twenty natural laws, being Creator's model for independent thriving. They also facilitate free societies, unlike anything the world has ever witnessed!

Ditch the damn 'matrix.' It is a leach. It tenaciously clings to our willingness to be mind controlled, and your conscious ignorance is crucial to its success. It, therefore, does all in its power to ensure that ignorance prevails. It trades on your ignorance. It knows that your mind is supremely free, and you are its gatekeeper; a creator, designer, fact checker, assigner of values, entrepreneur and facilitator. You are the spiritual conductor of your life, precisely as nature intended. Wake up to the dynamic power of consciousness and your spiritual prowess, and you will be instrumental in changing the course of human history, never to go back. The more our faculties are shown united, the simpler conscious understanding becomes.

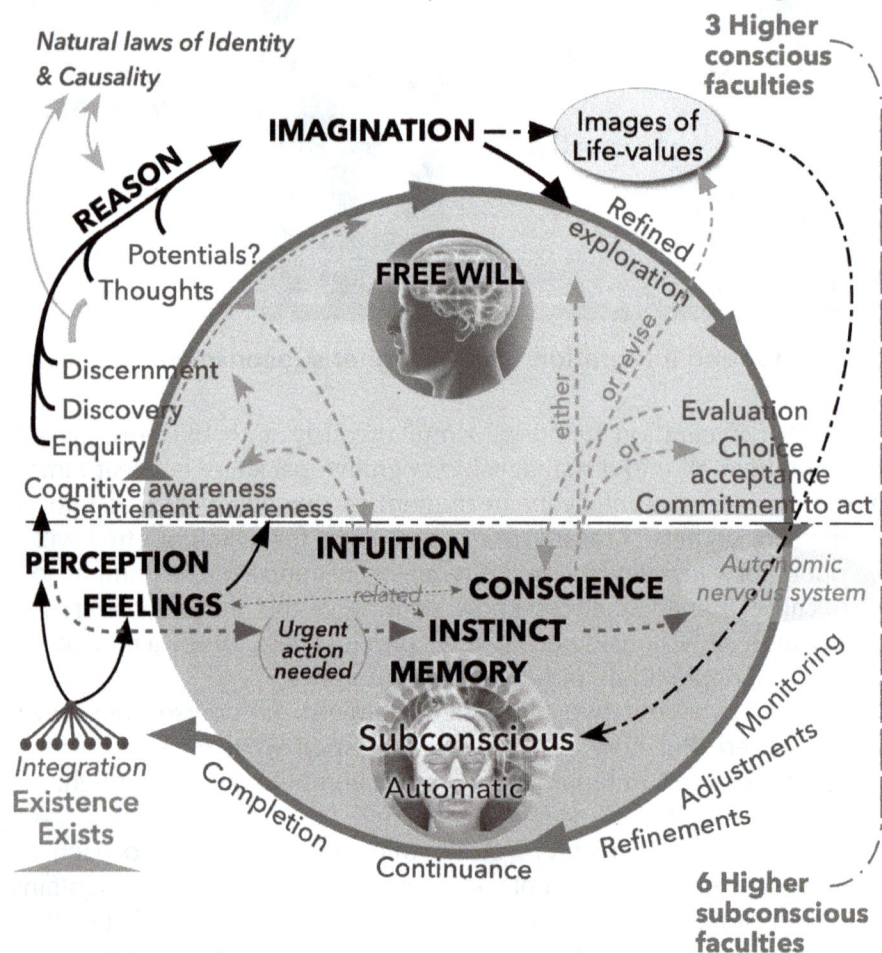

18. Nine higher faculties of the Value Transfer Loop

Diagram 18 shows the complete Value Transfer wave, now in its repeating 'loop' format, which is our whole conscious process. These added complexities were not shown in Diagram 5 in Chapter 2.

I highly recommend that you bookmark this page/diagram. It will refresh your memory of the entire process without reading many pages. Study it carefully. It is a treasure trove portraying unbelievable complexity in the simplest form.

Chapter 7

As shown in circular form, the 'process' of our consciousness is entirely objective of life itself, which for self-preservation and longevity is unalterable. The orderliness of our mental faculties joins forces with biological order to endorse the real meaning of the word 'law.' Encrypted in the 'nature' of every man, woman and child, natural law (ius naturalis) cannot be erased. (Chapter 10 describes these twenty natural laws.)

As no doubt you've guessed, they speak of a method, system, logic, process, order, equality, and harmonious cooperation. Our task is to learn, use, and profit from them, materially, mentally, emotionally and spiritually.

Diagram 18 also shows the multiple times that our two vocabulary's can be crossed over, even for relatively simple decision-making. Finally, material and spiritual reports are cognitively and sentiently received as awareness.

More subtle nuances appear. For example, uploading life values to the subconscious is shown in the (right-hand side dash/dot) arrow. Notice how it passes through the wilful commitment to act, thus allowing our prized values to generate emotions automatically. Notice how four of the higher faculties are cross related, also how instinct bypasses the whole cognitive process yet honours free will according to prior learned behaviours.

Benefits of Full Consciousness: Exercising our consciousness in life value terms is the greatest reverence and gratitude anyone can offer their Creator. Whoever attains this level of conscious enlightenment will experience a load lifting off their shoulders. They will realise they've nothing to gain from pseudo-intellectuals, new-age mystics, pretenders, imposters, blood-spilling authority, and soul-destroying spiritual bandits — all predators blasted into oblivion for eternity! Every soul-destroying intruder with ego-driven belligerence will hit a brick wall — namely, one's dynamic, impenetrable, whole, material, mental, and spiritual self!

The problem has been, and it remains, that no one teaches the study of life and how to build happiness. Yet, our struggle vanishes once we learn and practice these laws of nature. Life is recognised as a gift and lived accordingly; this practice is the path of self-mastery.

Sovereigns seek to gain knowledge and wisdom to be the best they can be in any situation. Therefore, they learn to live in a way that honours their power to cultivate happiness, inner peace and graceful strength.

Those who discover their beautiful spiritual aspects will also learn a profound truth. Every emotional chaos, or trauma originating from pulpits and parliaments of fiction, falsity, and irrelevance, will have been struck from their life without ever asking!

Conscious Ascendance

Spiritual independence, enlightenment, and empowerment will manifest as never before. Their world presents in a whole new light. Those who choose to master their lives through uploaded values will quickly reap benefits.

- 'Full consciousness' puts our most fervent desires on auto-pilot. Mental strain is reduced to near nil, while emotional joy excels.
- Choosing valued goals will soon become second nature.
- Fears of independence vanish.
- Confidence grows, and self-esteem increases.
- Tranquillity, joy, power and peace prevail.
- Emotionally rewarded, these people become humbly proud of their achievements and happiness.
- Focus on life shifts, not to abandon material things but to spiritually enrich them.

Taking charge of our power to bring health, mental integrity, and joyful happiness in every present moment slashes our mental workload to the core. As ignorance fades into oblivion and one becomes more accomplished, tranquillity, joy, power, and peace flood one's life beyond anything dreamt possible. Freedom of mind, Clarity of mind and Peace of mind are free to all of us.

- Joy in life relies on choosing our actions in spiritual terms.
- Kids can be taught the principles of value correspondence from an early age.
- Massive roadblocks are demolished due to erroneous beliefs and conscious ignorance.
- Perception is shown as a truthful, multi-purpose faculty.
- Beliefs translate to knowledge, or they evaporate.
- Imagination assumes a vitality very different from anything taught.
- Free will is sandwiched between two different functionalities of the subconscious mind, smashing the common belief that consciousness is awareness.
- Our subconscious mind upholds our goals and ambitions without further effort.
- Mental stress vaporises.
- Intellectual prowess is greatly enhanced.
- The entire process can be (sufficiently) taught from early childhood, offering untold benefits for every man, woman and child. Further education expands the founding principles, as later shown.

Chapter 7

- Spiritual blessings include peace, efficacy, tranquillity and emotional harmony.
- Emotions resolve as never before. We can mastermind them in advance.

No better model of ethics or morality exists or is as simple. Both are ours for the taking; a richly spiritual life ours to exercise with humble and reverent gratitude. Nothing approximates. Nothing touches the Creator's supremacy. There is no opposition, competition, or cost, nor can there ever be. In the Bible book of Romans we read—

"And be not conformed to this world: but be ye transformed by the renewing of your mind, that ye may prove what is that good, and acceptable, and perfect, will of God" —Romans 12:2

Humanity is now awakening to this realm of conscious spiritual intent. I trust that you now picture a life grander than ever conceived or dreamt, individually and socially — that you are now awake to our Creator's vision for your life. Picture it. Feel it. Those who transcend the material world that has long ruled humanity will understand their responsibility to engage in spirituality and embrace its totality, thus engaging with their specialist mentor. Because life is what you are, you are your path to spiritual success. All else is a distraction.

Your connection to spirit is sure when you stand in the glory of creation as its partner. If you're already feeling this connection and feeling spirit embrace you now, offering love for you and your life, then you've got it! Please accept what you know and comprehend with eternal gratitude. Your search is over.

Walk with your specialist friend every moment hereafter. Love is the most incredible energy in the cosmos. Much more than grace, benevolence or compassion, it is a way of being — respectful to self, spirit, and all others. Enjoy peace daily and your connection to a symbiotic family of spiritual beings here on earth. You will be a catalyst in humanity's spiritual ascendency — in planet earth's recalibration. Take charge now. Your life and your spirit will soar.

Christina Puchalski, MD, Director of the George Washington Institute for Spirituality and Health, contends *"spirituality is the aspect of humanity that refers to the way individuals seek and express meaning and purpose and the way they experience their connectedness to the moment, to self, to others, to nature, and to the significant or sacred."*

According to Mario Beauregard and Denyse O'Leary, researchers and authors of The Spiritual Brain, *"Spirituality means any experience that is thought to bring the experiencer into contact with the divine (in other words, not just any experience that feels meaningful)."*

Conscious Ascendance

Do you see? All three authors confirm that life values are crucial to spiritual accomplishment. Moreover, if spirituality is our connectedness to nature and the significant or sacred, then our consciousness, being the same, is spiritual, even though it deals in part with physicality. With our material goals spiritually enriched, our subconscious mind and spiritual values are our given pathway to success.

Self-governance: When today's accepted notions of ethics and morality overturn, you'll see that our Creator has modeled the (natural law) principles of ethics, morality, and natural justice, smack in the core of our conscience and emotional reporting systems, exactly where they belong!

You can quote me right there, because in the core of your very being, is found Creator's perfect model for personal freedom and the means for free organic societies. The Creator's will is self-governance within natural law. All else is an abomination!

What happens if we fail to accept life's challenges and let others push our barrow. What if we decline mental effort because others have studied history, social sciences or philosophy and we have not? Look at today's society for your answers. When we refuse to take charge of our life, governments swoop in and assert their claim of authority. They call us 'useless eaters', which, they claim, accords them sovereign status after that. With their assumed power to control your life, they do all necessary to topple all challenges. Accordingly, many believe a 'sovereign' influences society or civilisation via a claim of authority. In wielding power to direct large groups of people, these (make believe) 'sovereigns' usually rely on genealogies in asserting they have a 'divine right to rule.' They trace their lineage to some bloodline or historical figure, like Jesus, Mohammad, David, etc. But since we are all equal, no cultural birthright or heritage gives anyone the right to rule or make such a claim. No sovereign status can derive from there.

Our failing to strive for self-mastery and sovereign standing is all that governments need to assert their claims of authority and bogus sovereign status. We automatically sacrifice our sovereignty by admitting their 'ruling position' is valid or that a nation is sovereign.

"Your perspective on your position determines your power or prison" — Richard Yiap

By abdicating from responsibility and forfeiting all claims to our life, we let governments take charge of what we have forsaken. By sacrificing love, truth, freedom, justice, and prosperity, we lose any means of reclamation and redemption. Meanwhile, all who prostitute individual values thrive because nothing opposes their evil.

Chapter 7

Sovereignty is little more than an ethical mind engaging in moral activities and accepting responsibility and liability for one's actions. These people apply life values such as diligence, discipline, respect and integrity, all in pursuit of practical, moral and spiritual thriving. Every mental and emotional reward signifies success. Skills of personal excellence, spiritual accomplishment, and emotional rewards testify to their advancement. Joy and happiness are their rewards.

In other words, what individuals do with their God-given talents to develop self-mastery, allows for the development of valid sovereign status. Sovereignty is a philosophy of and for life, not an outcome. A true sovereign embraces their embodiment of natural law, morality, ethics and natural justice, one whose example leads other people into more significant states of freedom. That example is their badge of honour. None else is needed. To maintain this success, they must act with honour and integrity in defending the right of all people to self-develop precisely as they have.

Sovereignty requires dedication — not unlike mastering painting or the piano. It requires precision and skill, but infallibility is not needed, however. Instead, sovereign people consistently reflect on their own experiences to see what can be improved and how mastery can be grown. That is why we have conscience and emotions. Sovereignty is masterly enacting a fulfilling life, accepting no external authority and issuing none. Therefore, no acclamations, certificates of achievement or nobility status are warranted.

Whether dimly aware or fully realising their most significant potential, sovereign people know what is possible when they learn to communicate with their souls. Moreover, they recognise that situations improve with a dedication to the truth, wise planning, and honourable cooperation with others. One earns the title of Sovereign through mental application, diligence, discipline, and the constructive pursuit of a moral existence.

Nothing excels! Pay no more attention to that which is not in your life's interest. Accept your blessings. Learn to use them. Creator has your back, all the way. Values express our love of life, and our gratitude, for those values touch the very heart of our soul. Choose values that uphold your spiritual life, and not only will you summon a life force beyond your conscious ability, you will also have assured its delivery and expressed gratitude for its love of your life. Your future is what you project that it should be. Many say you are already 'sovereign' because you are alive. Do not be hoodwinked. True sovereignty has been exceedingly difficult in the past because 'individuality' is trashed, and (collective) societal presumptions are substituted; rule most particularly. Ethics and morality suffer accordingly. Metaphysics is impaired, and so is the science of psycho-epistemology; but no more.

Conscious Ascendance

Sovereignty is a lifelong pursuit, its measure no less than ever-increasing degrees of competence, skill, and benevolent power. Time is unimportant—progress results from true sovereignty and natural law as partners in life. Nothing else compares.

Sovereigns dedicate themselves to gaining competence and self-mastery through work, self-reflection, and self-discipline — perfection not demanded. One infraction or mistake is not a disgrace, provided one takes steps to correct it. Self-mastery embraces acts of restitution. We learn through mistakes. Thus we may develop an exemplary attitude toward life, a spiritual mindedness resulting in ethical thought, just actions and behaviour, including the willingness to correct errors. Unless that drive is willingly engaged and upheld, no sovereignty will emerge.

Sovereignty is not automatic; thus, no one can effortlessly claim it. Neither can one grant sovereignty to another because until it is self-actualised, it does not exist. Sovereignty is responsibility

The truth is that if we each took to developing self-mastery seriously, or self-sovereignty if you prefer, authoritarian powers would be rendered obsolete in short order. This platform of personal benefit can usher in a new sociological and political foundation, more ethical and moral than any employed in the past. Peace-loving, organic societies are not only possible, the likes of which the world has never witnessed, but nature urges us to institute them!

Social emancipation is possible thereby. Those who awaken to these discoveries, and embrace them, will break through the strangleholds of ignorance and complacency as though they never existed. As fully connected beings, they will experience vital energy of spirit and become sovereign facilitators of a new age, unlike anything previously thought possible. This knowledge strengthens our connection with the Source of All Creation.

Some say true sovereigns are duty bound to slowly and carefully educate the people so they can one day be sovereigns in their own right. Superficially this is a noble thought, but the word duty is a mind trap, wide open to authoritarian misuse. No claim or document or the fact of one's mere existence grants sovereignty. Character is the only means, but unless one acts the way Creator intended, no sovereign being will emerge.

To enable the transformation of our humanity, we must fully understand it. Such knowledge is more than grasping the power to think for ourselves, discern truth from disinformation, and stand firm for what we know is right. We must also understand the role of values and that their graciousness permits no compromise. Our achievement and unparalleled success lie in honouring that nature will not be cheated.

Chapter 7

Natural law theorists have long believed that we each possess an innate morality and that it prescribes natural law. They offer the 'ten commandments in the Bible as support. But as you now see, the reverse is true. Natural law is innate and immutable, whereby it prescribes one's morality out of sheer necessity. Natural law is factual, not a theory, hence my phrase 'existential natural law' is my direct replacement for 'natural law theory.'

We must deal with the consequences of our actions, just as nature obliges we learn from our feelings. If we fail, consequences redouble, and we get hit once more. That shows how nature upholds our values, ethics, actions, and morality, without overruling our free will.

That truth is utterly profound. Why? Because 'independence' removes the whole subject of morality from the collective domain ruled by governments and puts it into the private domain, where it rightfully belongs. Now the herd mentality is smashed completely!

I began this chapter by stressing that it is prudent to understand how the higher faculties process values to serve our desires and ambitions. That deeper understanding makes no mistake about how the entire conscious process works for our most fabulous self and wellbeing.

- Most of today's beliefs concerning ethics and morality overturn.
- Present natural law theories holding that morality determines natural law are inverted.
- All (today's) 'collectivised' jurisdictional claims over ethics and morality are invalidated.
- Authoritarian governments are rendered obsolete. Self-governance under natural law is their replacement. Nothing excels.
- Natural law now has immutable teeth that no one ever suspected.

Some matters concerning personal consciousness remain; however, the groundwork for a new social foundation is now established.

Conscious Ascendance

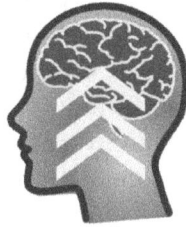

8. Independence and individual rights

The first two chapters laid the groundwork for human consciousness. Following chapters described its completeness, save for two aspects not yet revealed. Nevertheless, they explained how consciousness works, why it does so, and what benefits it delivers, according to our respective individual choices. Full consciousness might perhaps be described as the technology of consciousness.

This remainder of this book examines some of the personal and societal applications and outcomes of conscious enactment. Only then can (existential) natural law be set forth for the benefit of Man, both now and for thousands of years to come. Appropriately, therefore, this chapter explores our express need to functionally apply consciousness to all that we do, always remembering our independence one from another. It is essential to correlate our autonomy and right to life with societal matters that may influence our choices to be independent of the State. Examining how our choices impact society raises a fundamental question. Can freedom abide by societal constraints without sacrificing what makes our consciousness function?

For centuries, politicians and many others have sought to promote the 'collective' as far superior to 'individualism.' Although entirely unfounded, the most common method has been to propagandise the idea that individual concerns are selfish, greedy, and inhumane, an assault on the 'common good' or public wellbeing Humanity has tragically fallen for this insulting collectivist language and ideology. The result is that we are each submerged into a collective soup having no life of our own. It matters not what name we give its ringleaders, be it globalists, futurists, new agers or young global leaders, the dissolution of our singular essence and destruction of our independence is satisfied. So we are demeaned. Our creative power is compromised as though our lives utterly depend on a collective mass over which we have no say. How many people grasp that "we" and "us" are nothing but mental diversions splashed on the front page of our minds?

The State, thus constituted, pretends to favour those in need. It steals the farm and gives a few pieces back on its terms. Therefore, any independence that supposedly threatens governments' central planning and dominance must be denounced, if not outlawed. The constituted authoritarian rule prescribes the social order, demanding that perceived or actual challenges are denied.

Individualism and independence are the rudiments of organic, symbiotic societies, opposite authoritarian control.

History informs us that control over the mind has long been considered essential for societal peace and harmony. Moreover, when thought is manipulated, resistance to rule diminishes markedly. People readily give in to authority, never understanding their authentic power. They will customarily accept their position and that life is at the mercy of forces beyond their influence. Yet we each are the 'first cause' in our lives.

Sadly, many New Age beliefs hold that 'energies' prevail along with synchronistic manifestations, propounding that we should 'surrender to the universe.' Psy-ops of this calibre delude gullible people.

All we need do on the contrary is realise that instead of bowing to fake realities, each one of us has the power to take charge of our lives. We need not compromise our desires or surrender them; we can spiritually enrich them. Every man and woman can develop their power as individuals, in contrast to a herd mentality hell-bent on submission to a state of affairs fashioned by others.

Every man and woman can change their will and direct the source of their energy to their express purpose; all diversions and coercions are negated thereby. The secret is knowing that one's power is individual, independent from that which others may exercise. When you creatively exercise your independent power to satisfy your life, other people will manifestly benefit. Positive outcomes result. Nothing is lost, and society benefits accordingly. Success testifies your method and your means. Your 'win' lifts others. It reminds them of their inherent power if they choose it, whereby they too may cultivate the power to assist others. Thus communal benefit arises out of 'independence' automatically.

Symbiosis is advantageous to two different organisms living in close physical association and gives power to both. The more you develop your independence, the more it will catalyse, expose and reduce oppression.

So the question arises. Will you sacrifice your energy to passivity, drudgery and boredom fertilising oppression, tyranny and wars? Or will you use your energy to multiply your power? Since your creative power is individual and independent, the more you develop it, the less fear you will experience.

Collectivists have long hammered the notion of family, group, community and social support. That is good since it is our vital self-interest to uphold and support those around us. The problem is that collectivists will do all possible to foster group identity at the expense of being independent. Authoritarians fear independence like they fear hell itself. Their fear arises from their particular inadequacies simply because they know nothing about their mental, emotional, or spiritual abilities. And because state authority fears even one dissident who advocates independence, our door to freedom is slammed shut, forcing us to adapt to a legally contrived environment as though animals, all escape routes blocked.

Collectivists and authoritarians firmly intend that you remain passively inert, utterly ignorant of your power, because, like a malignant, infectious disease, your entrapment helps their cause immensely. Passivity spreads and multiplies in populations. The irony is that those who fiercely project the quality of independence, particularly in sport and entertainment, allow us to escape our fears of independence. Accordingly, millions adore heroes and heroines from all walks of life, including artists, musicians, and movie stars.

If people correctly understood the truth, they would not fear at all. Instead, we would see that the more independent we become in ourselves, the more genuine heroes and heroines are not our relief from fear or stress. To the contrary, we would view them as like-minded celebrants of their intellectual and spiritual advancements, as we are of ours.

Others do not shape free individuals. They generate and shape every thought and energy-pulse of their self-chosen objectives. Free thinking and the desire to benefit also enhance the freedom of others. Strong will exists to discover life through imagination and creative power, for without, freedom withers and dies. As free individuals imagine and creates, their work naturally spills over to the benefit of others. Free individuals know that the greatest good comes from liberating all individuals to pursue their highest aspirations. To walk through that door to human progress is to divorce oneself from the collective mindset.

Recall that an infant's mind lacks the cognitive ability to enquire, discover and make choices. Their motivation to act is subconscious, primarily from emotions. The cognitive mind is bypassed, as the dashed

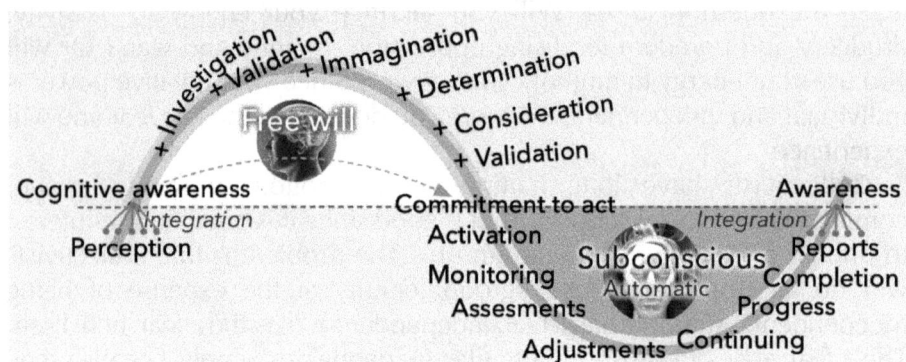

19. Cognitive progression through childhood

short circuit line through free will in diagram 19 shows This cognitive bypass is referred to as the 'natural law of allowance.'

Progressively throughout childhood, the perceptive faculty increasingly prompts enquiry and investigations, which induce material and spiritual value choices. In other words, the cognitive mind progressively adds new abilities, as the + icons in diagram 19 illustrate, but not necessarily in that order. Instead, each comes into play to assist the development and refinement of other considerations. The cognitive process progressively assumes its proper waveform, and the (short circuit) 'law of allowance' self-cancels.

The wave's subconscious part never changes, meaning the emotional feeling mechanism remains unchanged from infancy through adolescence to adulthood. What changes observably is that the child learns to transition from 'emotional incentives' to 'reason-driven incentives and spiritual motivations.' Free will and value selection progressively take centre stage as a result. The law of allowance has served its purpose. Joy and happiness are the end products in both cases.

Our transition through adolescence is a smooth progressional transfer of motivation, lest it should be.

Initially, our automated subconscious mind sustains our lives. It's so doing allows for our cognitive development from day one.

Progressively, thereafter, our cognitive mind assumes free will and responsibility to establish the values upon which the subconscious mind relies.

Over time, free will becomes the author of our lives, emotions, and spirituality. The subconscious mind moves to the back seat as our cognitive faculty takes the steering wheel.

Of those three points, our human sciences say absolutely nothing. For

Chapter 8

that reason, let's look at this mental transition through adolescence in more detail.

Science has recently found Peter Pan neurons' contribute to the rapid growth of the amygdala during childhood. This population then declines due to rapid emotional development in adolescence. Science has no explanation for this phenomenon, but the mind shift just described and the Value Transfer process point to it. They show that as the cognitive mind progressively learns to evaluate data and form judgements, its decision-making ability becomes the leader. The subconscious mind properly becomes (free will) value-directed, lest it should, whereby the mind sequence shifts from perceptual to cognitive (free choice) motivation. Joy and happiness, which arose from emotional motivation to act during infancy, are replaced. Value-based mental motivation to act delivers emotional responses in adulthood.

It is a tragedy that many people never make that transition or do so only in part. There are several reasons why this changeover is not known.

Emojis, memes, the 6 o'clock news, billboards, television and Hollywood endlessly assail our subconscious minds with image values of some kind. As a result, consciousness is trapped, forcing our existence into a state of animality. At very best, we wrongly blame emotions for untold torment and suffering when in fact, (so-called negative) feelings merely report the failure to value-coordinate our two minds.

Self-mastery through value-based, responsible free-will decision-making cannot be over-emphasised. Failure effectively arrests our consciousness at the animal level, leaving us open to rule as though herd animals. Untold mental suffering results from multiple statutes, laws, commandments, acts, undisclosed legal contracts and executive orders.

Failure to master our minds engenders adult reliance on feelings for motivation. The alternative is to shift from emotional promptings to reasoning about the value of life, thus choosing wisely as adults. So we author our emotions instead of them calling the shots.

Let me return to the Law of Allowance to explain this difference better, because this law is the most beautiful and gracious of them all, showing more than mere cognitive childhood development.

During infancy and early childhood, the subconscious mind is the motivating force behind our actions. As our cognitive abilities increasingly become prominent, free will becomes our motivating force. We switch from feeling motivation to intellectual motivation and empowerment. Free will picks up the baton and begins conducting the full consciousness orchestra.That is how it should happen. That is how Creator intended that it happen. Our two minds swap places in the complete conscious sequence, usually during the period of adolescence, as the dashed lines in diagram 20 show. Follow the arrows, and you'll see that the adult cycle is near identical to the childhood cycle.

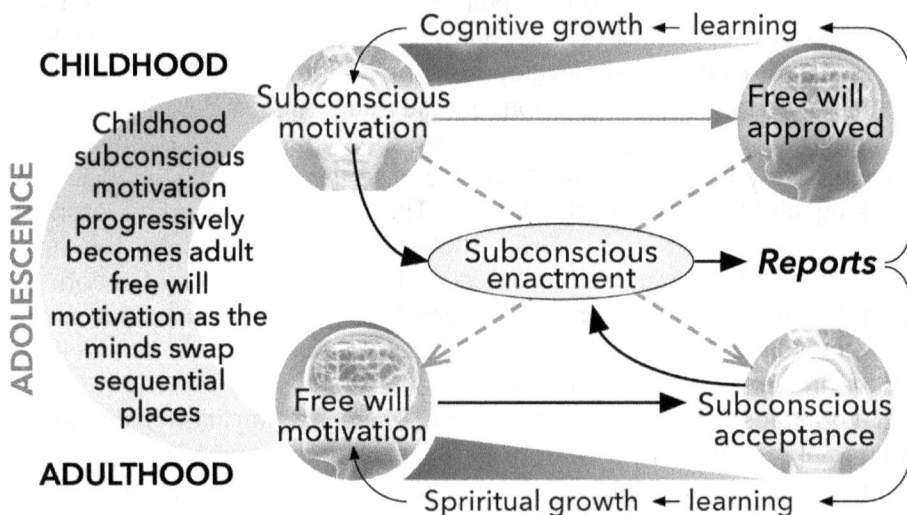

20. Mind switchover – Motivation change through adolescence

The main difference is that spiritual growth replaces cognitive growth, both resulting from learning.

That motivational switch-over is what Jesus spoke of—

"When I was a child, I spake as a child, I understood as a child, I thought as a child: but when I became a man, I put away childish things. —(1 Corinthians 13:11).

Nevertheless, the Law of Allowance does not entirely cancel. Creator has allowed it remains for learning, and mental maturity, to grow and become habituated through choice, according to one's abilities, throughout our entire adult life. At our own pace, we each consistently amass high percentiles of truth in our intuit database, fostering more excellent reliability and certainty with the least effort.

That is the most beautiful and precious gift, without a doubt. But unfortunately, the unmitigated tragedy is that conscious ignorance does not merely conceal it, but that millions of people suffer as a result. They are mentally and emotionally locked to a state of infancy yet forced to deal in an adult intellectual realm.

It could be said, and perhaps should be said, that this mental stranglehold accounts for nine tenths of control wielded by the so called 'matrix.' If so, this knowledge of full consciousness is farewell to mind control of that ilk and good riddance.

The remedy is to learn the role played by values, our discernment

Chapter 8

process and the role of emotions, in short, the complete conscious process.

The story you are now about to read describes how this book came into existence and how you have the same powers of discovery.

When I became aware that governments were not governments and that neither the common law nor natural law theory offered any remedy, consciousness appeared to be the only way forward. But, like 99.999 percent of the population, I had no idea what consciousness was, much less how it worked. Was it mere awareness, as most people believe? Was it some unified energetic field, such as unity or group consciousness, we can supposedly reach into like an enveloping fog? Was it a Christ consciousness — whatever that means? What is our 'higher self'? Is it our subconscious mind, divinity, or a whirlwind of thought or intuition that descends from the ether to awaken us? I did not know, and neither did most people.

I did not know that my resolve to smash through ignorance was the passion I needed to succeed. In truth, it triggered my subconscious mind to search and find information beyond all that I knew ten years back. Nevertheless, the answer came to me some two years after I authored 'Law from Within,' and that is what I want to describe now.

I speak of our astounding ability to petition our intuitive skills to obtain beneficial information concerning a particular quest. The method involves asking your subconscious intuit abilities to search further than your cognitive mind can reach. Whether writing a book, a poem, a piece of music, artwork, or just seeking greater enlightenment, the subconscious mind will assist, provided your passioned request champions the value of life.

I've already explained how we can exercise our consciousness to ensure good health and rid ourselves of fear. I further described how to upload life values, or spiritual values, to the subconscious minds to enrich all our material desires and pursuits spiritually. I learned how the Divine mind has ensured that we each possess unlimited power which we can access. Now, roll all those capabilities into one bundle and reverse it. Instead of uploading our values, let's solicit that our subconscious mind finds values and downloads them. Let's learn how we can petition the subconscious mind's assistance as our mental partner – our buddy.

By uploading your values for subconscious acceptance and orderly priority, you now work as a team. Your powerful buddy has access to a vast array of resources, beyond your cognitive ability, including from the Source itself. Our intuition faculty tells us how we can draw on that information automatically. So let's combine these two abilities into one. Let's suppose that you seek something very dear to your heart, much as I did when I desired to know how consciousness works. Remembering that our subconscious mind is our (behind the scenes) working assistant, we must stick to the formula that we know will work. In short, conscious requests of this kind must focus on our particular passioned desire to attain or achieve a life-supporting goal. Our requests should entreat the subconscious mind to discover and present image information that is otherwise unavailable to us.

At no time must it appear that we are telling our subconscious mind its job. We must not constrict its search path. It must be allowed to find answers in its way. So we should define the broad compass of our (valued) search without specifying the form, method or process of that enquiry.

When I began this study, I sought to know what consciousness is. I did not specify awareness, group consciousness or channelling. I left those gates wide open. My most startling revelation was discovering that the subconscious process sandwiches free will. That comprehension came from being intuitively informed to follow the process of enquiry, investigation and decision-making that we correctly use repeatedly. In other words, my earnest desire to uncover the fullness of consciousness came from the simplest of intuit information, which later, through more exhaustive investigation, blew my mind completely. In short, I learned exactly how I had learned, as never explained before.

The secret that I discovered is to choose an open and unrestricted pathway. For example, if you desire a new abode or some means to serve your family's needs and growth, and money seems to be the problem, forget the money. Instead, petition your subconscious mind concerning your family's requirements for alternate accommodation; for betterment. Answers may take weeks, months or more. But, persist with passion, and you will succeed.

The answers you get will likely surprise you. For example, intuition may guide you to make a career change that, through events and promotion maybe, will bring about your new accommodation without worry. Or you may receive intuit information concerning your line of work that leads to an idea worth millions to its developer. Who can know where from or how your solution might eventuate?

So it is that we can begin asking our subconscious mind for ideas and suggestions concerning how important life goals might eventuate. Communion of this kind is not a passive meditation technique, where one divorces from intellectual thought to allow (subjective) information to flow.

This technique is not opening the mind to sundry suggestions, impulses, or energies, nor is it a form of meditation or summonsing the law of attraction. Neither is it 'channelling,' as known. Instead, it is a

Chapter 8

deliberate, conscious request that the subconscious mind uses its image-matching capacity to reach beyond your cognitive, investigative ability. You are not submitting to all and sundry suggestions, impulses, or different energies. You are deliberately requesting information from a source devoted to your life's success! I'm talking of spiritual communion.

First, determine what information you want concerning a particular part of your project. Define its context, why you seek it, and your passion for it. Be specific in terms of life, not physicality or your bank account. Next, picture your subconscious mind advancing your project and your life. Visualise it searching on your behalf and picture receiving an answer.

- **First:** visualise what information you seek in its proper context and broad terms.
- **Second,** picture using the information as though you had already received it.
- **Third,** visualise the benefits that will result. Picture triumphant success. Feel its enveloping warmth.

You will have projected your future and taken charge of your success. You've summoned power beyond your cognitive ability and expressed gratitude for its love of your life. And that has touched the very heart of your soul.

All that remains is to authenticate or validate the (image) hints that you receive, then transform the answers into the practicalities of your life. Then, polish this technique, and outstanding results will flow.

I trust you now see the tremendous power of having both minds on the same page. That is how this book came into being – beyond all knowledge of consciousness that I have read and researched at great length.

Of course, you cannot act out your visions like you did when uploading your values because you have no answers yet. So instead, commit to preparing to use the information when it arrives. Build a framework in which the new data will fit. For example, you might sketch out what chapters come before and after in a new book. Or, you might prepare the background in a painting. If greater wisdom is your goal, read related matter and carefully discern its truthfulness and relevance. Focus on your intentions in context, which will offer (visualised) clues to your subconscious mind, like using keywords for websites. What happens, in neuroscience terms, is that your valued request creates an impetus for your neurons to join. These neuron-firing triggers create an antenna that will find the information you seek.

Advanced learning is now possible. The aim is to explore beyond the mural of present reality as though the subconscious mind is one's assistant, searching behind the scenes to fulfil your request. This method dramatically enhances our creativity and freedom. Much like value-directed visualisations, upload your values; now, the information intuitively downloads.

When answers begin popping into your head, know with certainty that your two minds are indeed in full communion, united in service of a spiritual being, spiritually living in a materialistic environment.

Success is reliant on your values and your passion for advancement. If the answers you get do not fit perfectly into your work, adjust what you've done, or revise the information. Perhaps a whole new thought train emerges and sparks more questions. Take time. Think, and you will succeed. You're a winner — even if your answers do nothing but doubly confirm what you have already done!

This technique works absolutely! This whole book is my evidence. Initial findings shocked me since they controverted many common beliefs, plus much I had been taught. However, hours and days spent researching, cross-checking and validating information reinforced my initial findings robustly. My understanding grows continuously.

Once the mind switch during adolescence is understood, it becomes evident that our transition from childhood is more intellectually dependent than age dependent. This observation explains that 'individualism' is the principle of being independent and self-reliant. It refers to self-centred thoughts and actions, self-reliance, egoism, and self-mastery. Do not let 'egotism' mislead you, which most people refer to as 'ego.' Egoism and egotism are opposites.

Individualism in the political and social sense is our freedom of action, free from collective or state control. It is free enterprise through our (individual) right to support and uphold our life and to pursue happiness within the equal rights of all others.

Rationality does not guarantee that we are reasonable individuals. We can think, speak and act reasonably and justly, for example. Alternatively, we can work in ways that inadvertently or purposively fail to respect our lives as separate individuals.

If we are to free ourselves from dictatorial rule on a global scale, we must refuse to have others master our minds. Remember that free people have no ambition to become absorbed in a greater mass. No desire or oppressive necessity exists. Nothing attracts their surrender of self. Nothing entices their joining a delusional fantasy where 'everybody has everything,' yet nobody is recognised, much less credited as the source. Necessarily, human progress results from divorcing oneself from the collective mindset.

Ayn Rand made a fundamental distinction that helps define individualism and independence. We can learn much about a society by studying what we are as individuals but nothing concerning ourselves from studying our societies. She also said, and I concur, that there is no such thing as a collective brain or a collective thought. We can reach a joint agreement, but our reasoning precedes that agreement, and that reasoning is for each one alone. To repeat, no such thing as a collective stomach exists or a collective mind.

There you have individualism in a nutshell. We can share or transfer the 'products' of our body and spirit, but never can we share the private functions of our body and soul. That reinforces that we can change the content of our consciousness, but we cannot change its process.

As human beings, we each are independent, one from another. Independence means being singularly alive in body, mind, and spirit. Since no communal mental faculty known as consciousness exists, we each can do, think and say things independently and differently from other people. This separateness marks each one of us as an independent living human being. The separateness of human beings is the natural order of the world.

Independence is fundamental to our biology, psychology, and praxeology which studies human action and conduct. Independence is essential to our lives, thoughts, feelings, and activities.

Of course, people depend on others for many things. They succeed and benefit from passive or active cooperation with others. Such cooperation can be given or withheld. It is not automatic, which again testifies our independence as individual personalities.

'Collectivists' fear independence because they do not know the power of full consciousness. Consequently, they cannot rely on their mental, emotional, or spiritual abilities, whereby they desperately cling to group support. They accept authoritarian rule because it forgives their dependency on others. The state relieves the vacancy in their mind, and they feel comforted. All seems well. Yet, we are intellectually abandoned in more ways than we can count. We're left to fend for ourselves without understanding what is essential to survival.

The choice to be free is one we each must make. But first, we must know what that choice is. Then, we must know how to exercise it and learn how to protect it. From that understanding, we can reach out to others whenever and however we choose. Finally, once sure of our independence, we can stop riding a collective life raft rotting from mental bankruptcy.

Solutions to private and public problems require logical and critical thinking. We profit from rejecting what is unworkable or biased, recognising that our mind functions independently, no matter how pressured to accept common beliefs and thought trains.

Independence of that order is power — precisely what propagandists and collectivists wish to nullify or eliminate.

Your power issues are forth from two sources. First, your ability to think and apply logic to events and information; to reason from A to B to C; to analyse, deliberate and evaluate. Your second power source is imagination, the capacity to project your thoughts into the future, to conceive and invent what has not yet manifested. Without such visualised conjecture, likely your desires will never exist. But that merely scratches the surface. Imagination is visualisation for the express purpose of impressing our desires and life-sustaining values on our subconscious minds.

That is precisely where your independent power manifests.'Some people want to say that power is a neutral object that can be used for good or evil. That isn't true. Your deepest power is alive. It's personal. It's stunningly energetic and dynamic. It connects with your deepest understanding of what is true and good and right. But it never sacrifices itself on the altar of what others insist is good and true and right. It never deserts you for an abstract ideology someone else has devised. That ideology was formulated, in fact, to separate you from your power.' —Jon Rappoport [13]

That explains why no one teaches the consciousness process! However, when you independently exercise your creative power to achieve what you most desire, your deeds will positively affect others. Your win lifts them, reminding them of their inherent power if only they choose it. The more you develop your independent imagination, the more it catalyses for exposing and reducing oppression. Your creative power is yours, individually and independently. The more it grows, the less fear you experience. Your robust future, happiness, and freedom lie in your knowledge of consciousness and using it to the full.

"The boughs of no two trees ever have the same arrangement. Nature always produces individuals; she never produces classes." —Lydia Maria Child

Independence removes the whole subject of morality from the collective domain that governments uphold and puts it into the private domain where it rightfully belongs. Barring accidents, immoral or unjust acts confess our guilt and testify our agreement to effect necessary remedy.

Wrong and evil do not disappear — they are uncivil or criminal deviations from the cause and purpose of life. Evil is not the equal of life nor an equitable competitor. Wrong and evil are gutless, nuisance-like diseases, manifesting as abusive aberrations. They require correction and justice nevertheless. Criminals require remediation.

Those who uphold their life respectful of others do not. Instead, they grasp the Natural Laws of Respect, Integrity, No Trespass, and the Law of

Chapter 8

Just Consequence; all described later. They choose to live according to natural law ethics because such are Creator's keys to success.

It becomes evident that Group or unity consciousness will not substitute for our nature or being. Thus a new life-supporting wholeness emerges. Your life is Creator's intention and endowment, meaning it is long past time to steer independence back on course. That is not the independence of one state from another, such as the (American) 1776 'Declaration of Independence.' Instead, our separation from those who violate our right to life.

Free to make that choice, we each are obliged nonetheless. We must learn what freedom is, how to exercise it and how to protect it. From that understanding, we can reach out to others whenever and however we choose. But first, independence means being singularly alive in body, mind, and spirit.

The subject of 'rights' is usually considered a political matter, not a matter of consciousness. But if conscious thought drives our actions, then our 'right to action' is intimately related to consciousness. Freedom pertains to each (independent) living man, woman and child, which demands that we each have the right to life.

A right is a moral principle defining and sanctioning a man's freedom of action in a social context. —Ayn Rand [14]

'A natural right in the strict sense is that which is naturally under a person's control, his body with its faculties of movement, feeling, thought, and speech. By extension, a natural right is what a person brings under his control without violating any other person's natural rights.' —Frank van Dun [15]

Observe the profound accuracy of those statements. The first quotation speaks for itself. No ambiguity exists. The fundamental (natural) right is our right to life, specifically to uphold and sustain our lives.

A 'right' is one's freedom of action. It is not one's action. Neither of the above quotations says that one has a natural right to a thing, an outcome or a product — to an education, welfare or health care, for example. We each have the natural right to seek an education or health care, but no right to demand that someone provide it. Consequently, the right to life is not the right to a product, service, or outcome. It is your entitlement to freely seek such things, including creating, building, or developing them.

The right to act in support of your life forbids that ever be curtailed, denied, or deprived. If it is, then your life is trespassed or violated.

No collective life exists; thus, no collective human rights can exist. Rights can only be 'individual rights,' and no act, decree, or legislation of Man can alter that fact.

Conscious Ascendance

Accordingly, the source of individual rights is not divine or congressional law but the Law of Identity. Nature impels each man and woman to sustain their lives through their efforts. To fail is to impose that one or more other people step in to assist.

The Universal Declaration of Human Rights (UDHR), to which Australia is a signatory, was adopted by the United Nations General Assembly, in December 1948, at the Palais de Chaillot, Paris. This document purportedly enunciates the rights to which all individual human beings are inherently entitled, which guarantees liberty. However, understand that 'liberty,' is social and exists only as the structure that a society determines or permits. In contrast, 'freedom' is singular.

So although that document is hailed worldwide as celebrating human liberty, freedom is categorically denied. Article 29 (3) states—'*these rights and freedoms may in no case be exercised contrary to the purposes and principles of the United Nations.*'

Article 30 states—'*Nothing in this Declaration may be interpreted as implying for any State, group or person any right to engage in any activity or to perform any act aimed at the destruction of any of the rights and freedoms set forth herein.*'

All disputes and disagreements with its 'permissions' are forbidden — no one is allowed to challenge the United Nations stranglehold of the freedom subject.

Consequently, your born (living) nature and your right to life are subject to United Nations permission — all counterclaims denied. You are a chattel, an enslaved person with no natural right to life; only your government granted permission subject to UN approval; individual rights denied outright! You live according to granted permissions despite you never elected any United Nations members! You have no freedom and no rights, 'liberty' is your best hope.

As defined and written, these so-called 'Human Rights' are not rights. Under 'maritime law', we each are just a 'person,' a legal persona, a mask. Legally, we are dead. That is why today's legal systems refuse our flesh and blood living being? Dead legal entities have no ability to action anything. How then can they possibly have rights?

It is therefore incumbent on us all as independent beings to preserve individual rights and interests, our responsibilities, and personal 'executive' decision-making ability concerning the conduct of our lives.

In the United States Declaration of Independence, Thomas Jefferson carefully chose the distributive plural of the word 'laws' to include both the laws of nature and nature's God. He thus declared that all men are equally endowed by their Creator with unalienable rights, which means "*the laws of nature, and of nature's God*" constitute our unalienable right

Chapter 8

to life. That our rights are of nature, so they are inherent, intrinsic, and immutable.

The natural rights of life and liberty are unalienable —Bouvier's Law Dictionary, *1856 Edition.*

Alfred Adask explained unalienable rights clearly—

"It is impossible for any individual to sell, transfer or otherwise dispose of an 'unalienable Right.' It is impossible for you to take one of my 'unalienable rights.' It is likewise impossible for me to even voluntarily surrender, sell or transfer one of my 'unalienable rights.' Once I have something 'unalienable,' it's impossible for me to get rid of it. It would be easier to give up the colour of my eyes or my heart than to give up that which is unalienable." —Alfred Adask [16]

Accordingly, Unalienable Rights are immutable and impossible to erase. They are our right to action, specifically our immutable right to live and sustain our lives, drawn about us within the equal rights of all others. No directive, proclamation, or anyone can erase this fact.

Rights are not separately granted or bestowed. Our right to life is immutably inherent in life and inseparable from our nature. It is the right to think and act, to use and exercise our faculties to support life. It is the right to live free from molestation and to protect that right. Every abrogation, or refusal of these facts, represents death in some form.

The right to life is not 'self-ownership,' as many will claim. One cannot separately own what they already are. For that very reason, every man, woman and child has the unalienable right to sustain their life. The difference between 'self-ownership' of one's life and one's 'unalienable right' to life is unmistakable. The first is one's claim. The second is oneself.

Once categorically asserted that we each have the inherent and unalienable right to live, and so sustain our life, protecting the equal rights of all others, all counterclaims are self-cancelled. Disagreement is rebellion against life, self-confessed evil. All trespass, violation and aggression of our right to life are thereby outlawed.

The right to life is the right to act and sustain our lives through actions. As regards the fruits of our labours, it is the right to work, to produce or earn that product.

Ayn Rand made a fundamental distinction in saying that our right to life is the source of all rights by which property rights are their only implementation. No rights are possible without property rights. We each must sustain our life through our efforts, without which we've no right to the fruits of our labours, thus no means to maintain our lives. Very importantly, our property right is our right to act. It is not the right to be granted education or health care; instead, our right to seek such things. Efforts to pursue and earn from our actions are our only guarantee of success.

Individual rights are now crystal clear.

- We have the Unalienable Right to act in support of our life. (*Una*lienable means *una*ble to be removed.)
- We have the Inalienable Right to the product of our efforts, to the fruits of our labours. (*Ina*lienable means with*in* the product.)

Ownership of one's efforts may transfer to another, whereby the inalienable right to that product' exchanges for value.'

Because individual rights belong only to flesh and blood living beings, both are divorced from today's legal jurisdiction. Our right to act, and right to its product, cannot apply to inert fictional legal entities; because they cannot action anything. Unalienable and inalienable rights are categorically denied any authoritative misappropriation by anyone, government included. Group rights are not possible, nor does any need exist, due to all having individual rights and protection.

Free will undeniably ties rights to consciousness since exercising your rights is your choice entirely. So let's explore that connection.

We must be free to uphold and sustain our lives. That means we each must have the unalienable right to act and the inalienable right to that which our labours produce.

The converse is a crime against humanity. To forbid our right to life and property is theft. To forbid our free choice prohibits free thought, thus violating our conscious process.

Now think as 'authoritarians' do. If you desired to dominate and control the people of your country, surely you would see that overt control of people's actions surreptitiously controlled their minds? Would you not use propaganda and political correctness to maintain a state of apathetic ignorance sufficient to refer to them as sheeple or useless eaters? Moreover, if the vast majority of people fell for this ruse, the tyrannical sociopaths and psychopaths who orchestrated this crime would feel justified in claiming an elite status or some unique bloodline. Whose consciousness is denied?

So let's join 'rights' to 'consciousness' and witness what is possible. But, first, let's agree that until we abolish artificial law, our right to life cancels and we are enslaved to fake legalities.

As flesh and blood, free-born independent living beings, conversely, our right to life is innate and immutable. Inalienable and unalienable rights are co-dependent since they both reference life. You cannot have one without the other! The simple truth is that a producer who does not own the result of his effort, whose production is usurped or stolen, does not have the right to think, make choices and live. State denial of property

Chapter 8

rights effectively turns men and women into state-owned property. As Rand[10] said, those, who claim the right to 'redistribute' the wealth produced by others claim the 'right' to us as their property.

Does this explain why the United Nations authoritatively rule human rights, in total contravention of its (Article 1) statement *"all human beings are born free and equal in dignity and rights"*?

Do you see how that document begins with the word 'free' in Article one, then swaps it for the word 'liberty' in Article twenty-nine? That done, it trusts that no one will notice the profound difference between freedom versus liberty, nor 'individualism' versus 'collectivism,' notwithstanding some permissions thrown in for comfort's sake?

Do you now see why states rule that 'equitable title' be separate from' legal title'? Do you see that when claiming to own our own lives, we concede that ownership of our lives is up for grabs? Once you have grasped that rights uphold your life, 'ownership' of your life is irrelevant. Your life is what you are. It is not a separate (independent) entitlement that you or anyone else can claim. To claim another's life as governments do, they mask it, transform it into a fictional entity, a persona, a legal entity, a citizen. That is today's condition, a crime that should never be.

Does that help explain why the Thomas Jefferson Memorial in Washington DC has the word INALIENABLE engraved in twelve-inch high letters, despite that Jefferson used the word UNALIENABLE?

Countless similar examples have destroyed the lives of millions. Most result from wide-scale public ignorance of what consciousness is and on what it depends.

Conversely, individual rights protection is crucial to thrive and prosper absent limits. Fortunately, the more we strive to develop our consciousness, the more our rights are categorically denied authoritative misappropriation by anyone or any group (government) for any purpose.

Now observe what that means in practice.

- When your actions preserve other people's right to life, your own rights are guaranteed.
- Actions that violate other's rights, forfeit your own, and freely confess so doing.
- Your free right to choose is the deciding moral factor.

Virtually everyone who knows of the American Declaration of Independence credits that document as the most definitive expose of our individual rights ever written. So it is. Its protections of our lives as independent beings, not social animals, are clear, unequivocal, and unambiguous.

So why is that document not today's definitive standard? What error or

149

omission has allowed our right to life to be usurped, overruled, rejected, reviled, repressed, stripped from existence and denied practical utility?

There seems to be only one answer. Nothing on the political horizon of 1776 could have suggested that it might be essential to protect the essence and nature of the (declared) protections inherent in the document. Jefferson said so himself, did he not? *"We hold these truths to be self-evident."* His conclusion, in retrospect, suggests that our right to life, liberty, and the pursuit of happiness are so self-evident and unquestionable that no need to protect those rights existed.

History has subsequently exposed that upholding our right to life, and the vital need to protect it, are two distinctly separate issues. Seemingly, that fact was not self-evident in 1776. Admittedly, Jefferson offered that "whenever any form of government becomes destructive of these ends, it is the right of the people to alter or to abolish it." Sadly, that allows the horse to bolt before the gate closes.

In retrospect, it is essential that declared right be protected by right! If ever America's revered 'Declaration' is revised, an additional clause is needed to protect our protected right to life. For example—

> *"To secure the certain, unalienable right to life, unless all men created equal, unequivocally ensure their right to life, and their unalienable right so to do against all cancellation, violation, or usurpation, they will have neither."* —Kenneth E. Bartle.

Individual rights demand protection for humanity to be free. Do you see what few people have ever seen? Because life is what we are, we each have the immutable right to its continuance. That means all dispute with that position is self-extinguished.

Life is axiomatic, meaning every attempt to refute it must use it. All refutation is self cancelled thereby. 'Life ownership' does not enter this picture. Life exists or does not exist. And when life exists, so too does the right to live.

Nature requires that we respect our own life and the lives of all others. Freedom and respect are reciprocal. Endorsing other people's right to their life ensures our own. Our insistence on their protection ensures ours.

Freedom, respect and individual rights are inseparable. Full consciousness delivers incontrovertible evidence. Neither of our two minds can violate the process of the other; thus, respect for others derives from self-respect.

Are you beginning to see how 'rights' and natural governing laws immutably encrypt in our human nature, all erasure denied? If so, you'll also see that whoever claims the right to override your decision-making process is claiming the right to treat all human beings as animals. Your

Chapter 8

defence comes from knowing how consciousness works and how your innate rights are inseparable.

Now plundered rights and goods across centuries and denial of full consciousness are laid bare for all to see. This chapter has shown the need to functionally apply consciousness to all we do since we are individually independent of others. We must also become separated from the state necessarily.

At the beginning of this chapter, I asked whether freedom can abide by societal constraints without sacrificing that which makes consciousness function? The answer is yes, resoundingly. However, it remains to discover how consciousness determines our ethics and morality.

Conscious Ascendance

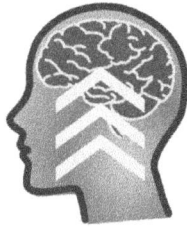

9. Alive - Conscious - Spiritual

Suppose you can comprehend the finely governed process that upholds and protects your life, even reporting your progress, and that you have the unalienable right to choose what values you want to have supported and protected. If so, you will understand Creator's blessings like never before. If you grasp likewise that your upholding others' right to life protects your right to life, you will appreciate Creator's desire that friendly societies develop and flourish. This chapter shows how esteemed personal and societal benefits await your acceptance with the least effort.

That advantage requires we first focus on our authentic being. There is no need to abandon today's advantageous societal goals; instead, we must cancel all belief in the imperative need for a state to overrule free will. Natural law governs the consequences of our actions; thus, no prior commands demand. Necessarily, therefore, we must abolish artificial law. Jointly, our task is to implement natural law inherent in our nature and protect it perpetually. Failure denies our right to life and holds us slaves to fake legalities, all the while today's monstrous criminal fraud hails as morally legal.

Such is not a demanding task. Indeed you've already accomplished a great deal in recognising truths in what you have learned here. Have you begun to compile your list of life values? (There's a blank page in the Appendix for you to use.) The sooner you start packing values into your life, the faster you benefit. As your picture of life grows, you'll notice it becoming ever more straightforward. Smiles of joy will become commonplace as you realise that natural law is not what you have to learn; it is your teacher instead. You will glow with a feeling of protective love, unlike anything you've ever felt. Peace of mind will prevail.

With individualism and independence established, it becomes essential to understand what responsibilities and duties fall to each of us. Ethics and morality are of prime importance since they are products of our free conscious process. Their bonds and obligations point to the foundation from which natural law emerges. Your increasing knowledge steadily positions you as one of the founders of the most influential societal revolution in human history, all based on human consciousness, spiritual values, and the natural laws of self-governance.

'Service corporations,' aka 'governments' hold a knife to the throat of humanity to prolong the 'legal life' of the state, and we, like sheep, unknowingly vote to sharpen it. Conscious nescience is the culprit.

Conversely, knowing 'values' drive full consciousness teaches how 'spirit' interacts with itself in objectified, life-enriching form, fully as Creator intended. That drives the knife at our throat through any evil that holds it, without mercy!

Ethics, morality, individual rights, and natural justice are essential learning before earth and heaven can resound with absolute joy. For that, Creator's lessons are blessedly shown within natural law as gifted!

Ethically, morally, and spiritually, the Natural law of Allowance obliges that we recognise and accept the same rights for others and their ability to progress at their pace according to their choices and skills. It also chastises our failure to do so. Nothing surpasses this spiritual invocation, personally and societally. Altogether, this suggests a science, or code of ethics, devoted to how men and women should think of life values and life itself, respectively, of self and others. Its premises are straightforward.

- **Life:** Nothing is more pertinent to every man, woman, or child on earth than life itself. Life is the base reference for all that concerns it. Life differentiates ethics from its lack and morality from immorality.

- **Virtues** are attitudes, life values, or developed character traits that enable us to act in life-supporting ways that foster and master our potential. These uphold our spiritual essence.

- **Respect:** Respect is the voluntary endorsement of the vital need to support one's life through the lawful exercise of one's faculties. The same applies to not hindering or harming the lives of others.

This crossover point in the Value Transfer Wave, in which our cognitive thoughts and intentions cease, and subconscious enactment begins, shows that ethics only concerns thoughts. At the same time, subsequent actions are the province of morality. Ethics and morality are therefore modeled right in the heart of our entire conscious process, in sequential order. What better could we ask than to have such guidance encrypted in our nature, all assisting decisions that support our lives and societal dealings with others? The difference is unmistakable.

- **Ethics is personal.** It concerns our thoughts and intentions
- **Morality is social.** Actions manifest our morality.

Yet we've all been brainwashed to believe the exact opposite. So, for example, 'morality' concerns our thoughts and intentions, while 'ethics' refers to rules of conduct for professional business practices such as medical and legal services. That error needs correction.

The relationship between private ethics and public morality is now apparent.

- **Ethically:** Life demands our deliberate choice to support and sustain it, never sacrificing its supreme value to anything lesser. Thoughts, desires and goals that uphold one's life are ethical—those that don't aren't. Ethics apply to thinking and deliberation before choosing an action. Thus ethics are expressly divorced from morality.
- **Morally:** Life impels that we never act to deprive another of their life or the means to support and sustain it. Actions that respectfully uphold the lives of others are moral – those that don't aren't. Morality applies to committed action, not to thoughts that precede it.

That distinction allows ethical and moral education to be formulated, written, and taught across all curricula, from preparatory school onwards. Ethics deals with the means of determining a moral course of action. As the author of our efforts, we originate our morality, or its lack, and are fully accountable for both.

Those premises are often respectively described as ethical intelligence and moral intelligence. Actions affecting ourselves are primarily ethical (or unethical) since no one else is involved. Actions and behaviours that affect others are moral (or immoral) principally since they manifest in the public domain. Therefore, the (crossover) point at which we commit to action is where our ethical thoughts and considerations cease being private. Our behaviour then affects others, and this demonstrates our morality. Our intentions and values transfer from our private domain into society, where they are now open to public scrutiny. Thus morality may be newly defined.

Morality is the conscious will to live according to one's nature, never depriving others of the same opportunity.

Grasp that vital importance. Remember how the subconscious mind delivers a perception report concerning our actions and how emotions are broadcast. So we each are a living, breathing, walking advertisement of our ethics and morality, not only as a visible image, but one that others sentiently receive, to which they can emotionally respond.

Now consider the often repeated saying, *'service to others comes before service to self.'* Does it? Your freely chosen, value-based ethics are a service to yourself without question. However, since ethical thoughts eventually transpose into moral actions, what first served you is now your service to others. You've shown what is possible and upheld their choice to emulate your achievements. Of course, we may choose to assist others materially, but that is not our moral duty.

Here is the beauty of it all. 'Life values' are your ethics. They can be uploaded to the subconscious mind and put on autopilot. Thus your morality shifts to autopilot. Your moral service to others is now automated. Do you see how graciously you are blessed? Your values, spirituality, emotions, ethics and morality can all be automated, and you are in complete command.

Question; what written statute or purported law can achieve even one-quarter of that? None!

Morality is the enacted manifestation of one's ethical principles. Immorality, conversely, manifests a lack, or refusal of ethical considerations, lack of moral discipline, or lack of justness.

This understanding suggests a science, or code of morality, describing how men and women should act and behave, based on ethical principles about oneself and the lives of all others. Its premises are equally straightforward.

- **Precedence:** Morality is the product of our ethical or unethical choices and intentions. Ethics harms no one but ourselves. Immorality harms others.

- **Virtues:** Virtues, attitudes, values, and developed character traits that foster and master our material and spiritual potential are the source of our enacted morality.

- **Respect:** Respect for others is our enacted morality, entirely conducive to 'individual rights.' Without such character, we hinder or deny the right to life of all others and all respect for life.

- **Justness:** Justness is the sum of just actions, the testament of our morality. Justness unto ourselves inevitably manifests as justness unto others.

Necessarily, such a code of morality would be independent of human opinion, rule and authoritarian decree. Howls of protest would undoubtedly follow, such as— *"How on earth will immoral behaviour be arrested if we are our own moral governor?"*

The answer lies in the Natural Law of Just Consequence. Every instigator of an immoral action publicly confesses guilt through their action(s).

So the question is answered. One's immoral or unjust actions self confess one's guilt and liability for remediation. Once guilt is established, the particular trespass or violation of another's life is unquestionable. The formula is straightforward. It is as though Creator said, *"I've perfected societal governing within your very self, precisely so that you may translate its Natural Laws into your societies."* Morality is not a social mandate, nor is it 'collective.' We each are accountable for our morality or lack thereof.

In sum, free will, life values, ethics, morality, and justice encompass all. Each of us is a unique and precious being governed by the natural laws of our nature. Our right to live is exclusively independent and immutable. Our singularity, beautiful uniqueness, and the natural order of our life, ordains boundaries separating us from others. Our rights, words, deeds, works, and property are separate from another's and other things. Nothing could be simpler or more in tune with nature herself.

Morality is the enactment of self-mastery that honours and ensures freedom for others. To that extent, it secures our freedom.

- **Ethics** are our personal benchmark.
- **Justness and morality** are our social benchmark, the sum of just actions and testament to our morality.

So now we have an answer to the question — *'how can uniform moral uprightness be achieved if each chooses their own?'* As a collective, we cannot, as history has long proven, but we each can as individuals. Everything in our nature and its governing laws urges that we should. When ethics correctly ascribes to the thought process and morality to behaviour, implications become clear.

- Ethics and morality are removed from the (collective) 'political domain' and placed squarely in the individual, 'private domain'.
- We must ensure that our unalienable life rights and inalienable property rights are protected; morality demands it. Such protection arbitrates just restoration when needed. Without rights protection, so too morality is unprotected.
- Convivial society results from moral actions in aggregate.
- Independence, one from another, enters with respect for each other.
- Co-operation amongst equals, or one's likes, results in mutual benefits.

Those who prize ethics and morality as spiritual progenitors of life relish these steering virtues because others learn of respect and unceasing justness from joint dealings. Moral actions are the flip side of natural justice.

Conscious Ascendance

Our actions testify to our authorship, for which we are wholly accountable. Our behaviour testifies that we admit to its consequences. Absent accidental behaviour, every immoral or unjust act confesses our guilt and our agreement to effect necessary remedy. That is the foundation upon which 'natural justice' depends.

Many people find that idea opposite to that taught. Nonetheless, legal prevention of wrong behaviour is to enforce morality legally. Today's legal system is the premise of enforced prevention, despite initiated force is immoral and the source of gross injustice. Innocent people are punished for victimless crimes as though morally justifiable. It remains that forced denial of our choices violates free will, which is immoral and unjust.

Spiritually based ethics are none less than spiritual life values we put on autopilot. To automate our life values is to automate our ethics, which, as mentioned, instantly puts our morality on autopilot as the Creator intended we should. That achievement has profound implications.

- All of today's beliefs concerning ethics and morality overturn.
- All 'collectivised' jurisdictional claims over ethics and morality are invalidated.
- Authoritarian government switches to self-governance under natural law.
- Present natural law theories that hold morality determines natural law invert. Natural law then has a truthful vitality, immutably and factually grounded in our nature, that no one ever suspected exists.
- Natural law, in common to all people, now has teeth no one knew, which cannot be denied or erased!

As free societies form in ways you've never imagined, a profound spiritual swelling will arise in your heart that words cannot describe. There can be no dispute that we each have an inherent and immutable right to life's continuance as Creator intentioned, without refusing one's life. All argument is self-extinguished upon its utterance.

Life is yours to live! Full consciousness and natural governing laws are the means, and Creator has your back all the way! A complete understanding of the conscious process is the path forward. It is your vision of success and the only means.

Justness is firmly encrypted in our nature and manifests in our ethics and morality according to our choices. Step outside those boundaries, and there is no justness. As 'justness' works personally, it works for society. Our actions may or may not serve 'justness' upon others. Unless we justly and morally deliver to others, we admit self-trespassing that we professedly uphold. So our actions confess the need for remediation.

Chapter 9

The conclusion is clear. Whosoever victimises another voluntarily gives up their rights for correction, remediation, and compensation. Such voluntary acquiescence remains until that crime or aggression is restoratively closed. That is the general principle of Natural Justice according to (existential) natural law.

'Natural justice' exists to remedy one's immoral or unjust actions. It is the practice of remediating 'injustice.'

So now, the difference between 'justness' and 'justice' surfaces.

- Justness is (first) served by each man and woman, not interfering with or denying any other person their ability to live and sustain their life.
- Only innocent individuals (persons) are free. One found guilty of injustice, or unjustness, cannot justly be considered to be a free individual, independent of the victim. Accordingly—
- Justice is served to offenders, as a correction, remediation, or restoration, in the measure of their offense, respectful of their causal actions.
- The tool of justice is correction, not punishment. Justice concerns the remediation of trespass.
- Offenders are thus returned to an ethic-based morality, moral unity, and acceptance of others' right to life. Compensation may be involved in some cases, although mitigating circumstances may overrule.
- Because no victimless crime can exist, no penalty applies.

Those points sum up the core principles of natural justice, which then permit the founding of convivial societies.

Offenders who trespass the law are those who choose to step outside the law and become outlaws, whence their actions bring the weight of natural justice to bear on themselves. The degree of sufferance caused by aggressors determines the degree of remediation or recompense necessary under Natural Justice. Morality thereby shifts from being a social convention to its proper place as the conveyor of justness originating from its fully accountable site within each (individual) living being. Truth is—

No one decides justice. It just is.

When each living being is enabled to become self-responsible, there are no mandated interests. Each is a self-regulator, having no prescription for others concerning their choice of religion, morals, politics, interests, desires, fashions, or any other. A society where each can freely meet, engage, or depart, absent subordination and regulation, would result in the most peaceful social order ever witnessed. Self-governance is irrevocably endorsed.

Conscious Ascendance

The road ahead is clear. If the world is to become free from rule of force and widespread tyranny, the phrase consent of the governed is highly controvertible. Why? First, it can never satisfy all, and second, governments that rule according to (statute) permissions, in practice, decree our 'consent.' Mind-controlled brainwashing is their trade tool, while insensibly, 'consent of the governed' approves it. We were given the alternative to this insanity centuries ago—

"Nature, to be commanded, must be obeyed." —*Francis Bacon*

That quotation takes us right back to Chapter One, which stated—

- Animals adapt to their environment, as their nature has determined.
- As our free will determines, we alter the natural environment to serve our purpose.

Natural laws govern our actions and behaviour, whereby Creator consents to self-governance indubitably. Nothing can alter that fact; hence nothing more is required.

Organic societies properly founded on the 'nature of those self-governed,' ensure that consent is universal!

'Constitutional law' then acquires absolute power to protect Man and nothing more. The Majority vote for new legislation becomes a thing of the past. When all people are free to choose, no contrary legislation is permissible. All rules that abrogate free will are outlawed. Consent is universal since those who refuse have no alternative but to agree to arrest for causing harm. Although unprecedented and never witnessed in all history, this endowment strictly provides 'individual rights,' freedoms, living identity and 'natural justice' are upheld and forever protected. No better precedent exists than self-governance supported and protected as encrypted in our human nature.

Although never realised before, a revolutionary about-face of this magnitude is ours for the knowledge and willpower to achieve! Full consciousness and its natural laws are our passports to humanity's glorious future. Nothing less will suffice! Grasping the truth of our nature is now the battle for humankind. Nothing has precedence, is more relevant, nor is more urgent.

Recall Jeffersons statement from Chapter One of this book—

If a nation expects to be ignorant and free, in a state of civilisation, it expects what never was and never will be. —*Thomas Jefferson*

Conscious knowledge is our path to freedom and a state of peaceable civilisation in perpetuity. So now let's paraphrase Jefferson's statement—

If a nation expects to be consciously knowledgeable and free in a state of civilisation, it expects what should be, and protects it.

Chapter 9

Mankind is gifted with the lawful means to (universally) implement free societies on a global scale, as never dreamt before?

"That personal freedom is the natural right of every man; and that property, or an exclusive right to dispose of what he has honestly acquired by his own labour, necessarily arises therefrom, are truths which common sense has placed beyond the reach of contradiction. And no man, or body of men, can without being guilty of flagrant injustice, claim a right to dispose of the persons or acquisitions of any other man, or body of men, unless it can be proved that such a right has arisen from some compact between the parties in which it has been explicitly and freely granted." — Gen. Joseph Warren *(1775)* [17]

Two hundred plus years have passed. Freedom is still not understood. Humanity remains ignorant and ruled, thus not civilised, despite *"truths which common sense has placed beyond the reach of contradiction."* Conscious ignorance is the number one cause.

"Facts don't disappear just because they are ignored." — Aldous Huxley

Particular criteria are essential for developing freedom-based, organic societies, but not necessarily in this order.

- Human life is supreme; all challenges are incompatible and potentially destructive.
- Nature preserves and upholds free will as immutably fundamental to life; all violations destructive thereof.
- Free to function according to their nature, all people are fully accountable for the consequences of their actions.
- Free will, choice, and self-governance, within the equal rights of all others, precludes all forms of societal domination and control.
- Independent right to self-defence is self-evident and self-defensible.
- The unalienable right to life and inalienable right to the fruits of one's labours apply to all people.
- Unceasing protection of the Creator's 'natural existential laws' is vital; all cancellation and usurpation forbade.
- Ethics, morality, and respect for others are essential, derived from Creator's existential natural laws.
- One's living, flesh and blood identity is one's only identification; all else is cancelled.

Cooperation: As fully individuated, free, independent beings, 'cooperation' with others facilitates beneficial results from synergistic teamwork. We must question whether cooperation is our free choice, or will persons of authority dictate involuntary cooperation?

Conscious Ascendance

The difference is clear, as General Warren phrased it—

"One is in perfect accordance with a natural personal liberty which constitutes the chief element of the happiness of human beings, the other violates it and is the chief cause of the Bedlam-like confusion which pervades all ranks and conditions of mind." —Gen. Joseph Warren (1775) 17

In determining the ground rules very carefully, we should question whether involuntary cooperation is possible. Should it not be called servitude? The answer lies in the previous discussion concerning how free will ultimately determines the consequences of our actions and how they affect others for better or worse. As Warren insisted, natural laws—

"teach us that our own happiness depends upon a proper respect for the happiness of others and that therefore we should not make social arrangements which require compulsion or the violation of the natural freedom of any individual."

Further—

"there must be no arrangements which depend for their success upon agreement on verbal rules or processes for agreements of opinions, tastes or interests. There should be, instead, preservation of the liberty of each person to differ in these and all other respects."

To disagree with Warren's position is to disavow one's nature. Indeed, as elsewhere shown, respect for freedom matched with voluntary cooperation, based on mutual exchange of value, produces almost unbelievable benefits, primarily unknown in enterprise and trade that presently suffocates from cut-throat competition.

Does any or all of the above demand government? Yes, but not as we have ever known it. Self-governance is entirely possible within the realm of natural justice, which, as natural existential law informs, is the maintenance of the 'natural order.' As a result, humanity can advance rapidly and exponentially since unbounded benefits, and just protection of our right to life are in-built.

Rulers have long known human freedom is a fact of nature. However, because nature disavows and denies rule, authoritarians ostensibly had no option but to invent 'legal entities' to circumvent nature and thus rule. That fiction, or should I say fraud, prevails to this day. These tyrants must maintain conscious ignorance if authoritarian domination and control are to survive. Our only remedy is to smash through centuries of ignorance concerning how consciousness works.

Mystical dreams about raising vibrations, or ascension, are inadequate, to say least, once grasped that our cognitive mind is in complete control of our values. Because spiritual values are imperative, the ball falls in our court of rationality, logic, assessment, and evaluation as independent living beings.

Just think of resultant benefits if competition, primarily due to government registrations, burdensome taxes, and multiple other regulatory demands, were smashed. Think how our opportunities would blossom from living in a free society where rights and justice are fully protected. Industries would quickly bow out of crippling competition and focus on market cooperation, precisely as human nature models for us to copy. After all, our bodies and mental processes testify to cooperative enterprise across the board, complete with reporting and corrective systems to ensure success. Conversely, the more we cling to pretences that smash the integrity of our lives, so natural law certainty will deservedly sink our efforts.

There is no conflict between orderly governance (natural laws) and free will. That teaches us we must never violate the other's function; else, self-deprivation or destruction inevitably follows. Likewise, to violate another's right to life is to sacrifice one's own.

Just as we can advance or fail ourselves but cannot change our natural processes, we can contribute to or fail society but cannot change the natural law process. Nature's gift to humanity is beyond compare. Free will and natural law are inseparable from individual rights. No invented laws or statutes match this achievement, and never can they!

Freedom and respect morally constrain us. Therefore, no (invented) supplementary rule is necessary. Had Man studied how consciousness works to preserve our freedom instead of society rule; conscious fidelity would have been long known and practised; individual rights indispensable. That is the only path to freedom and a state of peaceable civilisation. Full consciousness is the path to success.

Society-as-symbiosis: Symbiosis means interaction between two different organisms living in a close physical association, typically to the advantage of both. Society-as-symbiosis describes a convivial society of independent flesh and blood human beings living according to those principles, wherein respectful and responsible interaction is mutually advantageous.

Such societies spring from free and independent people who all respect the equal rights of others, just as natural law works within ourselves. They live among their likes, according to their free choices as responsible and caring people, and all respect natural law in their mutual dealings and interactions.

Freedom prevails to the extent that each treats others peacefully and fully respects their rights, work, and property. They live together as independent beings without being urged to any joint enterprise or social interaction, not unlike a commune.

Other people's uniqueness, individuality, personal integrity, and property are fully respected, with nothing but their humanity in common. Individual freedom allows opportunities, facilitates negotiations, actions and outcomes, yet allows free exit. Individuals are lawfully free to pursue their goals separately or to collaborate with others.

Such convivial, symbiotic order has no organisational or statutory purpose—no leader, director, or governor. No authority exercises direction, rule, or control. No government exists because such forfeits the nature and integrity of their symbiotic society. Nothing establishes rulers or the ruled. No individual or group owns it, rules over it, or is responsible or answerable for its success, yet all contribute.

No common goal exists, but education offers moral guidance. Specific direction and influence may exist, such as from elders and those of great wisdom, but there are no positions of power to exert influence or command anyone. The natural laws of societal orderliness prevail.

Whoever steps outside this natural law paradigm chooses to be an outlaw. Initiated force, fraud, or coercion are arrested, such actions confessing a perpetrator's agreement to suffer all consequences. Thus natural justice, remediation, and recompense accord with natural law. All problems resolve through diplomatic negotiations or an appointed judge or arbitrator.

No mixture of collectivism and individualism is possible! No social, organic order can wage war! Societies of this kind may take a generation or two to accomplish. Still, if we do not start now, we risk authoritarians will forever prohibit us from starting.

Today's path to a state of peaceable civilisation requires we embrace life, respect, individual rights and freedom as just described. Statism and statute law then becomes redundant, with safety rules remaining.

No ruling body may exist to which anyone must bow, because free societies spring from the independence of constituents, each according to their free will, who all respect the mutual rights of others as natural law.

Remember that freedom means complete separation from government coercion, not freedom from your landlord or your employer. Freedom means independence and separation from the coercive dictatorial powers of the state and nothing else.

Spirit is our connection across all boundaries and barriers. It transcends race, religion, gender, culture, nation and education. It unites all discrepancies in mental understanding and ability, not to produce one unified entity or collective consciousness, but instead to coalesce as a spiritual force uniting all independent beings.

Chapter 9

Could anything be more simple or clear cut insofar as we each are responsible for the building of society?

This new-found knowledge encourages many more people to drink from the fountain of freedom, and guide others to do the same. In short, we are each blessed with a model that explains how science works to uphold and sustain our lives, from which, natural laws readily translate into our societies. Once that is accomplished, all conjecture, subjectivism, theories and consensus opinion are removed from consideration. Life is vastly simplified, and becomes self supporting.

Fortunately, science is slowly awakening to the interconnectedness of our conscious and subconscious minds as our spiritual essence. This will assist transitioning from the 'collective,' to 'independence' and freedom. The more this path opens up, the easier our life becomes. When our unalienable rights are truly honoured and protected, a voluntary, symbiotic community will follow.

Given this new understanding and appreciation, enlightened people know that collaboration with others is one of the most beneficial forms of adaptation available. As described above, cooperative enterprise opens opportunities for material and spiritual advancement like no other. Dynamic consciousness makes no demands save our integrity, values, honesty, truth, and respect for others. To accept all responsibility, and accountability for our actions is to respect natural justice. We suffer no authority and issue none. Sovereign individuals rightfully, humbly, and lawfully insist that all challenges to our unalienable right to life be referred to Creator, not to a court of law.

Revised Education is imperative and Urgent

- Science has failed mental acuity, hence philosophy.
- Philosophy has denied psychology.
- The psychology of consciousness has failed us.
- Human consciousness, thus abandoned, allows collectivism to fail society.
- Society has degenerated into a disaster condition almost beyond repair.

If you can grasp that totality, it is clear that present-day education concerning consciousness is vacant, utterly inept, dare I question, corrupted? Learning the truth of our nature is now the battle for humankind. Nothing but a drastic transformation in conscious ability will rid ignorance and correct today's social obscenities.

Only a healthy reappraisal of consciousness will free destructive patterns and thrust us into a healthy state of collaboration with each other and our ecosystem. Until then, we will keep polluting our environment and minds, killing and destroying like an ignorant bunch of mindless automatons until everything is dead.

Neuroscience is extremely valuable, but life is hindered until reason is spiritually explained. Tragically, most science is flawed at the basic life-level of enquiry, unable to creatively project our spiritual nature as our Creator intended. That rejects the spiritual value of mental content, which is why we possess consciousness. Therefore, a mental regenerative educational program is urgently demanded across all curricula, founded on spiritual values.

This transformation will result only from understanding that truth, reality, and values are the keys to a future we have never dreamt possible. After that, natural laws will awaken personal, psychological and philosophical understanding. Then, awareness, conscious knowledge, discernment, truths, and emotions become vibrantly clear and fully connected. That allows empowerment to emerge from our nine higher faculties beyond anything human sciences have ever explained.

Spiritual consciousness then comes alive. The potency of spiritual values and their vital role in our mental and emotional wellbeing will challenge commonly held beliefs across all human sciences and sociologies. New-agers, libertarians and voluntaryists are thereby challenged to reappraise their premises. This revision calls to question almost every precept taught concerning humankind!

Nothing demands omniscience or infallibility. The subconscious mind asks only that one chooses important life values within the limits of one's present knowledge and understanding. Emotions exist to prompt the expansion of our expertise and values. The subconscious mind wants you to express your actions and goals in ethical, moral, and life-sustaining spiritual terms. It wants that you superintend you, not for pets, possessions, position, money, dogmas, beliefs, governments, or ideologies to own you. Our choice is explicit, and maybe you have now reached some conclusions of your own. Here are some ideas that flooded my mind when these revelations initially came home to me..

"It's a very thorough package. *My whole focus narrows to the word 'value' yet my field of endeavour expands to the cosmos. That is awesome, because it's no longer about service to self versus service to others, is it? I was born into this world with unique gifts. With that glimpse of the divine and access to it, I can make the world a more beautiful and wholesome place. I've no fears or feelings of inadequacy any more. The more I affirm the love, esteem, and trust with which I view myself, the more I show others how they may do the same, my family included. They are free to explore their own talents as far as they wish. All they need do is put their own life as #1 on their priority list."*

Chapter 9

"At *last I'm beginning to understand that the 'matrix' is a lie*, *if not mind control. People believe it to be true. After all it rings with reality and daily smacks us in the face, and so it's never challenged. We're fed limited concepts of just about everything, but that short changes what I'm capable of. Full consciousness changes everything. I'm beginning to challenge everything from science to politics, medicine, media, money and more. I'm seeing more hogwash than I've ever seen, and seeing straight through it. The cool bit is that my power depends on none of it. I can choose my path and spread my wings, and not be controlled by any 'matrix' mural posing as reality. Of course that is tangible, but knowing what I now know, my spirituality is not for being short-circuited, least not from this point on."*

"I'm speechless! *Just look at the numbers. If fifteen prime life values can be uploaded to my subconscious, each taking no longer than three minutes, then in forty-five minutes I've turned my whole life about face. Okay, first I had to discover how, then make a list of life-values, then let my imagination run, and then put my passions into action. So what if that took a week or three? Does time matter when my life is on the line? And what about my kids? If I can show them what's possible with value choices, it wont be forty-five minutes or three days out of their life, it will be forty plus years of joyful happiness added."*

"Knowing *that free will is locked in* *blows my mind. I can't stop smiling because respect is called to attention constantly. Just thinking of how all my faculties are dynamically united in processing what I choose to value — is — well — I'm just speechless! I know that beyond my enquiries and choices, the process is automatic? OMG."*

"A *treatise on consciousness from infants through adolescence* to *wise elders, all based on the divinity of life, is stunningly remarkable to say least. That any attempt refute it must use that which it is and thus self cancel, is astronomical. Nothing compares in all history."*

Human sciences have not yet recognised our inherent ability to respond to today's crisis. Their closed perspective obstructs a greater understanding of ourselves, our conscious and spiritual abilities, and our place in the physical and spiritual universe into which we are now emerging.

Life demands our most profound consideration and resolute response. It vitalises a deep understanding of our purpose in being alive at this time in human history and brings us face to face with our destiny.

For that, we are all blessed. We can open to our power and potential. There is nothing to be feared. I trust you will have now used some of these suggestions and learned of your power from your own experience. If so, you must surely recognise that consciousness and natural law afford our most significant opportunity for intellectual and spiritual advancement and survival as a species. Nothing has surpassed it, nor can it. It remains that we will have neither fulness of freedom nor the right to self-govern if we do not responsibly act upon that right. Nature invokes that we each claim our rights to life and property upheld through education and natural justice.

Freedom demands that we each act to uphold and protect it responsibly. Freedom is not automatic. It must be fought for and defended! It is the only condition in which our consciousness operating system can function as it should. Freedom requires acting upon our knowledge of natural law with its incumbent responsibilities as outlined in the next chapter. That means exercising our right to self-mastery and protecting the same rights for all others. Nobody can do it for you.

Importantly, natural laws are not an add-on. Instead, they are the only inherent facilitation through which consciousness can function. Precisely because natural laws govern the consequences of our behaviour, none limit our free will, nor can they. Instead, they inspire us to be more conscious of how we do things, and that 'invitation' facilitates 'cooperation.'

Perhaps you've already glimpsed a critical element not yet mentioned. First, recall how it became essential when choosing life values to nominate and select the same values on which the subconscious mind relies. 'Diligence' offers a classic example. It uses that value when auto-piloting your car, and you use it when hand digging to plant a tree. In the next chapter, you will discover that many natural laws embrace the essential life values to which you will gravitate. Cohesion results, and it is nigh unbreakable. Simple biological correlations merge into conscious ethical considerations that eventually register as life values and transmute as natural law. The whole of life is one value-charged parcel that full consciousness makes impossible to ignore.

Once you understand that respect for these natural laws is 'spiritual,' we learn that 'Spirit' is the origin of both nature and humanity. Our lives are spirit in action. As the consequence of God's free creative act, nature serves as the living theatre in which we each freely act and develop as moral beings, as spiritual beings. No priests need to stand in for God. Our blessed capacity to live a virtuous life in which morality is our outward expression of spiritual freedom is our' here and now' soul connection to our source Creator, the testimony of our spiritual reverence.

Enacting moral law as the spiritual extension of our freedom serves nature's God and fully reveres our creation. I trust that you now understand what responsibilities and respect fall to each of us.

Chapter 9

Conclusively, natural law innately and immutably exists in support of our free conscious process. Moreover, natural law is the progenitor of ethics, morality and justice, not vice versa, as natural law theory teaches.

That inversion has mammoth implications. Natural law is personal, first and foremost. It ethically facilitates our most excellent mental, emotional and spiritual efficiency. After that, it manifests as morality that reciprocally upholds the rights of all others, and ours. Natural justice falls sweetly into place sequentially; whence freedom blossoms forth as the only possible outcome.

All of it derives from our conscious process. When practised and confirmed, the door opens to petitioning knowledge far beyond one's present moment comprehension. The conclusion should be self-evident, the vastness of it all, how most is fully automated, and how its natural governing laws apply socially. You are fast becoming a founder of the most significant societal revolution in human history, all based on human spiritual consciousness.

This book has revealed what centuries of bogus ideologies have concealed. You now know how perception interfaces reality while the remainder of your subconscious interfaces spirituality. You've learned how to tune your conscious and subconscious minds to a state of harmonious cooperation devoted to your wholesome success. Conscious knowledge now rescues you from multitudes of bogus beliefs that grow like poisonous weeds on infertile banks of conscious ignorance. Most importantly, you can now take deliberate charge of the autopilot driving your subconscious mental processes, thereby flooding your life with unbridled joy.

Will this raise our consciousness? No, it is perfect, just as Creator endowed, but we must learn to use it fully. Once understood that value assessments should be impressed on the subconscious mind so that our (emotional) mentoring system reports in exact accord with our choices, mental and spiritual prowess skyrockets. Value validations, being emotions that appear in milliseconds, show that no better mentoring system exists.

Self-mastery will be vividly transparent to those who choose to practice it. You can be better today than you were yesterday and better again tomorrow. Self-appraisal is the only standard of judgement worth having. What others do and what they achieve belongs to them. Once understood how beneficial this practice is and how efficiently it may develop on a broad scale, all forms of domination and control will fail regardless of fraud-based benefits. Vacant ideologies, religious misdirections, and legal fictions will wither and die from lack of support.

Conscious Ascendance

That delivers an opportunity to entirely divorce from societal domination and control that has damnably beleaguered humanity's entire history. You now know that your nature is Creator's model for free organic societies, forbidding political power and endless tyranny. Natural law theory is now obsolete; thus, bogus philosophies and erroneous teachings flounder in their false inventions, having nowhere to turn but to the only court of appeal that is relevant.

Everything is in place for the institution of free societies founded on natural law. Thus given, we now have an opportunity to declare our correct political status as individual, living, sentient beings under the protections of a 'constitution' founded in our nature and Creator's natural governing laws as bestowed. No contrary position or argument holds merit or legitimacy, nor can it!

This key to personal freedom, and social liberty, is unprecedented in human history, a sociological and political foundation more ethical, moral and just than any the world has ever witnessed, all courtesy of nature itself!

Awaken to your dynamic powers. Thrive like never before. Unfold the blueprints for humanity's glorious future. Personal and societal revolution is yours to enjoy. Creator backs all who take up this transformative challenge. Remember always—

To be knowledgeable and free in a state of civilisation is to expect what should be, and protect it.

'I am'

The short Ayn Rand novel, 'Anthem,' [18] published in 1938, deals with the professed values of our entire civilisation. The central character, Equality 7-2521, begins a process of self-discovery and self-fulfillment that cogently expresses the difference between a collectivist society and a friendly society founded on the individual self, right to life, and autonomy. Forcibly held captive and controlled, he escapes. Prior taught to think and speak of himself as 'we,' tears of deliverance flow when he discovers the word 'I.' A complete understanding of the phrase, 'I am,' leads to his profound grasp of how humans are stripped of their nature. In books found after his escape, he learns that individuals live with the immutable right to pursue their happiness in freedom, never to be group enslaved. So he proclaims—

"I know not if this earth on which I stand is the core of the universe or if it is but a speck of dust lost in eternity. I know not and I care not. For I know what happiness is possible to me on earth. And my happiness needs no higher aim to vindicate it. My happiness is not a means to any end. It is the end. It is its own goal. It is its own purpose.

Chapter 9

*Neither am I the means to any end others may wish to accomplish.
I am not a tool for their use. I am not a servant of their needs. I am
not a bandage on their wounds. I am not a sacrifice on their altars.
I am a man."* —Ayn Rand [18]

Anthem is about us, an incredibly powerful expose of fascist slavery, with freedom its vital counterpoint. It most poignantly expresses totalitarian slavery that the author hoped Man would avert; namely, at the crossroads of his consciousness, he should come to his senses, grasp what fails his life, and what redeems it.

Our conscious abilities are bountiful beyond measure; they hold and reveal natural laws as our gifted invitation to live in wholesome spiritual fullness, our unalienable (free will) right to choose our course and purpose in life a blessing without compare. No better model of ethics or morality exists or is as simple. Both are ours for the taking, a richly spiritual life ours to exercise with humble and reverent gratitude.

The institution of free, organic societies adequately founded on the nature of those governed is now in your hands. Nothing has precedence, is more relevant, or more urgent. Nothing past has described consciousness so fully or natural law so specifically. Now blessed beyond anything taught, humanity may excel as never before.

This knowledge requires we declare our correct political status as independent, living sentient beings under the protections of a 'constitution' as nature and its governing laws effective prescribe. No contrary alternative suffices, nor can it, since that would trespass what Creator has already consented!

What better could we ask? No one has yet witnessed a world where everyone moves freely through life with radiantly clear knowledge of their true potential, spiritual purpose, and genuine connection to the Source of everything. Peace-loving, organic societies are now possible beyond anything the world has ever witnessed.

Freedom, creation, joy, abundance, sovereignty and natural justice are for us to institute—all else contrary consigned to history. So will arise an unprecedented, intellectually and spiritually advanced human civilisation, in which all are Creator blessed and protected.

We all should have been taught the process of full consciousness from childhood. Then we would have learned the natural governing laws that Creator has encrypted in our very nature, no less than His blessed invitation to live life to the fullest possible. As you grasp the totality of this automated orchestra under your baton of free will, smiles of deliverance will beam with delight. Desiring nothing but the development and flourishing of friendly, free societies, we will find it painful even to remember the dark age of conscious ignorance that festered where your mind's wings should have grown.

Please, do not put this book on a shelf to gather dust. Instead, place it where you can flick to a page, read a short passage and entertain that idea for a week or more. Repeat that exercise frequently.

You will very soon understand the finely governed process that upholds and protects your life in tune with the values you choose to support. You will appreciate Creator's invitations like never before.

As one of the most emancipated beings on earth, your mental, emotional, and spiritual life will soar to the heavens on wings of joy.

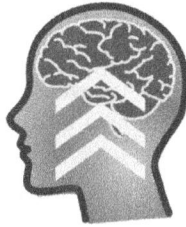

10. The twenty natural laws

This book would not be complete without listing the natural laws with a brief description, including their application.

They are written in sequential order, since orderliness defines the law. Second, they are written for your express study. Each law concludes with references to its source, not its chapter or page number. I invite you to follow the given clues, find the page numbers of those topics and pencil them in the margins of this chapter. Not only will you have read this book, but your cross-referenced study will also boost your knowledge considerably.

There are correlations and links I've not mentioned because you should discover them yourself. They will considerably enhance your abilities and confidence, allaying all fears in the future.

This chapter bridges the gap between personal natural law and natural societal law. A third book ('Navigate to Freedom') will deal with natural law as it applies socially and societally. It will comprehensively unite both books as though one complete, indivisible work.

The most comprehensive understanding will result from reading this book first. I desire that your excitement and vitality flourish from practising what you learn here and from subsequent study or research. So let's begin.

Many patterns of physical and mental order exist, and their interconnected orderliness constitutes the natural laws of our being, which altogether serve to uphold and sustain our lives. Order, in this sense, means to structure in an orderly fashion.

Conscious Ascendance

Our heart (hydraulic) and lungs (pneumatic) work cooperatively like two individuals. A similar relationship exists between our kidneys and liver. Our body has levels of organisation that constructively build on each other, such as different cell types and tissue types that make up organs to form different organ systems. Our hearts and lungs differ, and our conscious and subconscious minds work cooperatively for the same purpose. Values are communicated between them, much as blood conveys nutrients to our cells and organs. Accordingly, human consciousness is an orderly value transfer system that connects physicality to spirituality.

All the separate systems are interconnected; thus, the function of one system induces the tasks of all others as one indivisible entity. Cells exist independently in every tissue, organ and system. Additionally, our various mental and emotional faculties are all independent, yet each is a cooperative part of the whole. There is an orderliness of interconnectedness and interoperability, which is what the word 'systems' conveys. So we can be sure that what is good for us is what is complete or perfect for each of us, according to our nature.

Such orderliness or law governs our functioning, the cooperation of our systems and faculties and the independence of each. Without it, we could not function at all. We could not live. Life supremacy is the bottom line. This mutual commitment to upholding life is the bond or obligation that defines ius naturale, known as natural law.

Grasp that natural law is not about crime and justice but concerns the beauty and fullness of our spiritual life in a material realm, and you will have advanced more in two milliseconds than humanity has in two centuries.

It gets better! From empirical research and logical reasoning, natural existential law is fully authenticated and validated from its encryption within every man, woman and child. No legislator, authoritarian dictator, or even Satan can erase it! Natural law does not prescribe, rule or command, nor is there a need. In governing the consequences of our actions, it guides us to honour the natural order, but to receive that counsel, we must seek it and choose it.

Every virtue has a positive consequence, and every trespass of life has a debilitating result. Fortunately, every man and woman has free choice to know in advance of any action what likely outcome will result. Our reasoning faculty and conscience exist for a good reason. Evidence is indisputable. If we ingest toxic food or poisons, we pay the price, however high that be. Likewise, if we hold toxic thoughts, propaganda, or bogus ideologies in our minds, anxiety, stress, and trauma are certain.

Chapter 10

Emotions applaud our actions or reprimand us. Incentives are decisive, and so are penalties. Every effort testifies our morality, whereby every step that trespasses natural law self-confesses transgression. Natural justice will then take its course in free societies, insisting on correction and remediation, including possible recompense. Nature has ordained morality within the confines of respectful free will; thus, no additional laws are needed. Just as our heart protects our lungs and vice versa, similar patterns of natural order protect our two minds. Free will falls wholly within that protection because Creator sandwiched it fully inside the subconscious process for mental efficacy and freedom. No invention of Man is more beneficial, more committed, or more protective.

Society is nothing but an aggregation of individuals, equal in nature and uniquely diverse in expression. What applies to one applies to all. Just as our creative ability and emotional and spiritual joy may skyrocket, stress diminishes to near nil simultaneously. Consequently, thriving power, expansive freedom, joy, peace, harmony, and spiritual attainment are enabled globally.

Collectivism is denied, but collaboration and cooperation are not. Indeed both are reinforced.

Observe the profound difference. Authoritarian rule denies the concept of the individual and replaces it with a oneness called society. It packs every unique human being into this collection to be treated identically with all others as though a herd. But you are *not one of all others*, never were a collective, and never will be. You are *one with all others*, a single individual that all together counts in aggregate. Authoritarians use subtle trickery of words so that collective control commandeers herd responses and denies individuality. Your consciousness is arrested and suffocated, even if your body is not.

Existential natural law is your only escape because it already exists within you. Its natural laws are complete in themselves, immutable and enduring. They are vastly more potent than 'natural law theory' because each is fully validated and authenticated, unquestionably established as factual, and completely objective of life itself. Existential natural law replaces natural law theory.

Natural law protects free will from all interference save what we permit. Responsibility for self-governance is ours independent from others. Once we understand how we function bodily as a whole while preserving the individuality of each constituent member, we see how the same principle can work in free societies indisputably.

Conscious Ascendance

Now your preliminary study into natural law can begin. Diagram 21 shows how the twenty natural laws fall into four groups having five in each, clockwise from law number 1. Each one connects to all others, which reinforces their wholesome unity. Additionally, each law has a counterpart or supporting law found diametrically opposite—for example, 3 points to 13 and 6 points to 16.

Ten Fundamentals of Natural Law

We should study each with its diagonal counterpart to grasp their relationship relevance and source in our nature. Natural law emerges from the ten fundamentals below, each applicable to all twenty natural laws listed after that.

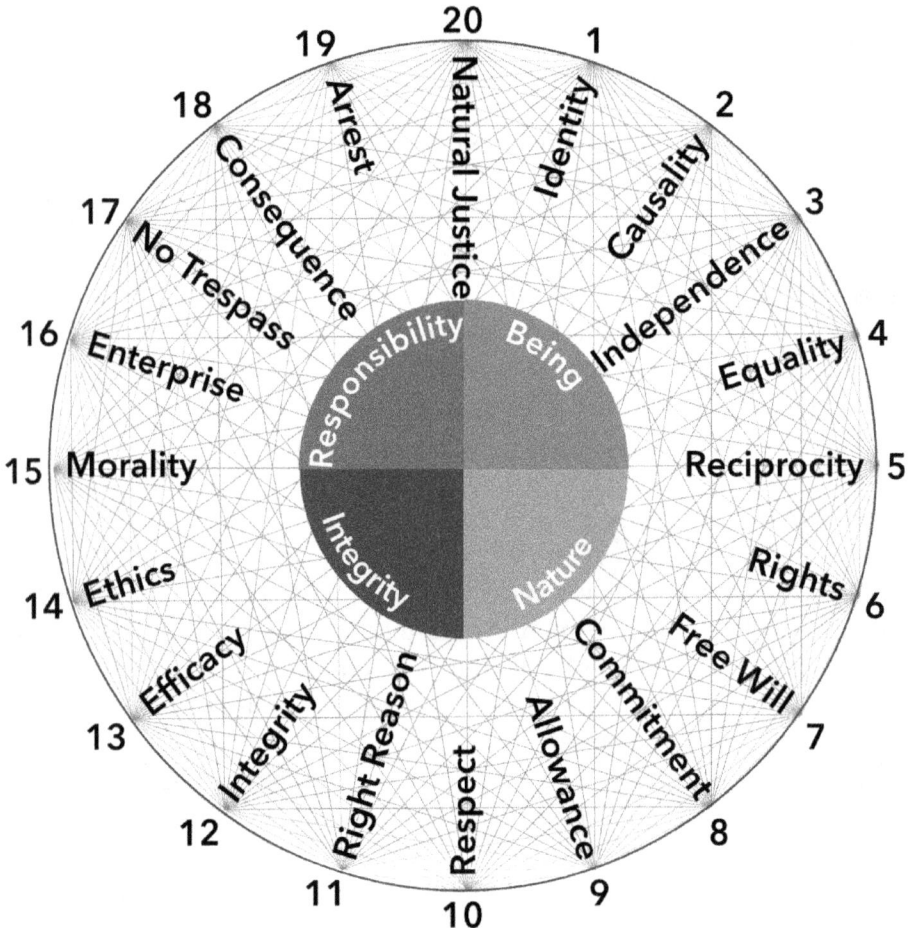

21. The twenty natural laws

176

Chapter 10

1. **Natural Law is to be respected; not obeyed.** Natural law cannot be obeyed or disobeyed. It has only to be respected. Every living man, woman and child has free will to respect natural law, treat it with hostility or contempt, or even refuse it. All consequences are one's own, whether for good or evil.

2. **Natural law is *of* Man; not *for* Man.** It is inherent in our human nature and immutable. It cannot be subtracted from or added to; thus, any contravening law is trespass from the outset, therefore denied. Completeness leaves no gaps; zero, zilch, nada. We ignore natural law at our peril. It follows that values, ethics and morality all emanate from within individual men and women, in every country and culture, each according to their choice, corresponding with the right of all others to choose. Natural law does not rule in the usual (positive) law-book fashion; rather, it exists within our nature as life-sustaining moral guidance, always accessible.

3. **Natural law is objective,** not subjective. Natural law does not refuse subjective opinion, but such is irrelevant if it offers no spiritual or life-sustaining purpose. Therefore, actions that respect natural law are objectively lawful. They uphold life objectively and serve justice, therefore. Activities that do not are unlawful and unjust, mitigating circumstances admitted.

4. **Natural law is immutable.** Natural law is intact. No one or any construct can overrule it without such action confessing the unlawful power or force so to do.

5. **Natural law upholds independent human life**. We are each one, independent from others. Society is many. Free societies are the aggregation of independent living beings, all species-equal, unique in expression and thus individuals. No (common) lung, organ, brain, stomach, mind, or consciousness exists. The individuality of human life cannot fuse into one unified entity therefore, without us each sacrificing our unalienable right to life to a (mass)' collective' with no life and no consciousness.

6. **Natural law grants no authority.** Natural law permits no jurisdiction for one individual to command another. This jurisdiction is amply testified by neither of our two minds being able to overrule the other. The principle of integrity, and one's unalienable right to life, is evident. Natural law grants no permission or authority for one to trespass upon another's life.

7. **Natural law refuses all authority.** Free will is the overseer of acceptance and refusal. So that it is protected, natural law denies all

orders and all authority save its own, whether from a partner, neighbour, pulpit, parliament, congress or any other.

8.   **Natural law admits no trespass.** Whosoever knowingly initiates the use of physical or coercive force, or fraud against others, negates and paralyses the victim's means of survival. Self-initiated trespass actions forbid other people's free will right to choose. So doing relinquishes one's right to choose—therefore, such 'outlaws' are not free. It follows that the right to exercise force to arrest such assaults is morally justifiable. Murder and self-defence are opposites.

9.   **Natural law seeks integrity.** Natural Law, and Positive Law (statutes), apply to different things, so they cannot be alternative systems of rules applicable to the same thing. The natural orderliness that governs our being is complete and without lack, entirely given to maintaining our life with immutable, undivided, wholesome integrity. Natural law obliges that we act in spiritual accordance with the same integrity of purpose that upholds our bodily life. Spiritual integrity is vital to sustaining and enhancing inestimable joys that result from living a life of moral integrity! Consciousness facilitates that end.

10. **Natural law supports our life** respectful of all others. Integrity, lawfulness, and justice are the foundation and culmination of natural law, the total expression and manifestation of body, mind and soul, respectful of life. Therefore, when our (consciously initiated) actions outwardly manifest honesty and integrity found within, without which our mental and bodily life could not exist, the orderliness and morality of societal structures are obliged to correspond. All that remains is to arrest initiated violence and trespass. Nothing less will suffice. Nothing more is needed.

Tragically, so long as human and sociological sciences refuse to study human consciousness in the manner here described, these laws remain hidden. Remember that the primary purpose of these laws is a thriving life within the equal rights of all others. Each law relates to the other nineteen, implying that the brief descriptions below are purely a (note form) introduction. Jurisprudence and natural law students are requested to study these laws, their source, and their interdependence in more detail.

As previously mentioned, each law's sources should ideally correlate to their descriptions, most found in chapters two through seven inclusive. As suggested, you may pencil in relevant page numbers for each law in the margins. Alternatively, you may pencil the law number next to relevant text passages in each of the chapters. By so doing, you will make connections in your mind, all to your great advantage. Moreover, any later study to refresh your mind will be faster, more direct and more thorough.

The Twenty Natural Laws

1 Natural Law of Identity

A thing is what it is and that as the thing is, it acts; conversely as the thing acts, it is.

Identity is the core tenet of objective ethical morality. Whatsoever has no identity cannot be consciously identified. It has no valid ethical or moral import. Devoid of any life value, nothing of worth offers. Except for (chosen) actions, there are no facts of random occurrence that could have been different, as against facts that must be. An entity's nature determines what it can do and dictates what it will do for any given set of circumstances.

Application: We are each prompted to identify the fundamental nature of ourselves, the true identity of what life is, and what life ought to enact. Pretense is self-defeating. Unless we act according to the reality of nature, our choices and actions are flawed before they begin. Founding premises are that > Existence exists, Man exists, Man has an identity, a nature, and all are knowable.

We gain no material or spiritual benefit from whims, fancies, or ideologies having no life-upholding foundation. Neither can society. The Natural Law of Identity applies to the nature of Man himself, our every thought, consideration, and personal interaction with others, politics, and society.

Source: This law derives from existence itself — from your reality — from every constituent of physical matter, their separateness and existent interrelationships — every man, woman, and child — every tissue, cell, organ, system, and faculty of our physical, mental, and spiritual being. (Reference chapters 1 and 2.)

2 Natural Law of Causality

All action is caused and determined via the nature of the entities that act; no real entity (thing) can occur through chance, or without cause; a thing cannot act contrary to its nature.

The two laws of existence, and identity, must exist before our consciousness can identify what exists. The process of thinking, and the contents of one's thoughts, are two separate things. Efficacy of our mind depends entirely on existent reality, our discovery and using both these laws.

Application: Nothing can act contrary to its nature. Accordingly, committed actions reveal our moral nature; our ethical or unethical thought intentions do not. The responsibility lies with the actor, therefore. Restoration of the natural order, i.e., natural justice, will focus on rehabilitation, remediation, and compensation, concerning an action, not apportioning blame. Natural justice focuses on actions and consequences, not the perpetrator's intention. The laws of identity and causality apply to personal ethics, especially the natural law of justice.

Source: As described in the Natural Law of Identity (above). The Law of Causality is the inevitable consequence of the Law of Identity.

3 Natural Law of Independence

All men and women are unique and independent, according to their nature of equally being Man, qua Man.

We are each an independent element of the human species, indisputably. We each are capable of doing, thinking, and saying things independently from what others are doing, thinking, and speaking. Such marks us as separate living beings, despite all being equal in human nature. Our separateness as human beings is the natural law of the world. This law is fundamental to our biology, psychology, and praxeology (the study of human action and conduct); to our lives, thoughts, feelings, and activities.

Application: Independence, and one's unalienable right to life, are inseparable. Societal constructs and dealings should uphold and protect both. Our life, our every breath and heartbeat, are witnesses and testament to our (individual) being, without which we cannot exist. Independence cannot be refuted but can be refused. The natural law (or order) of one's nature governs every single body function. Mental, subconscious, and emotional methodologies share the same goals, but their content is uniquely independent. All body and spirit functions are private in their source. We can share experiences of life and value exchange, but their origin is always individual, inviolate in nature, belonging to each alone. These laws are immutable in every particular man and woman's being. None can be erased, save through death. Independence is undeniable.

Source: Separateness of all biological constituents necessarily contributes to life's fullness, satisfaction, and resoluteness. Likewise, our free will (cognitive mind) (8%) must be independent of the automated subconscious mind (92%) to ensure authentically effective psycho-epistemological functioning.

Chapter 10

4 Natural Law of Equality

All living beings of the Homo sapiens species, are alike in nature and faculties, equally endowed.

Appearances and traits materially differ, but the property which defines uniqueness is equal in concept to all. Differentiating characteristics that define individual essence serve not to diminish equality but to emphasise its broad compass, including the individuated faculty of a free mind we each possess. This union of individual faculty with unique free expression testifies that all living beings are equal, yet all are independently separate in body, mind, and soul.

Application: Without equality and independence, one's right to life and property, freedom, and convivial society have no meaning. The union of one process testifying to equality, with particular free expression (independent content), should properly be the core of our business and societal structures, taught in all curricula from infancy.

Source: The non-hierarchical nature of every single tissue, cell, organ, system and faculty of our physical, mental and spiritual being without exception, despite unique differences. Processes occur sequentially, and all are contributory. No element or function is hierarchically superior, more dominating, or authoritative. All support life equally.

5 Natural Law of Integrity

The state of being whole, undivided, integrated, ethically intentioned, and committed to one's life, fully accords with the natural laws of one's nature.

Integrity manifests within us as the truthful, honest, holistic cohesiveness of our physical, mental, emotional, and spiritual faculties. Integrity's founding premise is spiritual, namely the upholding of our life. Integrity is our core value, the sum of every derivative value, desire, and spiritual goal supporting the totality of life itself. Integrity underscores the whole of our physical, conscious, subconscious, emotional and spiritual being.

Application: Integrity founds fundamental respect for the lives of others. It is the primary tenet of all personal, social, business and contractual dealings, to be taught across all curricula. Integrity's indubitable and resounding success fully endorses the proper embrace of the same ethic in all personal and societal intentions, actions, and goals. Conversely, lack of integrity results in diminished quality of life, in some form and to some degree. (Refer also to the law of Just Consequence.)

Source: Interdependency of the natural laws of identity and causality.

Truthfully precise subconscious reporting, faithful surveillance, monitoring and adjustment of all bodily functions and mental and spiritual processes.

6 Natural Law of Individual Rights

Every man, woman, and child is an independent living being, having individual, immutable, and unalienable right to his or her life, free and independent from any trespass, usurpation, or violation whatsoever.

Our right to life and sustenance is unalienable, immutable, and inviolate. One cannot live without performing the self-sustaining actions of living or without the right to act in support of their life. Right to the fruits of our labour is inalienable and inviolate.

Application: Unalienable right is our right to act, to live and sustain our life, within the rights of all others. Inalienable right is to the product of our action(s); entitlement (or belonging) to that which our efforts have produced, including improvements and cultivations, made to the land.

Our body, thoughts, actions, and emotions are ours individually; this true for all others equally. Individual Rights are moral principles that restrain society members from interfering with another's activities. Rights belong only to individuals, to every him, and every her, singularly. No collective rights can exist. Individual rights impose no obligations on one's neighbors except to abstain from violating their rights. Individual Rights of Man preside over all other life forms. The Natural Law of Individual Rights pertains to every unique living (human) being, every politic and society, and all personal, business, and societal dealings with others.

Source: Independent Life. The separate contributory functioning of every biological and psychological constituent. Maintenance of independence within equality, including the natural laws of No Trespass, Allowance, Just Consequence, Respect, Reciprocity, Commitment and Natural Justice.

7 Natural Law of Free Will

Free choice of thought and actions of any and all Living Being's, are guaranteed inclusive of the responsibility, liability and accountability, naturally and inherently flowing therefrom.

Free thought requires wilfully choice of its content. That fuels the database of our subconscious mind, which in turn powers conscience and emotions. Without free will, no mental, emotional, or spiritual growth is possible. That subconscious mind protects our cognitive free will, and vice versa testifies free will is inviolate and protected.

Application: Free thought imparts full responsibility for our actions, which confirms this law is inherent within our individual right to act and bear the consequences. There are no exceptions, escape routes, let-outs, excuses, or pardons for refusing to exercise free will, and none for overruling it. Individual rights, free will, respect, and responsibility, are inseparable. They must be upheld and protected.

No one can command free will, even Creator; otherwise, there is no free will, consequences inescapable. Therefore, no Man-made construct overruling our enacted responsibility is permissible. (Witness decisions given in the Nuremberg Trials.)

Free will imparts and embraces the essence and vitality of every natural law herein described. Those who claim free license to overrule free will, regardless of asserted authority, mastery, or divinity, are imposters, renegades, pirates, or psychopaths. Their claims are false, without merit, value, or substance! Free will is unimpeachable and indestructible. Nothing can override free consent, thus confirming that torture or traumas that violently and criminally force submission are neither free agreement nor consent! Because consent is (secretly) obtainable without the victim knowing, e.g., through propaganda or misguided ideology, mental vigilance is essential, per the natural laws of identity and causality.

Source: Free will is inherent, confirmed by you reading these words. It is fully supported, preserved and protected through automated subconscious functioning, upheld by specific material and spiritual values, initially of your choice. Human life is not possible without free will.

See the natural laws of Identity, Allowance, Causality, Commitment, Independence, and Equality, and their diagonal counterparts shown in the natural law (flower) diagram.

8 Natural Law of Commitment

To live is to commit to action(s) and bear the consequences.

Commitment is the willed intention to achieve a particular outcome or result from a chosen action and bear responsibility for that action. Commitment authors the consequences of our efforts, regardless of what thought or evaluation prompted it (mitigating circumstances accepted). Moral responsibility, and accountability, are expressed through actions. (Refer also to the Natural Law of Just Consequence.)

Application: This law falls squarely within all personal, social and business dealings and the jurisdiction of natural justice. Our volitional consciousness enables free choice, including the commitment to act, necessarily incurring its consequences. Our nature offers no automated alternative, as happens for other life forms.

Source: Our biological, psychological and spiritual nature. 'Life' itself, its material, mental, emotional, and spiritual maintenance, preservation and accomplishments, satisfaction, joy and happiness.

9 Natural Law of Allowance

Every man, woman, and child (including infants and those mentally handicapped) are endowed to venture forth and progress at their choice and pace, in service of their life, but are not absolved from refusing so to do.

Our subconscious mind may fully function, including for emotions, even though the cognitive mind is unable but not unwilling to perform at its fullest potential. Infants, young children, and those who suffer from a mental handicap are enabled to choose their actions and experience the emotions of success or failure. At the same time, they progressively grow as best possible in cognitive mental stature, understanding, and spirituality. This law allows for lessons of support and correction and for those teachings to be freely woven into the tapestry of our conscious and subconscious minds, thereby facilitating and stimulating mental growth and development.

This law accommodates maturity in which students learn to master their fulfillment in life. It permits learning and spiritual maturity to become habituated throughout adult life. That is its purpose and function. It is the window through which habituation of the learning process enables consistently higher percentiles of truth to amass in our intuit database, fostering more excellent reliability and certainty with the least effort. (See the Natural Law of Efficacy)

Application: This law applies to every living being of the human species. Ethically, morally, and spiritually, it endorses that we each recognise and accept others' rights and ability to progress at their pace, according to their choices and skills.

This law speaks of graciousness, politeness, integrity, gratitude, and respect. It facilitates the development of mental competence, consistent with choice and without penalty. It enables ever-increasing mental efficiency over time, making clear that mental and emotional growth requires a whole and prosperous life. No (purported) law ever invented can match what this natural law allows, and never will it. Man's laws can only trespass it.

This law should underscore all personal, educational, business, and societal dealings with others; the foundation of all education, cooperation, collaboration, relationships, marriage, and parenthood. This law is particularly relevant to schooling at all levels, including adult education. Devotees and students of Steiner, and Montessori education, will recognise its potency in a flash!

Source: Emotionally motivated actions in infants (emotionally reported subsequently) progressively induce cognitively triggered actions through childhood and adolescence, outcomes emotionally rewarded or (advisory) censored. In sum, a progressive mind switch occurs from (infant) emotional motivation to (adult) cognitive motivation; all supplemented emotionally.

Abuse of the Law of Allowance:

Abuse of this law occurs far too often, yet its victims, who mostly believe they've suffered an unfortunate consequence, rarely understand that, indeed, they caused it. Mental abstention, apathy, indifference, or lazy refusal to exercise one's mental faculties does not result from an impaired or debilitated faculty. No excuse is permitted, and no allowance for choosing to be mentally vacant, deprived, or retarded. Harmful consequences that inevitably result are of one's free choice in such cases, as justly deserved.

The Law of Allowance does not and cannot compel self-initiated development, for that would trespass free will. Instead, it justly allows the full consequences of one's choices for better or worse, whence the (parallel) Natural Law of Just Consequence adjudicates all outcomes. Therefore, abuse of this law falls within the jurisdiction and jurisprudence of Natural Justice.

10 Natural Law of Respect

No man, woman, or child can uphold their unalienable right to life without correspondingly respecting the equal right to life of all other living human beings.

Eating nutritious foods, exercising, sleeping, and bathing respect our bodies. Likewise, exercising thought, choosing life values and revitalising our hearts by relaxation and meditation respect our minds. We respect things of beauty through travel, visiting galleries, or reveling in the great outdoors. Diligence, honesty, and commitment appreciate our efforts. Our life entirely depends on self-respect for natural order, welfare, and governing laws.

The lesson begins at home from an ethical standpoint. Respect encompasses all aspects of our lives and our chosen values. Self-respect, and respect for others, should be one's core principle in life, physiologically, psychologically, emotionally and spiritually.

Application: Respect manifests through moral actions to become the primary factor in all matters concerning natural justice. Disrespect represents immoral actions. To uphold natural law is to show respect. Trespassers show contempt for life. Respect, and its relationship to natural justice, should be the core ethic taught in all curricula, from infancy onwards.

Respect necessitates that Individual Rights be instituted, thence protected from all trespass and violation. Whosoever disagrees with this fundamental fact of life should take their petition to Mans Creator, not to an (irrelevant) court of legal jurisdiction.

Source: 'Life,' as the supreme value. Virtues and spiritual Life-values. Health, hygiene, emotional satisfaction and spiritual accomplishment. All twenty natural laws. All perceptions, feelings and emotions, including conscience. Every constituent, organ, system, process, and faculty of our being, without which we could not exist.

11 Natural Law of Reciprocity

Respect for one's individual life, and reciprocally for the right of all others to live, ensures one's freedom, so too the right of all others of the human species.

Moral discipline asserts that where the rights of all other individuals are respected, no one can offend another through any application of their own. Freedom to live according to one's nature and personal choices applies to all; otherwise, it is not freedom. All contrary claims are anti-life. Any quarrel is with Creator and none other.

Application: Aggregate success of every constituent and faculty of our being guarantees continuance and maintenance of the (societal) environment in which each singularly prospers. This law applies to every unique living being, every politic and society. The institution of this law cancels every Man-made statute or directive that violates Creator's invitation to live. (Refer also to the Law of No Trespass.)

Creator has ruled that our independent life is conditional upon maintaining a societal environment guaranteeing that each life may prosper. However, such protection cannot ensure that each will thrive, which is the prerogative of free will. Therefore, we must translate this law into a free convivial society, thereby upholding reciprocal individual rights to life, property, and freedom.

Source: Reciprocity endlessly manifests within our nature. Our successful outcomes propagate more successful inputs to the continuance of life itself. No escape offers, save death.

12 Natural Law of Right Reason

Reasoning discovers truths that are not self-evident—to adapt material existence to life-sustaining purposes.

Reasoning is the intellectual ability to logically think through connected steps in search of truths that are not self-evident. Rational beings understand themselves through reason. They consider cause and effect, truth and falsehood, ethics and morality. Reasoning facilitates our ability to change attitudes, traditions, and institutions and convert beliefs into knowledge within free will and self-determination.

Application: This Law correctly applies to every unique living being, every politic, and society.

Source: Our human nature. Different constituent biological purposes, functions, interactions and interoperability. Volitional consciousness, including intercommunication and value transfer between our two minds, aka psycho-epistemology. All discovery, learning, logic, inquiry, contemplation, investigation, determination, evaluation, and commitment.

13 Natural Law of Efficacy

Related conscious faculties, permit efficacious functioning, correspondent with valid, truthful, value-based mental content.

Efficacy of thought and reasoning, accurate and speedy resolutions, intuition, life values, and emotional stability depends on whether our accepted mental data is truthful or corrupted. Those who place a high value on mental agility, truth, validity, and integrity will speed past those who must mentally wrestle every issue with a high degree of certainty and truth.

Application: This law teaches that we are responsible for our efficiencies, efficacy and success. Erroneous beliefs, fictional laws, mysticisms, subjectivism and perverted meanings will mislead authentic comprehension. Misconstructions of language and stolen concepts will hinder or cripple cognitive ability.

This law applies to every material, mental, emotional, and spiritual aspect of self, every goal and ambition. It also applies to every element of education, every politic, and every personal, business and societal dealing with others.

Source: The faculty of perception, our conscience, emotions and feelings. Cognitive mind's (word) concept vocabulary and the subconscious image vocabulary. Also, imagination, intuition, and subconscious mind programming for desirous auto-functioning. When data is misleading, corruptive or false, efficient mental functioning is severely handicapped, if not denied. (Refer also to the laws of allowance commitment, respect, free will, integrity and right reason.)

14 Natural Law of Ethics

Ethics, is the science of choosing life-supporting thoughts, values, and determinations, that when acted upon, outwardly express one's morality.

Ethics is the chosen code of principles governing the moral correctness of our behaviour and actions. Ethics is our moral guide to thinking and reasoning in a manner supportive of life. Consistent assessment and appraisal of life values should properly implant life-sustaining 'ethics' in the subconscious mind to always uphold moral actions.

Application: Ethics is the chosen code of principles residing within one's mind, governing life sustaining correctness. No one else is affected, whereby unethical thinking and reasoning occasions no harm to anyone but ourselves.

Resultant actions testify to ethical thoughts. Actions are moral, amoral, or immoral. These may, and almost inevitably, affect others, for which one is wholly accountable and responsible. Immoral actions may occasion harm to self and others. Therefore, there should exist a science of ethics within all education curricula.

Source: Ethics is inherent in the moral fibre of life itself. Truthful, honest, wholesome cohesiveness of all our biological faculties and our intellectual, emotional and value-based spiritual nature all testify to ethics. (Refer also to the Natural Law of No Trespass and the Natural Law of Just Consequence.)

15 Natural Law of Morality

Actions and behaviour publicly testify one's pre-conceived moral stature, and agreed moral accountability.

Morality and immorality are not innate; they result from each being's actions. Morality is not a social edict but a primary, personal requisite that properly pre-empts all our actions and behaviours. All accountability for its manifestation or lack arises from there, as Natural justice arbitrates.

Application: Our nature testifies that any immoral action, being a violation of another's right to life or property, does not break the natural law but instead reinforces and amplifies its necessity, thus cogently pointing to necessary correction and (or) remediation.

Immoral action, once proven, is confessed trespass of natural law, the perpetrator's guilt, and agreement to bear natural justice as a confessed outlaw. Outlaws are not free. They have consciously chosen to surrender their freedom, their immoral or unlawful behaviour providing ample evidence. (Refer to the Law of Natural Justice.)

Source: Every cell, tissue, organ, system and function of our body, and every mental faculty and process (not content), tasked to uphold every other constituent of our life. Every purpose, reason, collaboration, and functionality of our faculties exhibits their indubitable moral stature, without which 'life' cannot exist.

16 Natural Law of Cooperative Enterprise

Cooperative effort with others, will return more benefit than most individual's can achieve alone.

Strictly as body cells, systems, and faculties are not permitted to trespass upon another and cause harm, they are otherwise endowed to co-operate for synergistic benefit. Collaborative enterprise satisfies the natural law of no trespass in all respects while upholding the laws of equality, independence, right reason, efficacy and morality.

Application: Purposive actions among co-operating individuals require that individual rights prevail over any societal or business structure they may institute. Group rights are thereby ousted, eminent domain likewise. Business and contractual dealings depend on independence, voluntary cooperation, and everyone's unalienable right to life.

Source: The synergistic result of every individual biological and psychological constituent and faculty collaboratively working with fifty-trillion cells, two hundred cell types, seventy-eight organs and thirteen organ systems. Add two minds possessing nine higher faculties, all collaboratively supporting and maintaining life, all orchestrally free will conducted, conscience and emotions, plus intuition and imagination graciously assisting.

17 Natural Law of No Trespass

No independent living being has the right to trespass, or to violate another's life, or property.

This law informs absolutely no trespass of any other (volitionally conscious) sentient living being's right to life. Notice that respect for all others and no violation of the rights of others is effectively identical to the law of reciprocity.

Application: Two persons cannot be free and equal when one of them is controlling, managing, threatening, blackmailing, or extorting the other.

- Our right to act and live fully accepts the reciprocal right of all others equally.
- Trespassing another's rights self-cancels one's rights respective of any relevant action.
- No claim of right may negate, usurp, or overrule the unalienable rights of other living human beings.
- Independent rights of Man preside over all other life forms.

No form of eminent domain may hereafter exist. (Eminent domain means resumption/compulsory acquisition or expropriation; e.g., the power of a state or a national government to take private property for public use.) That is trespass, respective of our right to life and the fruits of our labours.

Source: Protective separation of heart from lungs, the blood/brain barrier, and organ protection via separation. The mental process is refused alteration of cognitive content. The subconscious mind is inherently forbidden to override our value choices. Subconscious process alteration is intrinsically prohibited. No attribute, constituent or faculty within our nature may trespass any other.

18 Natural Law of Just Consequence

Nature serves just consequence, whether respected or not.

This law justly allows the full consequences of one's choices, for better or worse. Whereas the Law of Allowance applies to alleviate or overcome legitimate impairment of some kind, the Law of Just Consequence precludes its abuse. No excuses apply, save mitigating circumstances.

This law mimics Francis Bacon's statement, *'Nature to be commanded must be obeyed.'* (Given free will, the word 'respect,' is more accurate than the word 'obey.')

This law does not prescribe that a consequence will be the exact measure of one's moral or immoral action, although it will, more often than not. Other people's efforts or mitigating circumstances may apply. 'Just consequence' means it justly belongs exactly to whoever caused it. That endorses natural justice. It permits what one chooses, whether for good or evil and makes no mistakes.

Application: This law applies to every unique living (human) being, every politic, and society. It is a core tenet of the science of ethics and the foundation of the Natural Law of Justice. Our moral obligation is to learn of this law and learn from it. It is the core of our conscience and emotions, not forgetting bodily dis-ease.

Chapter 10

Source: All actions have consequences. Aside from natural causes, commonly referred to as Acts of God, all actions result from choices made by people. We each are the author and practitioner of our efforts, just recipients of their consequences thereby.

19 Natural law of Forceful Arrest

Creator approved arrest of all initiated force protects Man's unalienable right to life.

Any initiated force that demands we act against our judgment negates and paralyses our means of survival. Whoever starts using coercive or physical force, for whatever purpose and to whatever extent, intends to harm or destroy our capacity to live, regardless of all claims to the contrary! Force, and mind, are opposites. Those who herd and rule men and women cannot claim the sanction of reason, as no advocate of contradictions can claim it.

Application: Without protection or self-defence, we are at the mercy of all who initiate force, including governments, fraudsters, blackmailers, tyrants, rapists, psychopaths, terrorists, thugs, warmongers and murderers. The precondition of a civilised society is the barring of physical force from social relationships. Nature has established that if men and women wish to deal with one another, they may do so through reasoned discussion, persuasion, and voluntary, un-coerced agreement. Security of each person and their property against predatory attack emerges as a most necessary condition of society. Protection of Individual Rights is the only proper function of a 'Protectorate,' a lawful substitute for government, including a Commission of Justice. (Refer also to the Natural Laws of Cooperative Enterprise, Allowance, Morality, No Trespass, Just Consequence, and Natural Justice.)

Source: Our instinct, bodily immune system, conscience, feelings and emotions. Subconscious ability to instantly switch between different modalities of corrective and remedial force.

20 Natural Law of Justice

Innocent, natural individuals are free. Proven trespassers of natural law are outlaws, perpetrators of deliberately enacted transgressions; voluntary bearers of natural justice.

Every individual is the author of their own internalised, thought-based ethics. Freely chosen resultant actions translate directly into moral justness or immoral unjustness served upon others.

Those, who (secretly) self-declare that others can be walked over, trodden on, and their rights ground into dust, have inwardly rejected morality. Correspondingly, their actions will outwardly broadcast that they require restorative justice, an imperative need to return to a state of natural order and its laws.

Application: Free persons do not commit crimes — those who have (prior) chosen to relinquish their freedom do. The full force of Natural Justice bears upon such perpetrators, being the only force they have the right to choose. Lawful remediation is now the path of natural justice. No legal instrument may be contrary since such contrariness upholds unjust and unlawful action.

Source: Natural justice is innately located smack in the core of one's conscience, and dynamic reporting systems, exactly where it belongs, for the exact reasons those faculties exist. They inform of justice or injustice, what is upholding one's life, or hindering it. Those approvals, or censure alternatively, respectively point to continuance or remedy concerning one's values, all subsets of life as the supreme value. No better example of natural justice exists than what the conscious process exhibits, innate and inherent within every man, woman and child.

Self governance through existential natural law

The remarkable difference between statutes and natural law is explicit, even more so when read in conjunction with its diagonal counterpart. In the simplest of terms—

- Our rights are upheld when our actions preserve other people's right to life.
- The converse is true also. Actions that violate other people's rights forfeit our own. Unlawful activities self confess we are outlaws, for which activities we are fully accountable.

That is how natural law governs without authoritarian rule while fully upholding free will. Self-governance is self-evident.

We must study the complete conscious process to discover the raw source of these twenty laws, their ramifications and personal and societal applications. As full consciousness emerges, authoritarian compulsion and force appear as the tyrants they are, marking the road to their abolition. Remember this—

"No problem can be solved from the same level of consciousness that created it," Albert Einstein.

Visualise your thriving ability with all fear gone—picture bountiful joy in your everyday experiences. Conceive expansive freedom, joy, peace, harmony, and spiritual attainment, personally and globally. What will be your choice? Will you follow today's path to destruction as sociopaths enforce, or will you trash conscious ignorance and thrive absent limits,

Chapter 10

thereby forbidding tyranny and vicious crime from ever surfacing again?

It should now be clear 'natural existential law' exceeds any other form of law known to Man. Therefore, spirituality's core principle and fruitful exercise are the greatest tribute one can ever offer their Creator.

'Existential natural law' is not a product of the human mind. It is the Creator's gift of how our mind functions, our personal invitation to prosper and thrive materially, emotionally and spiritually, as never taught before. No invention is necessary. Our discovery and practice are.

Until we awaken to the fulness of consciousness, its freedom and the right to self-govern and responsibly act upon all three, we deny ourselves and suffer the penalty. We each have that choice. This book has outlined what we must do to thrive as never known before. It has shown Creator's invitation to participate in a way never before described.

You are richly blessed. The path is now clear. All you need do is say yes to your subconscious mind and passionately mean it. You make the choices, and it will make the effort. Together, you will soar in the beauty and certainty of your nature and thrive absent limits!

Creator has your back all the way!

My Life-Value List

Prime values	Subset values - if any
Respect	
	15

Refer to Chapter 5 for revision concening how to choose

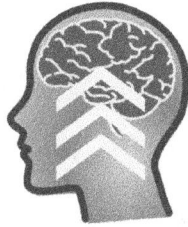

Appendix

Definitions

Today's (English) language and vocabulary have been twisted, polluted and distorted beyond sensible, logical and lawful comprehension; through poisonous philosophies and theologies, political correctness, legalese and mental corrosion resulting from unchallenged beliefs. Electronic communications, such as text abbreviations, have compounded these errors such that near enough is good enough. Laziness and apathy then forbid enquiry, exacting a devastating toll on critical thinking, understanding and communication.

This table defines words used here and on my website, explaining the human conscious process and 'existential natural law.' These definitions concern the conscious process. In my following book, I will expand this list to help people better use natural law to navigate their freedom in organic societies free from authoritarian dictates, statutes and commands.

Awareness, Cognitive; conscious recognition of material things, events, or circumstances.

Awareness Sentient; (Sentience) Sensory ability to feel or perceive feelings and emotions. Sentient consciousness — being consciously aware of an abstract feeling.

Consciousness: (noun) The systemic process of life-value transfer between the conscious and subconscious minds interfacing physicality and spirituality.

Consciousness, full: Consciously and consistently using the integrated sum of one's knowledge previously acquired from exercising volition; choice. ('Fullness' does not imply a finite measure).

Conscious Ascendance

Discernment: The mental process of discriminatory investigation leading to understanding; to usefully separates beliefs from truths, illusions from reality, pretences from facts, foolishness from wisdom, and ignorance from knowledge.

Ego: The acronym for egotism, as a rule — whereby 'egoism' is denied.

Egoism: Self-esteem, self-importance, self-worth, self-respect, self-image and self-confidence; worthy attributes arising from one's attention to their own wellbeing and responsible happiness.

Egotism: Being excessively conceited or absorbed in oneself; arrogance, egocentricity, egomania, self-obsession, narcissism, unwarranted self-adulation, vanity and conceit.

Epistemology: The theory of knowledge as concerns methods, validity, scope, and the distinction between justified knowledge versus beliefs and opinions.

Psycho-epistemology: The study of our cognitive processes as concerns value interaction between the conscious mind and the automatic functions of the subconscious.

Free will: A value-assessment tool enabling the establishment of values and benefits to advance life and reject what does not.

Human: (adjective) Relating to or characteristic of humankind, or Mankind; of or characteristic of people as opposed to God or animals or machines; (noun) a human being. (Hu man or hue man is a legal bastardisation of the word human that refers to the colour of man, the reference to a legal person. Both are denied within natural law.)

Imagination: 1) The forming of new ideas or images of external objects not present to the senses. **2)** To visualise one's values to transfer them from the 'word vocabulary' of the cognitive mind to the 'image vocabulary' of the subconscious mind.

Independent Living Being (ILB)© A copyrighted term used in the Copyrighted iDeed© process for biometric attestation of life, facilitating universal biometric ID that by nature certifies Individual Rights so cancelling any and all fraudulent (legal) identifications of that particular Individual. (ILB Identification commenced in America mid-2020 for American State Nationals.)

Individual: noun - A (single) Sentient, (volitionally conscious) Living Being having an unalienable right to life and inalienable right to property: all (incorporated) reference to a (legal) person (s) null and void.

Intellect: The faculty of reasoning and understanding objectively, especially concerning abstract matters, particularly distinct from feeling or wishing; capacity for knowledge and understanding; to learn, think and reason; build knowledge and comprehension.

Definitions

Intellectual discernment: Self-mastery; the tool of rational enquiry based on clarity, values and integrity of thought.

Intuition: An automatic search tool that works behind the scenes to enhance our mental abilities; Intuition delivers value-based insight before we act.

Law: noun (Natural law, God's law, Divine law, Laws of nature) Order, or orderliness; the natural order/orderliness of human nature. ("Law is not a prescription telling us how we ought to behave. Law is a natural fact, and law is natural law and nothing else." —Frank van Dun, Philosopher of law.)

Life values: Spiritual values or virtues: journey values that assist in accomplishing material and spiritual achievements. E.G., diligence, resilience, integrity, respect and honesty.

Logic: The art of non-contradictory identification.

Man: (noun) (plural men) 1) an adult male human being: 2 a human being of either sex; a person: God cares for all men.

Usage: Traditionally, the word man has been used to refer not only to adult males but also to human beings in general, regardless of sex. In Old English, historically, the principal sense of man was a human being. In the second half of the 20th century, the generic use of man to refer to 'human beings in general (as in reptiles were here long before man appeared on the earth) insensibly became regarded as sexist or old-fashioned. Terms such as the human race or humankind may be used instead of man or Mankind.

Mankind: (noun) [mass noun] human beings considered collectively; the human race: research for the benefit of all Mankind.

Metaphysics: The branch of philosophy dealing with the first principles of things, including abstract concepts such as being, knowing, identity, time, and space.

Natural Law: (noun) - As for 'Law.' From the Latin word Ius, which refers to a bond or obligation that arises out of a personal commitment made in a solemn speech; Law is an order of things. Accordingly, the term 'natural law' denotes a natural order of things. 'Law' also connotes respectability; law is an order of things that people ought to respect. The full human conscious process reveals twenty natural laws; hence 'natural law theory' is now (factually) superseded by 'existential natural law.'

Natural Law Definition: The set of universal, eternal and immutable conditions governing behavioural consequences of volitionally conscious beings: Absent compliance with these maxims inherent in the nature and state of Man, the peace and happiness of society can never be preserved.

Perception: From the Latin perceptio, percipio. The organisation, identification, interpretation and representation of sensory information necessary to understand it and its environment.

Person: noun - Per (centuries old) everyday colloquial language, an individual man or woman; a flesh and blood sentient living being; such definition repudiating or refuting all past, present, or future definitions, Law Dictionaries notwithstanding.

Person: Natural, i.e., Natural Person(n) - An individual person; this definition repudiates or refutes all past, present, or future definitions.

Philosophic materialism: The view that non-physical things do not exist, whereby spirituality is considered senseless. (The theory completely defeats itself because it belies the non-physical nature of thought from which it arises.)

Philosophic idealism: The idea that everything is an idea, energy, or consciousness. (Self-defeating since a brain's existence takes precedent.)

Power: The unalienable power and God-given right to freely use one's subconscious mind to attract the things necessary for happiness and success.

Rational thought: The learned process of logic and reason to advance knowledge and wisdom.

Reason: Mental ability to logically think through connected steps in search of truth that is not self-evident; to convert beliefs into knowledge within the realm of free will and self-determination.

Source: 1) A place, person, or thing from which something originates or can be obtained; the place something comes from or starts at or the cause of something.

Source: 2) Our allocated portion of the essential mind of God being the source upon

Thinking, mental activity. The mental process of choosing to consciously understand existent things, also theories, predictions, deviations and prognostications.

Thinking - Analytical: To abstractly separate constituent parts from the whole, so to study those parts and their respective relations; break down complex information, step-by-step in order to form an overall conclusion, an answer, or solution.

Thinking - Critical: The ability, and wilful intention to think clearly and rationally; to reason; to inquire, research, discover, evaluate difficulties and benefits; open or close the gate to all ideas, truths, postulates, beliefs, wishes, whims, propaganda, and indoctrinations of all kinds.

Understand:1) perceive the intended meaning of (words, a language, or a speaker) **2)** perceive the significance, explanation, or cause of, or be sympathetically or knowledgeably aware of the character or nature of

Definitions

(some constituent attribute, identity or idea) **3)** to comprehend, apprehend, grasp, see, take in. *(No legal connotation applies, as in "standing below or standing under another's authority.)*

Willpower: The conscious will to succeed, plus subconscious mind's empowered capacity to make one's choices happen.

Conscious Ascendance

Acknowledgements

To describe consciousness as never explained before is bountifully rewarding and damnably challenging because it uproots almost every accepted precept. For that reason I am profoundly grateful to several people whose worldwide works circle the subject of consciousness. Their passion and devotion to truth have greatly helped me see and understand human consciousness at full throttle.

Ayn Rand's Objectivist Philosophy is outstanding. Her consistency and adherence to principles heightened my grasp of life values enormously. Frank van Dun's assistance as a philosopher of law has been invaluable. His explanations of natural law cemented my understanding of how consciousness reveals the twenty natural laws encrypted in our human nature. Mark Passio's contributions to natural law are also outstanding. His passion and fire for truth express the urgency that this information goes mainstream now!

Many others have likewise assisted without their knowing. In particular, my thanks go to Craig Biddle from the Objective Standard, Larken Rose, Leonard Peikoff, Dr Bruce Lipstein, Joe Dispenza, Greg Braden, and Jordan Petersen. All of these people speak around or hint at what I describe, yet their observations and ideas together have a magnitude that few people grasp. Thanks to them and countless others, this book may never have been written.

My sincere gratitude goes also to my sons Scott and Craig. Their support is enormous as always, particularly regarding my health after my two brushes with death six years back.

The same applies to my colleague Max Emmons Taylor Jr. in America. Thank you sincerely, Max; your compliments, suggestions and many hours of work have greatly assisted my endeavours many times. Grateful thanks also to Linda Ray in Western Australia; your proofreading assistance over the past few years has been invaluable.

To all, please accept my heartfelt thanks for assisting in this work of monumental importance. I trust future generations will recognise that their benefits and joys are due in part to your many valued contributions.

About the Author

Following a multi-award-winning residential design career, Ken Bartle now researches and writes about how full consciousness delivers natural law. Superseding 'Law from Within' (2017), his expanded explanations from infancy through spirituality are now 'self-help' on steroids.

Residing in Australia since 1964, (Kiwi) Ken's long-taught ideology— *"A great house is not champagne and roses the day you move in — rather heartfelt gratitude the day you move out"* —strikes gold when applied to "life." 'Observational science' and deductive reasoning concerning consciousness shines as emotionally satisfying and demonstrably empowering. His masterful grasp of psycho-epistemology applied to natural law drives his passion but this book is just the beginning.

Although it describes consciousness for personal fulfillment and uplifting, it is important to grasp how these principles might apply in societal terms; how free organic societies may blossom through self-governance and personal sovereignty. That subject is for Kenneth's next book, *'Navigate to Freedom.'*

Bibliography

1. Sutherland, Stuart; National Library of Medicine; Consciousness: The last 50 years (and the next) Seth,Anil K: Website URL. https://www.ncbi.nlm.nih.gov/pmc/articles/PMC7058250/

2. Clark, Andy: What is Panpsychism? (Oct 2021) YouTube link; https://www.youtube.com/watch?v=b5DyJpQ0574

3. Frankish, Keith; Aeon; Why panpsychism fails to solve the mystery of consciousness: Website URL. https://aeon.co/ideas/why-panpsychism-fails-to-solve-the-mystery-of-consciousness

4. Goff, Phillip. Science as we know it can't explain consciousness. Durham University. Web URL, https://www.dur.ac.uk/news/allnews/thoughtleadership/?itemno=40191

5. Griffith, Jeremy. "The Book of Real Answers to Everything", Web address, Jeremy Griffith https://www.humancondition.com/book-of-real-answers/

6. Griffith, Jeremy. "Biologist Jeremy Griffith examines where the human race is headed." Web address, http://www.smh.com.au/national/education/biologist-jeremy-griffith-examines-where-the-human-race-is-headed-20141006-10qyvm.html

7. Hitchens, Christopher: Letters to a Young Contrarian Thinking. Web URL, https://www.goodreads.com/work/quotes/42824-letters-to-a-young-contrarian

8. Elder, Linda; (Article entitled) Defining Critical Thinking; Web URL, http://www.criticalthinking.org/pages/defining-critical-thinking/766

9. The Sydney Morning Herald: Shock discovery in Economic Man's mind; Website URL, https://www.smh.com.au/business/the-economy/shock-discovery-in-economic-mans-mind-20040412-gdipuj.html

10. Katz; Marvin C. A A Unified Theory of Ethics . Web URL, www.myqol.com/wadeharvey/A%20UNIFIED%20THEORY%20OF%20ETHICS.pdf

11. Grohol, John M, Psy.D. "Humans are governed by emotions." Web address, http://psychcentral.com/blog/archives/2005/10/20/humans-are-governed-by-emotions/
    Universal lighthouse radio; Scientists Prove DNA Can Be Reprogrammed By Our Own Words Web URL, https://www.universallighthouseblog.com/post/scientists-prove-dna-can-be-reprogrammed-by-our-own-

words?fbclid=IwAR3GDXPyHnmfkUaX2gU-Rappoport:Jon.

12. No more fake news. Jon Rappoport's Blog. Website URL, https://blog.nomorefakenews.com/2019/08/02/exit-from-the-matrix-your-power-in-a-decaying-world/

13. Rand, Ayn: New American Library, The Ayn Rand Lexicon. Individual Rights. "Ayn Rand Lexicon." "Individual Rights." Web address, http://aynrandlexicon.com/lexicon/individual_rights.html

14. van Dun, Frank: "Natural Rights." Web address, http://users.ugent.be/~frvandun/Texts/Logica/NaturalLaw2.htm

15. Adask, Alfred: "Unalienable vs Inalienable." Web address, https://adask.wordpress.com/2009/07/15/unalienable-vs-inalienable/

16. Warren, Joseph. The Objective Standard. Act Worthy of Yourselves': Joseph Warren on Defending Liberty; Web address, https://theobjectivestandard.com/2018/03/act-worthy-of-yourselves-joseph-warren-on-defending-liberty/

17. Rand, Ayn. "Anthem," Create SpacePublishing, Barnes and Noble, Web address, http://www.barnesandnoble.com/w/anthem-ayn-rand/1116684471

www.ingramcontent.com/pod-product-compliance
Lightning Source LLC
Chambersburg PA
CBHW071052040426
42443CB00013B/3310